Cash and Treasury Management

Tutorial

Aubrey Penning

Published by Osborne Books Limited
Tel 01905 748071
Email books@osbornebooks.co.uk
Website www.osbornebooks.co.uk

Design by Laura Ingham

Printed by CPI Group (UK) Limited, Croydon, CRO 4YY, on environmentally friendly, acid-free paper from managed forests.

British Library Cataloguing in Publication Data
A catalogue record for this book is available from the British Library

ISBN 978 1909173 989

Contents

Introduction

Qualifications covered

This book has been written specifically to cover the Unit 'Cash and Treasury Management' which is an optional Unit for the following qualifications:

AAT Professional Diploma in Accounting – Level 4

AAT Professional Diploma in Accounting at SCQF – Level 8

The book contains a clear text with worked examples and case studies, chapter summaries and key terms to help with revision. Each chapter concludes with a wide range of activities, many in the style of AAT computer based assessments.

Osborne Study and Revision Materials

The materials featured on the previous page are tailored to the needs of students studying this unit and revising for the assessment. They include:

- **Workbooks:** paperback books with practice activities and exams
- **Student Zone:** access to Osborne Books online resources
- **Osborne Books App:** Osborne Books ebooks for mobiles and tablets

Visit www.osbornebooks.co.uk for details of study and revision resources and access to online material.

1 Managing cash flows

this chapter covers...

In this chapter we will start by examining the differences between accounting to establish profit or loss (accruals accounting), and accounting for cash. We will see how these techniques differ and why each produces important results.

We then learn how profit can be reconciled with increase (or decrease) in cash over the same period.

We will then describe:

- *what working capital is*
- *what affects working capital*
- *how the 'cash cycle' of an organisation can be measured*

We will examine the main sources of cash, and the uses that it can be put to in a variety of organisations. We will see how different sources and uses of cash have different patterns of cash flow and explain how to identify them accurately.

We will also examine:

- *details of the people that we may need to consult when preparing information about cash flows*
- *the type of documents that will provide us with information that we need*

Lastly we will illustrate the format of the cash budget, which is widely used to provide information about the cash position of an organisation and is useful in the processes of planning, monitoring and controlling cash.

WHY CASH IS DIFFERENT FROM PROFIT

In your studies in accounting you will be concerned with systems that plan, record and monitor income and expenditure – the net result of which is profit (or loss). In this unit we have a different focus – we are going to examine how the fundamental resource of **cash** can be budgeted, monitored and controlled.

accounting for profit

Profitability is the amount by which **income** exceeds **expenditure**, and can be seen as the increase of overall wealth of the business. In order to account for the income and expenditure that are used to calculate profit we often use **cash-based receipts and payments** as a starting point, but then make substantial adjustments, by using techniques such as:

- taking account of amounts owed and owing, ie receivables and payables
- adjusting for accruals and prepayments
- depreciating non-current assets
- creating and adjusting provisions (for example provisions for irrecoverable debts)

The increased business wealth known as **profit** is reflected in the net result of all the assets and liabilities in the statement of financial position. This is the **'accruals' system of accounting**.

accounting for cash

Cash receipts and payments are normally recorded in a business's cash book. The balance of the cash book represents just one of the business assets (or liabilities, if it is an overdraft) that is shown in the statement of financial position. Throughout this book, when using the term 'cash' we will mean the cash book balances relating to business bank accounts as well as actual amounts of notes and coins.

In the same way, the cash receipts and payments that we will refer to throughout the text will also include amounts received into or paid from bank accounts. These transactions will include receipts and payments using cheques and BACS (direct payments, standing orders and direct debits), as well as notes and coins.

Receipts and **payments** are expressions that relate just to cash items, and do not incorporate any of the adjustments that are used to calculate **income** and **expenditure** when calculating profit (see above). We must be careful to understand the distinction between these two sets of terms.

the importance of 'cash'

A business needs to plan, monitor and control cash. We have just defined **cash** as the amount of **money** that the business has in a form that it can use virtually immediately. This is sometimes referred to as money in a **liquid** form, from which we get the idea of liquidity.

Cash is just as important to a business as profit, because:

- the daily operations of a business depend on being able to receive funds and make payments as they become due, and
- the survival of a business depends on having sufficient cash to meet its obligations

Unlike profit, which can vary if different accounting policies are applied, cash is a matter of fact. If a business is £10,000 overdrawn at the bank then the amount owing is not simply a 'book entry', but an issue that may require immediate action – depending on the business's agreement with the bank.

RECONCILING PROFIT WITH CASH

We have just discussed in broad terms how accounting for cash differs from accruals accounting, which is used to calculate profit. We will now use these ideas to see how a profit figure can be reconciled with the increase (or decrease) in cash over the same period.

There is no standard layout for an internal document that reconciles budgeted profit and cash, but we will start by using the relatively simple layout shown below. We will start with the profit figure and then adjust it for non-cash items to arrive at the change in cash. The order of the adjustments does not affect the outcome of the statement, and in an assessment you may be required to place the adjustments in a different order to the one shown here.

	£
Budgeted Profit for Period	X
Add non-cash expenditure used in calculation of profit:	
for example depreciation	X
Add cash receipts not used in calculation of profit:	
for example capital receipts	X
Deduct cash payments not used in the calculation of profit:	
for example payments for non-current assets	(X)
Adjust for changes in inventory:	
Deduct increase in inventory (or add a decrease)	(X)
Adjust for changes in receivables:	
Deduct increase in receivables (or add a decrease)	(X)
Adjust for changes in payables:	
Add increase in payables (or deduct a decrease)	X
Increase (decrease) in cash	X

Although this may appear rather long and complicated, it is actually following a logical approach:

- non-cash items that reduce profit are added back
- cash items that do not directly affect profit are accounted for
- adjustments are made for changes in inventory, receivables and payables

It is this last item that may need some explanation. If the current asset of inventory has increased it must be because more cash has been spent on inventory than is shown in the budgeted statement of profit or loss. Similarly, if receivables have increased, it is because less cash has been received from customers than is implied in the sales figure in the budgeted statement of profit or loss. Therefore adjustments are made by deducting the amounts by which inventory or receivables have increased. The opposite adjustment is made for a reduction.

Any change in payables is dealt with in a similar – but opposite – way. If you can understand the logic of this process then you should be able to deal with a range of items that require adjustment.

If you have studied Financial Accounting you will notice that the layout that we have used is similar to the 'Statement of Cash Flows' that forms part of the published accounts of a limited company. We do not need to know the layout of that formal statement for our studies in this unit.

We will now use a Case Study to demonstrate the use of this technique. In Chapter 3 we will return to the technique and show that it can be used alongside cash budgets.

FIRST TRADE: RECONCILIATION OF PROFIT WITH CASH

Jim First is planning to start a trading business. The following budgeted statement of profit or loss for the first four months of his business has been prepared:

Jim First: Budgeted statement of profit or loss

	£	£
Sales		22,000
less cost of sales:		
Opening inventory	0	
Purchases	21,000	
less closing inventory	(7,000)	
		14,000
Gross profit		8,000
less:		
Cash expenses	4,000	
Depreciation	1,000	
		5,000
Profit for the period		3,000

You are also provided with the following information:

- At the start of the period the business has a zero cash balance, and zero receivables and payables
- Jim has £25,000 to invest in the business during the first month
- Receivables at the end of the period are budgeted at £12,000
- Payables at the end of the period are budgeted at £5,000
- Non-current assets are to be purchased for £15,000 during the period
- Drawings totalling £2,000 are to be taken from the business

required

Prepare a statement that uses the budgeted profit of £3,000 and other information to calculate the expected cash balance at the end of the four month period.

solution

The statement can be prepared as follows, using the format shown earlier.

	£
Budgeted profit for period	3,000
Add non-cash expenditure used in calculation of profit:	
Depreciation	1,000
Add cash receipts not used in calculation of profit:	
Capital Invested	25,000
Deduct cash payments not used in the calculation of profit:	
Purchase of Equipment	(15,000)
Payment of Drawings	(2,000)
Adjust for changes in inventory:	
Deduct increase in inventory	(7,000)
Adjust for changes in receivables:	
Deduct increase in receivables	(12,000)
Adjust for changes in payables:	
Add increase in payables	5,000
(Decrease) in cash	(2,000)
Cash position at start of period	0
Cash position at end of period (overdrawn)	(2,000)

WORKING CAPITAL AND THE CASH CYCLE

Working capital is the part of the net resources of the business that is made up of current assets minus current liabilities.

You will have learned in your studies that current assets and current liabilities are shown on a statement of financial position. The total working capital shown on a statement of financial position is also known as 'net current assets'.

Working capital involves the circulation of the elements of inventory, receivables, cash, and payables, and the value of these elements will typically change on a daily basis. Contrast this to the way that non-current assets change only occasionally.

The circulation of working capital can be illustrated by the cash cycle:

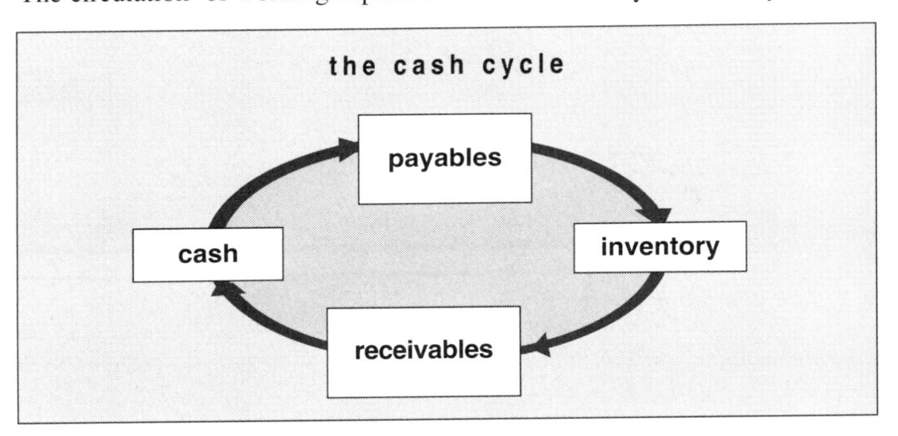

Note that the **cash cycle** is also known as the **cash operating cycle** or the **working capital cycle**.

The diagram above relates to a simple **trading situation**, and illustrates how payables (or suppliers) provide goods for resale on credit in the form of inventory. When the inventory is sold on credit this generates an increase in the amount of receivables. As the receivables pay the amounts owing to the business this increases the cash balance of the business. This means that cash is then available to pay the suppliers.

The same cycle applies to **manufacturing** organisations, except that the inventory that is bought must be turned into finished goods before it can be sold, by using labour and other resources that must also be paid for.

Suppliers will not usually want to wait to receive payment until the cash cycle is complete and the customers have paid their accounts. This means that businesses must plan to have sufficient resources available in working capital – in particular in cash – to pay suppliers on time.

calculating the cash cycle using sample transactions

Generally speaking, the shorter the cash cycle, the fewer resources will be needed, as the business is making better use of its working capital. We can demonstrate this by calculating the length (in time) of the cash cycle.

The cash cycle can be measured as the time from when payment is made for raw materials or inventory until the time that payment is received for goods sold.

Example 1: 5 month cash cycle

A firm receives raw materials at the end of April, and pays for them one month later. The raw materials are processed during May, and the finished goods are held in inventory until the end of August, when they are sold on two months' credit. The customer pays on time.

We can show the cash cycle for this example in the form of a time line as follows:

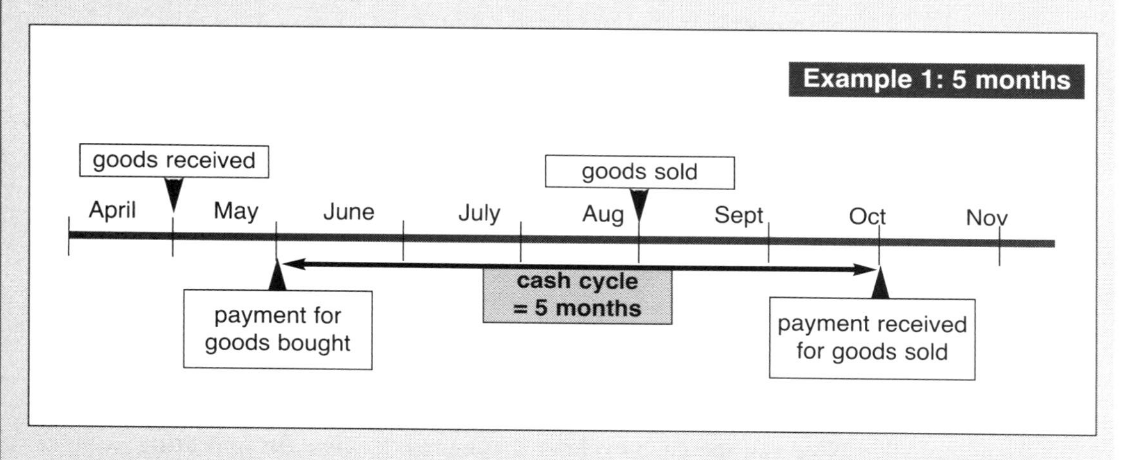

As we can see from the diagram on the previous page, the cash for the raw materials is paid out at the end of May. The money is received from the sale of the finished goods at the end of October. This gives a time for the cash cycle of five months.

Example 2: 2 month cash cycle

Suppose the firm in Example 1 had acted as follows: The raw materials that were received at the end of April were paid for on two months' credit. The finished goods were held in inventory until the end of July when they were sold on one month's credit, and the customer paid on time.

This would give a cash cycle time of two months as demonstrated in the diagram at the top of the next page.

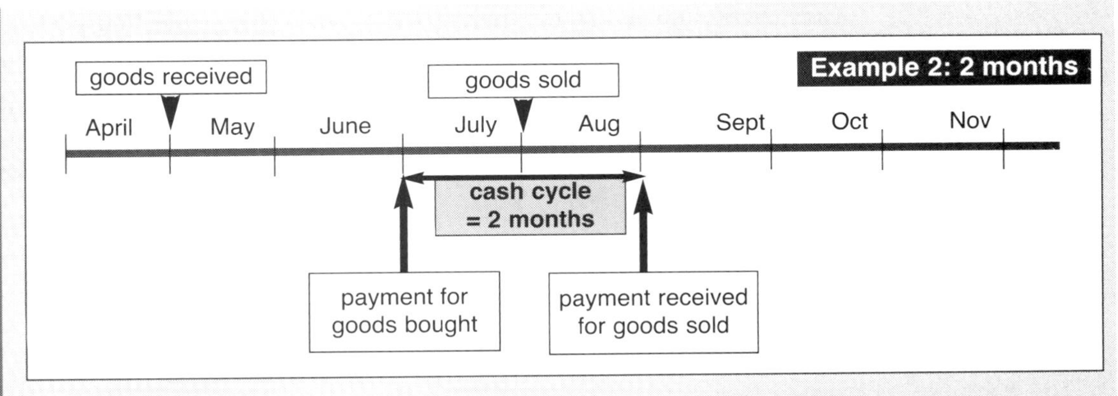

Now compare this two month cycle with the five month cycle seen on the last page:

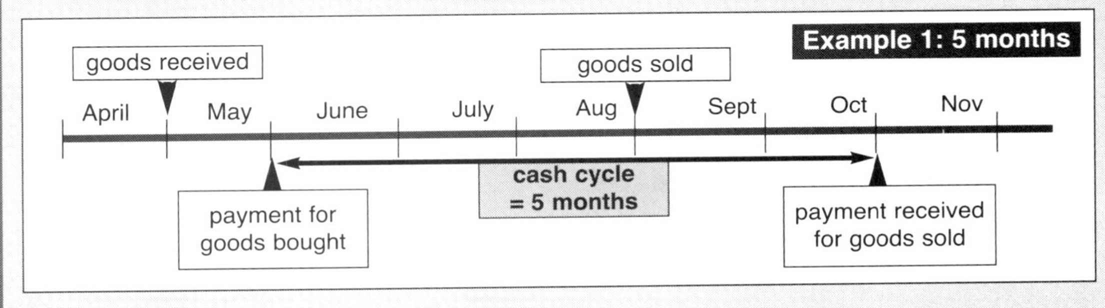

The business in Example 1 (seen above) has to wait five months for the cycle to complete and the money that it has paid out to come back in. In Example 2 the wait is only two months.

The examples above show only sample information about one set of goods. Because firms operate continuously the pattern would be repeating over and over, and this would affect the amount of money that the firm would need to tie up in the cash cycle. The longer the cash cycle the more money is tied up in working capital; the shorter the cash cycle, the less money is tied up.

calculating the cash cycle using average timings

An alternative way of calculating the cash cycle is to use average timings that can be established for inventory, receivables and payables. These will provide us with figures (in days) of:

- the average time that inventory is held (sometimes called 'inventory holding period')
- the average time that customers take to pay amounts due (known as 'receivables collection period'), and
- the average time that is taken to pay suppliers the amounts that are owed ('payables payment period')

Using these time periods, the cash cycle can be calculated as follows:

cash cycle = inventory holding period + receivables collection period – payables payment period

Remember that both inventory and receivables form cash inflows, while payables become a cash outflow. Payables payment period is therefore deducted from the sum of the inventory holding period plus the receivables collection period.

For example, suppose the following information is available:

A business has an average inventory holding period of 105 days, receives payment from its customers in 60 days, and pays its suppliers in 80 days.

This would give a cash cycle of:

105 (inventory) + 60 (receivables) – 80 (payables) = 85 days (cash cycle)

You may have come across the calculations for these performance indicators. They are often based on figures taken from the most recent statement of profit or loss and statement of financial position and are calculated as follows for a trading business:

$$\text{inventory holding period} = \frac{\text{inventory}}{\text{cost of sales}} \times 365$$

$$\text{receivables collection period} = \frac{\text{receivables}}{\text{credit sales}} \times 365$$

$$\text{payables payment period} = \frac{\text{payables}}{\text{credit purchases}} \times 365$$

Sometimes the figure for credit purchases may not be available, and in this situation the following alternative formula can be used:

$$\text{payables payment period} = \frac{\text{payables}}{\text{cost of sales}} \times 365$$

This will provide a reasonable approximation. However, if the figures for both credit purchases and cost of sales are available, then using credit purchases to calculate payables payment period is preferable.

The usefulness of these performance indicators and the cash cycle will be limited if the data used is not typical. For example using data including a seasonal increase in inventory levels would result in a cash cycle that was not representative of normal operations.

We will now use a short Case Study to illustrate the calculation of these performance indicators and the cash cycle.

Case Study

INDICATOR LIMITED: PERFORMANCE INDICATORS AND CASH CYCLE

situation

Indicator Limited (a trading company) has recently produced accounts, and the following are extracts:

Statement of profit or loss (extract)

	£	£
Sales		500,000
less cost of sales:		
Opening inventory	120,000	
Purchases	300,000	
	420,000	
less closing inventory	(80,000)	
		340,000
Gross Profit		160,000

Statement of financial position (extract)

	£	£
Current Assets		
Inventory	80,000	
Receivables	93,000	
Cash	17,000	
		190,000
Current Liabilities		
Payables		55,000

All sales and purchases are made on credit.

required

Calculate the average period in days of inventory, receivables and payables, and use these amounts to calculate the cash cycle. Carry out all calculations to the nearest whole day.

Note: use the closing inventory value to calculate the inventory holding period.

solution

inventory holding period $= \dfrac{\textit{inventory}}{\textit{cost of sales}} \times 365$

$= \dfrac{£80,000}{£340,000} \times 365$

$=$ 86 days

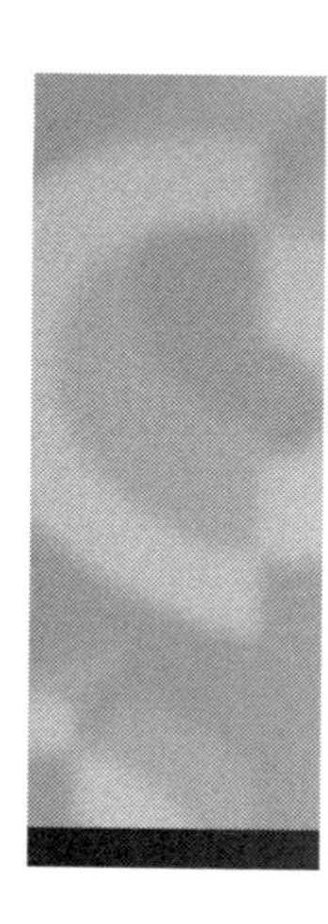

$$\textit{receivables collection period} = \frac{\textit{receivables}}{\textit{credit sales}} \times 365$$

$$= \frac{£93,000}{£500,000} \times 365$$

$$= 68 \text{ days}$$

$$\textit{payables payment period} = \frac{\textit{payables}}{\textit{credit purchases}} \times 365$$

$$= \frac{£55,000}{£300,000} \times 365$$

$$= 67 \text{ days}$$

Cash Cycle = 86 days + 68 days – 67 days = **87 days**

PRINCIPLES OF LIQUIDITY MANAGEMENT

The idea of **liquidity management** is very important, and much of this book is aimed at improving liquidity management in one way or another. Before we go any further it is worth explaining exactly what we mean.

Liquidity management relates to the management of working capital, including cash. It involves managing the level of all the elements of working capital – inventory, receivables, cash, and payables so that there are sufficient liquid resources available to meet the demands of the business. By liquid resources we mean cash or something that can quickly be turned into cash – hence the term 'liquidity management'. So a fundamental part of liquidity management is **having enough cash available to pay accounts when they become due**. These are sometimes called 'foreseeable obligations' and can be planned for. There are also unknown or 'unforeseeable obligations' that may arise without warning, and it would be prudent to make some allowance for the possibility of this occurring.

As we have just seen from our study of cash cycles, the amount of working capital needed will depend on the business and the terms on which it operates. Manufacturing organisations, for example, will need to hold large amounts of inventory, while businesses that sell to foreign customers will often have to give long credit terms and this will increase the amount of receivables. Each business must therefore plan, monitor and control the amount of working capital that it needs. While businesses must have sufficient liquidity to pay their bills, they must also guard against tying up too many resources in liquid assets like cash since this is wasteful. A large amount of unused cash sitting in a bank account is not the best use of resources – it could be put to better use by perhaps investing in equipment to make the business more efficient.

We will now look at two dangers associated with liquidity management.

overtrading

Overtrading occurs when a business attempts to expand its level of trading and then has insufficient working capital and insufficient cash available to support that increased level of trading.

Overtrading can occur when a business expands rapidly, because increased sales requires increased inventory and creates increased receivables. The increased value of payables does not wholly compensate for this and the amount of cash therefore gets squeezed. We will use a simple example:

worked example

Suppose a business is running smoothly, with working capital of £90,000 made up as follows:

	£
Inventory	50,000
Receivables	70,000
Cash	20,000
Less payables	(50,000)
Working Capital	90,000

If the sales level were to increase by, say, 50% that would probably cause inventory, receivables and payables to all also increase by 50%. If there are no further resources available for working capital then the total working capital would still be £90,000, and the results would be as follows:

	£
Inventory	75,000
Receivables	105,000
Cash	(15,000)
Less payables	(75,000)
Working Capital	90,000

Notice that the cash figure has moved from £20,000 positive to £15,000 overdrawn.

If the business had no overdraft facility it may try to survive by delaying payment to those it owed money and increasing the payables amount. This would cause problems with suppliers and would probably be unsustainable.

Overtrading can occur even if the business is profitable, and can result in the business having to cease trading.

Warning signs of overtrading include:

- rapidly increasing sales levels without increased resources
- falling profit margins
- inability to collect receivables promptly
- increases in irrecoverable debts
- deterioration of cash balances or increase of overdrafts
- attempts to delay payments to suppliers

Overtrading can be remedied by:

- reducing sales levels to a manageable level and / or
- increasing resources through increased capital

overcapitalisation

Overcapitalisation is the opposite of overtrading. It involves having more resources tied up in working capital than is needed.

It may be that high cash balances are being held without good reason, or perhaps high levels of inventory are kept and receivables are large since there is no pressure to manage them efficiently as there is no shortage of cash.

Although the results of overcapitalisation are not usually as dangerous as overtrading, the effect is to reduce profitability. This is because resources that could be used to generate profits (even if only by investing the money in a deposit account) are being used where they are not needed. The business may even have borrowed the money that is now tied up unnecessarily in working capital, and having to pay interest on it.

Warning signs of overcapitalisation include:

- high levels of inventory, receivables and cash
- payments being made to suppliers before they are due

Overcapitalisation can be remedied by:

- improved management of working capital
- using spare resources for profitable investments
- repayment of any unnecessary loans

further performance indicators

You will have probably come across the following performance indicators that are useful for managing liquidity.

- **Current ratio** $\dfrac{\text{current assets}}{\text{current liabilities}}$

This provides a simple assessment of liquidity; the higher the figure the more easily the organisation will be able to meet its short-term obligations.

- **Quick ratio (or acid test ratio)** $\dfrac{(\text{current assets} - \text{inventory})}{\text{current liabilities}}$

This excludes inventory from the calculation since it is not as liquid as other current assets, and the result is a ratio that forms a more critical measure of liquidity.

- **Return on capital employed** $\dfrac{\text{operating profit}}{\text{(non-current assets + net current assets)}}$

Although this does not measure liquidity specifically, profitability and liquidity are linked as illustrated earlier in the chapter.

- **Return on shareholders' funds** $\dfrac{\text{profit after tax or net profit}}{\text{total equity}} \times 100\%$

This is a measure of the profit attributable to shareholders.

- **Operating profit percentage** $\dfrac{\text{profit from operations}}{\text{revenue}} \times 100\%$

This shows the percentage of sales revenue that equals operating profit.

DIFFERENT TYPES OF ORGANISATION

In the following section we are going to examine the sources of cash receipts in an organisation and the uses to which that cash may be put. Throughout this section, and the rest of the book we will be referring to three main types of organisation. The types of organisation that we are going to base our work on are:

- **sole traders** – where an individual owns and runs a business himself or herself. The person will have invested their own money into the business, but they may borrow money from outside the business as well. They may work entirely on their own, or they may employ staff to help them, but these employees would not own any share in the business.
- **partnerships** – where two or more individuals own and run a business together. They will have invested their own money in the business and will share the rewards if the business is a success. The business may borrow money from those who are not partners and may also employ staff.
- **limited companies** – where a separate legal entity is set up with directors to run it. The capital comes from 'shares' that are purchased by shareholders who are the owners of the business that they have invested in. Limited companies are often larger organisations than sole traders and partnerships.

For studying this unit you do not need an extensive knowledge of these different organisations, since most of the cash receipts and payments are common to all types of business. A few sources and uses of cash are specific to certain organisations, and these will be highlighted when we come across them. All organisations will use a similar format for the cash flow statements that we will introduce to you later on in this chapter.

SOURCES OF CASH – CASH RECEIPTS

There are three main types of cash receipt:

- **regular revenue receipts**

  These arise from the operating activities of a business – the selling of the goods or services that the business provides.

- **capital receipts**

  These relate to the proceeds of the sale of non-current (fixed) assets – both tangible items like buildings or plant, and intangible assets such as investments.

- **exceptional receipts**

  These include 'exceptional' items such as the receipt of loans from the bank, or the proceeds of the sale of a major part of the business.

We will describe each of these three types in turn.

regular revenue receipts

For a trading organisation these amounts will be mainly the proceeds of the sales that the business has made. Other organisations may have revenue receipts in the form of government funding (for example in the National Health Service) or regular donations (for example charities). In this book we will concentrate on commercial organisations. The sales that these businesses make will be either:

- **cash sales** – money received immediately as the sale is made, or
- **credit sales** – where the customer is allowed time to pay

When we go on to draw up cash budgets we must be careful to distinguish between these receipts, and to calculate correctly the time at which the cash will be received.

capital receipts

Businesses dispose of non-current assets from time to time, and these transactions generate cash receipts that need to be accounted for. The disposal of these assets may have been planned to link with the acquisition of replacement assets.

exceptional receipts

Businesses need an initial investment when they start up, to provide them with the resources that they need to operate. They may also need further investment later on, particularly if they wish to expand their activities. Investment either comes from the owner(s) of the business, or through loans. For a sole trader or partnership business, capital is introduced by the owners of the business, and a limited company raises equity finance by the issue of shares to the original owners and to new investors. Businesses may also borrow money from banks, other institutions and possibly from individuals. Occasionally businesses may sell off whole sections of their operations, which will bring in cash.

All these transactions will generate major cash receipts, and will usually be planned well in advance.

USES OF CASH – CASH PAYMENTS

An organisation has to pay at some time for all the goods and services that it buys, as well as paying tax and rewarding the owners and those who have lent money. Cash payments can be categorised into:

- **regular revenue payments**
  Paying for the operational needs of the organisation, the goods and services that are regularly used
- **capital payments**
  Paying for the acquisition of non-current assets.
- **payments of drawings**
  These are drawings (for a sole trader or partnership), and dividends to the shareholders of a limited company. They may be regular or irregular.
- **payment of disbursements**
  These include payment of various taxes. Many are regular, but some can be irregular.
- **exceptional payments**
  These include major investments, such as the acquisition of a new business. Also included would be the repayment of substantial financing.

We will describe each of these five types of payment in turn.

regular revenue payments

The regular, operational revenue payments that a commercial organisation needs to make can be broadly divided into the following categories.

- **payments for goods for resale and raw materials**
  A **trading organisation** will need to purchase the goods that it wishes to sell. The amount and timing of these purchases will take account of the forecast sales, as well as the required level of inventories. Since the supplier may well offer to sell on credit, the timing of the payments will need to be calculated carefully. In the case of a **manufacturer** of goods for resale the planned production schedule will need to be taken account of so that the raw materials will be bought at the right time.

- **payments for labour costs**

  Apart from the smallest sole traders or partnerships, all organisations employ staff to carry out the operations of the business. This can include staff involved in the indirect (overhead) functions of the business as well as the direct labour force. Staff are usually paid in the same period that the work is carried out, but the complexities of income tax and national insurance may also need to be considered, and any overtime, bonuses or pay rises accurately accounted for.

- **payments for expenses**

  These are the other operational costs that are needed to keep the organisation functioning. Examples include rent, rates and insurance, communication costs, stationery, and all the other items that are essential for the smooth running of a business (or not-for-profit organisation). One item of expenditure that is not translated into a cash payment is the depreciation charge (loss in value) for non-current assets. Since this is only a 'book-entry' used to help establish profit, and is not actually paid out, it does not form a cash flow.

- **interest payments to lenders**

  When an organisation has borrowed money from an institution (or an individual) an agreement will have been reached as to the amount and timing of interest payments. For a repayment loan, the regular repayments of parts of the amount borrowed will usually be made at the same time as the interest payments. Payments will typically range from monthly to annually and will need to be planned and implemented accurately. Interest is different from ordinary share dividends in that an organisation will be committed to making interest payments in full and on time, no matter how poor its profitability.

capital payments

Capital payments may need to be made from time to time in respect of the acquisition of non-current assets. These may be made immediately the item is bought, or may be spread over a period of time, for example through a hire purchase or leasing arrangement. The non-current asset acquisition will have been planned through the capital budget to ensure that it is made at the optimum time for the business.

payments of drawings

Providers of capital for a business will usually expect their reward to be made in the form of a payment. The following are the main types of payment:

- **drawings by sole traders or partners**

  These are regular or irregular amounts taken out of the business in anticipation of profits earned. There is often no formal arrangement as to the frequency or amounts drawn, and the owners of the business may need to judge what are suitable amounts based on both their personal needs and those of the business.

- **dividends paid to shareholders of a limited company**

  These payments form the main reward for investing in the shares (along with the prospect of future growth in share value). For 'ordinary' shares, an interim dividend is often paid part way through the financial year, with a final dividend paid after the end of the year, when the profit figures have been finalised. Such payments are often made at the same times each year, although they can vary in amount, or may not be made at all if that is in the interests of the company. If the company has issued 'preference shares' then the owners of these shares will be entitled to regular dividends of amounts that are established from the outset.

payment of disbursements

Disbursements include tax payments – Value Added Tax for registered businesses, and Corporation Tax for limited companies, as well as PAYE payments to HM Revenue & Customs. Note that the income tax liability of sole traders and partnerships is the responsibility of the individual owners, and is not a business expense. It will be paid out of their drawings.

exceptional payments

These by definition will only arise occasionally, and could include the following:

- **payments for the acquisition of a new business**

  Businesses sometimes expand by acquiring other businesses and a payment for an acquisition would be considered an exceptional payment. Buying a business that is already operating can be an effective way of achieving rapid growth. The acquired business may be a limited company (in which case the shares would be acquired) or a sole trader or partnership, which would involve coming to a financial arrangement with the owner(s). Alternatively it could involve acquiring just a part of the business.

- **payments in respect of financing**

  Where a loan that was previously taken out is to be repaid in a lump sum, this is an exceptional payment. The timing will have to be carefully planned so that there are sufficient funds available to make the payment. The same sort of situation could arise if capital is repaid to the owners of a business.

sources and uses of cash – a summary

The diagram below summarises some of the main sources and uses of cash discussed in the last few pages. A Case Study follows on page 21.

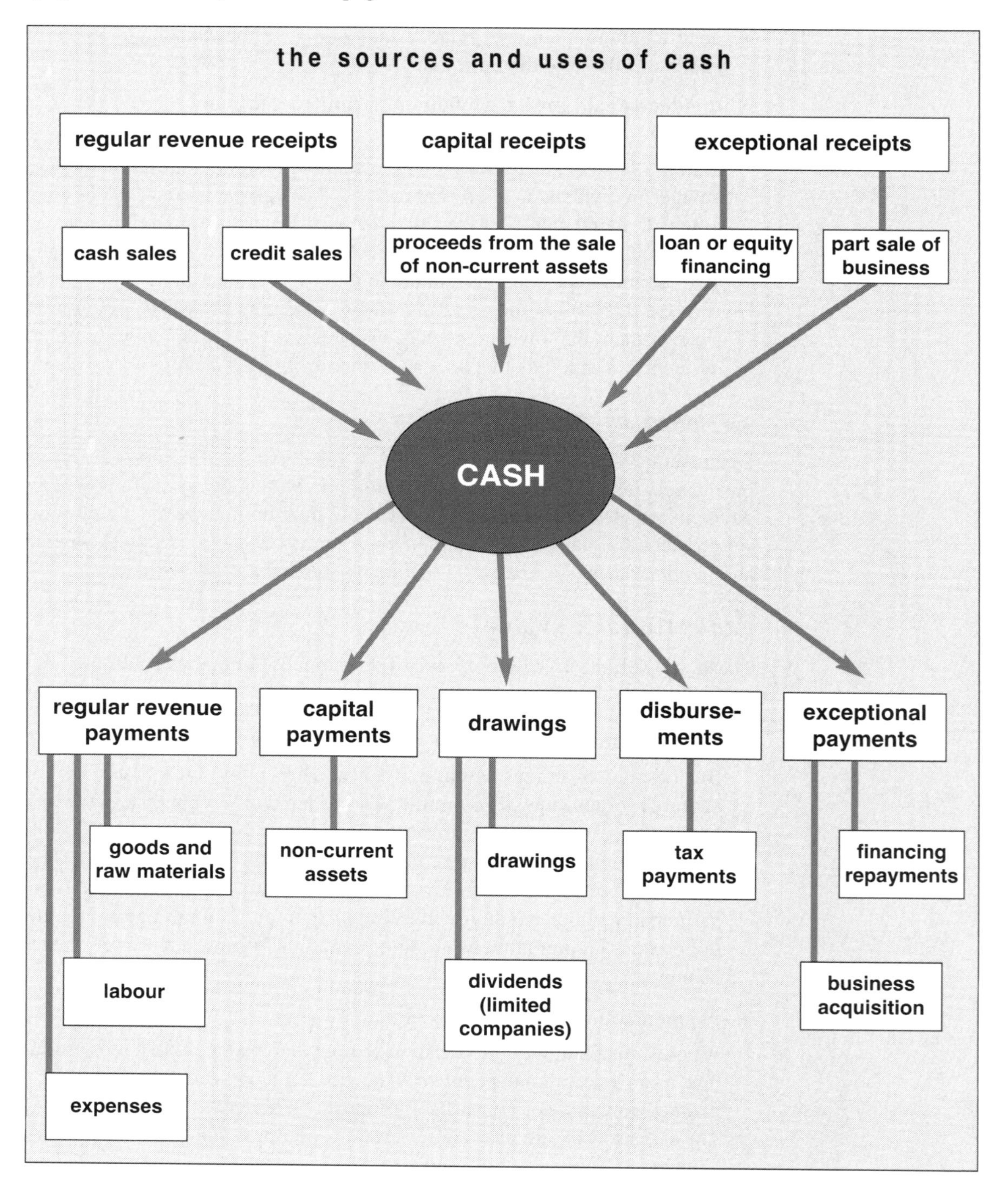

Case Study

BEE LIMITED: LIKELY PATTERNS OF CASH FLOW

situation

You are employed as an assistant accountant with Bee Limited, a company that trades online in artists' materials. As a first step towards examining future cash flow, you have been asked to analyse a list of types of cash receipts and payments that has been prepared for you. The analysis is to be carried out by completing two tables, shown below, which are to show the category that each item on the list falls into, and the likely timing of cash flows that arise from it.

Bee Limited – list of types of receipts and payments

1 Receipts from customers' credit card transactions
2 Payment of Corporation Tax
3 Payment of final dividend to shareholders
4 Payment for purchase of warehouse shelving
5 Receipt of bank loan
6 Payment for purchase of goods for resale
7 Receipt from sale of old office computer
8 Payment of staff salaries
9 Payment to buy shares to take over Cee Limited
10 Repayments of bank loan

required

Complete the following tables by ticking the appropriate columns.

Table 1

Number from list	Regular revenue receipts	Capital receipts	Exceptional receipts	Regular revenue payments	Capital payments	Payments of drawings	Exceptional payments
1							
2							
3							
4							
5							
6							
7							
8							
9							
10							

Table 2

Number from list	Likely frequency of receipts or payments		
	Regular monthly	Regular quarterly or annually	Irregular or one-off
1			
2			
3			
4			
5			
6			
7			
8			
9			
10			

solution

Table 1

Number from list	Regular revenue receipts	Capital receipts	Exceptional receipts	Regular revenue payments	Capital payments	Payments of drawings	Exceptional payments
1	✔						
2				✔			
3						✔	
4					✔		
5			✔				
6				✔			
7		✔					
8				✔			
9							✔
10				✔			

Table 2

Number from list	Likely frequency of receipts or payments		
	Regular monthly	Regular quarterly or annually	Irregular or one-off
1	✔		
2		✔	
3		✔	
4			✔
5			✔
6	✔		
7			✔
8	✔		
9			✔
10	✔		

Note that these are likely frequencies, but other frequencies are possible.

PEOPLE AND DEPARTMENTS TO CONSULT ABOUT CASH FLOWS

In a typical business there are a variety of people who may need to be consulted when planning, monitoring or controlling cash flows. Using the categories of receipts and payments shown in the diagram on page 20, we will now discuss briefly the personnel that are most likely to hold information or otherwise need to interact with those who are managing cash.

Since all organisations are different, the following can only be of a very general nature. Remember that the accounting systems of an organisation are affected by its organisational structure, its administrative systems and procedures and the nature of its business transactions. For example each organisation will have its own structure with the positions having roles and responsibilities that are geared to the organisation's needs. Further information on how the organisational structure works in a specific organisation will be contained in the policies and procedures documentation and in the individuals' job descriptions.

In the following organisation chart and the discussion on data sources we have used a limited company as an example organisation. Only limited companies will employ directors, but there may be people with similar roles in sole trader organisations or partnerships. In a small organisation several roles may be carried out by one person – a sole trader may even carry out all the roles himself or herself.

We will now outline a possible organisational structure for a manufacturing business, based on the chart shown below.

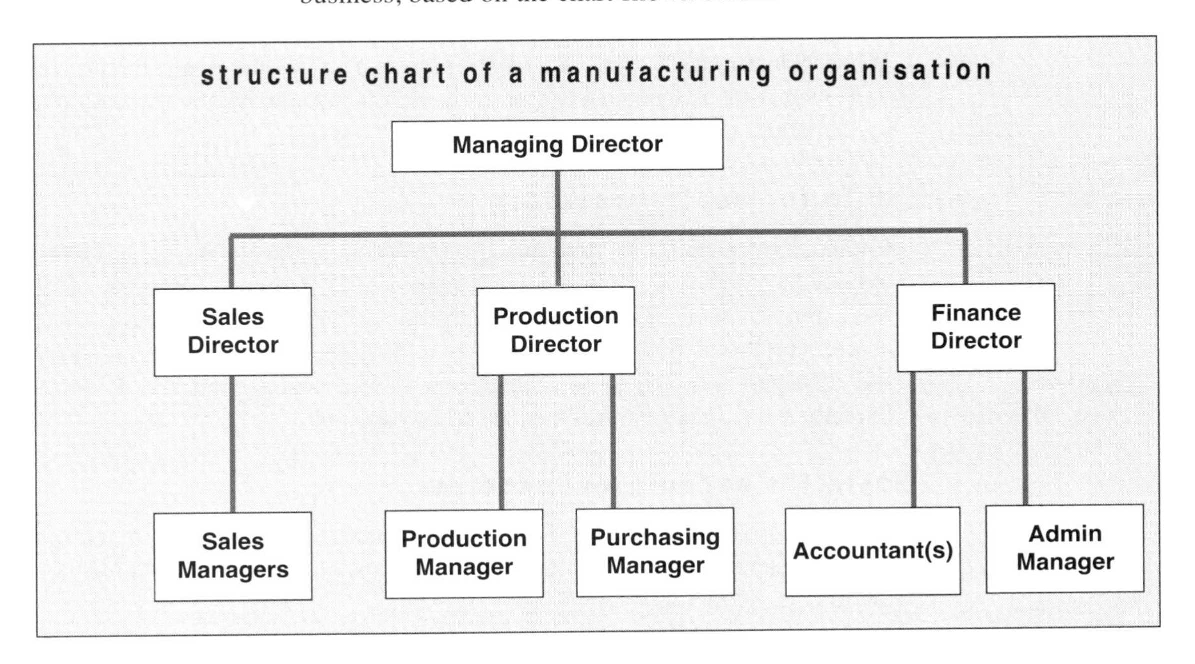

The directors and managers would be responsible for agreeing the organisation's budgets, possibly through a formal budget committee. The main budgets would typically include:

- sales budget
- production budget
- materials budget
- labour budget
- functional budget
- capital budget
- master budget (budgeted statement of profit or loss and statement of financial position)
- cash budget

In the next chapters we will see in detail how the data from the other budgets is used in the cash budget. At this stage we will just refer to how the individuals responsible for the budgets can help with providing data on expected cash flows. Throughout the following discussion, the individuals referred to may delegate some of their responsibilities to their subordinates.

data for regular revenue receipts

Data for sales receipts – both cash and credit – will come from the sales budget. The sales budget is prepared by the Sales Director (in consultation with the Finance Director). Cash sales will generate instant cash, but sales made on credit will also require information about typical credit periods. This information may be obtained from the Finance Director or his/her team. When planning cash flows it will be important to use reliable estimates of how long it takes customers to pay – which is not always the same as the agreed credit terms!

data for capital receipts

Capital receipts will only take place on an irregular basis, but the amounts may be large. The sale of non-current assets will usually be planned through the capital budget, in conjunction with the acquisition of new non-current assets. The Production Director is likely to have the required information on the disposal of production related non-current assets, and the Finance Director will usually control the sale of investments.

data for exceptional receipts

When exceptional items like the raising of finance need to be accounted for (through capital injection or loans), this will usually have been planned by the Finance Director.

data for regular revenue payments

The purchase of goods and raw materials is normally carried out by the Purchasing Manager. The materials budgets (both for usage and purchase of materials) will have been developed in conjunction with the production budget. The Purchasing Manager and the Production Manager will have worked together to ensure that the right items are acquired at the right time. The Purchasing Manager or the Accountant will have information on credit typically taken by customers.

The payment of labour costs related to manufacture will be laid out in the labour budget, and is controlled by the Production Manager. The Administration Manager (or Accountant) may deal with other salaries and wages that are agreed in the relevant functional budgets, along with expense payments.

data for capital payments

The acquisition of non-current assets will have been authorised in the capital budget, following proposals by the Production Director or Finance Director. The terms of payment will usually be set out in the budget following recommendations by the Finance Director's team.

data for drawings

In a limited company the Finance Director will usually have information on dividends. For a sole trader or partnership the owner(s) will decide on drawings.

data for disbursements

Taxation payments will be organised by the Finance Director or the Accountant.

data for exceptional payments

The acquisition of new businesses will be agreed by the Managing Director with the other Directors. The detail of the payments may well have been delegated to the Finance Director's team, who will plan and organise the relevant amounts. Any repayments of capital to shareholders or lenders will also have been planned at a high level in the organisation, and the Finance Director will have agreed the arrangements.

using data for developing cash flows

Later in the book we will examine the practical methods for converting data that has been developed for another use into a form suitable for cash flow documents. In particular we will see how to convert data that is based on accruals accounting into a cash form.

CASH BUDGET – RECEIPTS AND PAYMENTS FORMAT

The receipts and payments format of the **cash budget** can be used to monitor and control cash flows through each month (or week) of the budget period. It shows the predicted movement of the organisation's cash (typically the business bank account) by showing:

A the source and amounts of expected receipts – with an overall total 'Total Receipts'

B the amounts of anticipated payment for each type of cash outflow – with an overall total 'Total Payments'

C 'Cashflow for Month' (calculated as A – B)

D the opening bank balance ('brought forward') for each month (or week, etc)

E the closing bank balance ('carried forward') for each month, (C + D)

Note that the closing bank balance for one month is the same as the opening bank balance for the next month.

Negative figures are shown in brackets.

This format, with figures for four months, is illustrated below.

		January £	February £	March £	April £
A	**Receipts**				
	Sales	8,500	7,500	5,000	9,000
	Bank loan		20,000		
	Total Receipts	8,500	27,500	5,000	9,000
B	**Payments**				
	Purchases	3,000	2,800	3,960	3,000
	Wages	1,320	1,260	1,320	1,440
	Office expenses	1,800	1,800	1,800	1,800
	Insurance	1,200	–	–	–
	Non-current assets	–	24,000	–	–
	Total Payments	7,320	29,860	7,080	6,240
C	**Cash Flow for Month**	1,180	(2,360)	(2,080)	2,760
D	Bank balance b/f	10,000	11,180	8,820	6,740
E	Bank balance c/f	11,180	8,820	6,740	9,500

notes on the format

As you can see, the basic format can easily be tailored to the individual requirements of an organisation by inserting additional lines to deal with specific receipts and/or payments. Because each category of receipt and payment is shown separately, it can be used to monitor these specific items.

This format is an ideal application for a computer spreadsheet because formulas can be used to carry out the calculations and the results of any changes can be viewed instantly.

The strengths and weaknesses of this format can be summarised as follows:

strengths

- it gives a detailed picture of the inflows and outflows of cash within each month (or week, etc) within the budget period
- it shows monthly cash balances, and therefore allows peaks and troughs of cash within the period to be anticipated and managed
- it can be used to monitor actual cash movements as they occur, and to produce easy to understand variances
- it is ideally suited to the use of a spreadsheet model.

weaknesses

- it requires accurate information relating to the timing of each category of receipt and payment
- it is more time-consuming to construct than a cash flow summary statement (a reconciliation of profit with cash)

In the three chapters that follow we will examine in detail how this receipts and payments format can be used in practice, incorporating the complications that you are likely to come across.

Chapter Summary

- Cash is a simpler concept to grasp than profit. Whereas profit is measured by the difference between income and expenditure (which relate to accruals accounting), cash flows are simply based on receipts and payments of cash or bank transactions.

- A profit figure can be adjusted to arrive at a cash flow for the same period by using various data items in a logical manner.

- The amount of working capital that an organisation needs depends upon the length of the cash cycle. This is a measure of how much time elapses between the time that cash is paid for goods (or materials) and the time that cash from sales of the goods is received.

- Cash receipts in a business arise from regular revenue receipts (typically cash or credit sales), capital receipts from the sale of non-current assets, other disbursements and exceptional receipts from sources like financing.

- Cash is used to pay for regular revenue commitments such as materials, labour and expenses, as well as the acquisition of non-current assets and the occasional exceptional items.

- Various people in the business will hold information about cash receipts and payments, and they should be consulted regularly to utilise their expertise. These individuals will usually have helped to create the budgets that form the sources of the data used in the cash budget. While most organisations will be structured in similar ways and employ people in similar roles, it should always be remembered that structures and roles will have been tailored to the needs of the organisation, and this will have an impact on the choice of person who would need to be approached about a specific issue.

- The receipts and payments format of the cash budget can be complicated to produce, but it is an efficient tool for the purpose of monitoring and controlling the cash position of a business.

Key Terms

accruals accounting	the traditional system of accounting in which income is compared with expenditure to arrive at the profit over a period of time
cash accounting	the system of accounting for receipts and payments in cash or through bank accounts – effectively a part of a normal accounting system
working capital	the current assets minus the current liabilities of an organisation – also known as net current assets
cash cycle	the circulation of value through working capital as cash is paid out, and eventually received back again – the length of the cash cycle can be measured in days
liquidity	the ability of an organisation to pay its liabilities as they become due – it involves keeping sufficient current assets in money or in a form that will quickly convert to money
receipt	the inflow of money in cash (or into the bank account)
payment	the outflow of money in cash (or from the bank account)
revenue receipts/payments	receipts or payments of money that relate to the ongoing operations of the business, and not to items that have a long term economic benefit such as non-current assets
capital receipts/payments	receipts or payments of money that relate to the acquisition or sale of non-current assets in a business
exceptional receipts/ payments	receipts or payments of money that do not occur regularly or frequently
cash budget format	a cash flow format that shows opening balances, receipts, payments, and closing balances for each month (or week, etc.) within the budget period – the most suitable format for monitoring and controlling cash flows

Activities

1.1 The following planned information is provided regarding the next year for MF Supplies Limited.

Budgeted statement of profit or loss for year ended 31 December 20-5		
	£	£
Sales revenue		350,000
Less: cost of sales:		
Opening inventory	33,500	
Purchases	225,000	
Closing inventory	(35,000)	
		223,500
Gross profit		126,500
Expenses		42,500
Operating profit		84,000

- Trade receivables are budgeted at £65,000 at the start of 20-5 and £72,300 at the end of 20-5.
- Trade payables are budgeted to rise from £51,800 at the start of 20-5 to £54,000 at the end of 20-5.
- Non-current assets are planned to be purchased during 20-5 costing £33,000 and paid for immediately.
- Depreciation included in 'expenses' is £13,700.
- Corporation tax of £10,000 needs to be paid during 20-5.
- The budgeted cash position at 1 January 20-5 is £29,000 overdrawn.

Required:

Complete the following table to arrive at the expected cash balance at 31 December 20-5.

Use + or – signs as appropriate.

	£
Operating profit	84,000
Change in inventory	
Change in trade receivables	
Change in trade payables	
Adjustment for non-cash items	
Purchase of non-current assets	
Payment of Corporation Tax	
Net change in cash position	
Budgeted cash position 1 Jan 20-5	–29,000
Budgeted cash position 31 Dec 20-5	

1.2 The cash cycle illustrates the direction that cash flows in a business. Which of the following statements correctly shows the order of the components of the cash cycle?

(a) Receivables; Inventory; Cash; Payables; Receivables	
(b) Inventory; Payables; Receivables; Cash; Inventory	
(c) Cash; Receivables; Payables; Inventory; Cash	
(d) Inventory; Receivables; Cash; Payables; Inventory	

1.3 A firm receives raw materials at the end of January on one month's credit, and pays for them on time. The raw materials are processed during February, and the finished goods are held in inventory until the end of May, when they are sold on two months' credit. The customer pays on time.

Required:

(a) Draw a line diagram and calculate the cash cycle in months.

(b) Calculate the cash cycle in months if the firm bought on two months' credit but sold on one month's credit.

1.4 Complete the sentences shown below by filling the gaps with the correct words taken from the following:

reducing **too much** **insufficient** **longer** **shorter** **rapidly increasing**

Overtrading can occur when a business has [ ] working capital.

Overcapitalisation can occur when a business has [ ] working capital.

Signs of overtrading include [ ] sales volumes, [ ] profit margins, and [ ] creditor payment periods.

1.5 Kool Limited, a trading company, is comparing the working capital from the budgeted statement of financial position with the actual figures.

	Budget	**Actual**
	£	£
Current Assets:		
Inventories	20,000	50,000
Receivables	40,000	80,000
Bank	50,000	0
	110,000	130,000
Less Current Liabilities:		
Payables	30,000	50,000
	80,000	80,000

The following information has been obtained about the actual performance:

- The credit controller has been off sick, so no one has been chasing customers for the past few weeks. This has doubled the receivables.
- An order of £20,000 worth of purchases was delivered before the above statement of financial position date instead of afterwards as requested.
- An additional £10,000 worth of purchases was bought and paid for earlier in the year when a supplier offered a special price. The goods have not yet been sold.

Required:

Explain how each of the above pieces of information help to account for the differences between the budgeted parts of working capital and the actual figures.

1.6 A trainee in the accountancy department has made the following statements about cash management:

1. Accounting for profit involves comparing receipts with payments, whereas accounting for cash involves comparing income and expenditure.
2. If the cash cycle of one business is longer than that of another business that is similar in other respects, then the first business will generally need more working capital.
3. If goods are kept in inventory for a long time, and receivables are slow to pay there will be less cash available for other purposes.
4. Exceptional receipts should always be ignored when creating a cash budget.
5. A variety of people in the organisation should be consulted when creating a cash budget. The person to contact regarding a specific issue may vary according to the structure of the particular organisation.

Required:

Identify the statements above that are true.

1.7 Performance Limited (a trading company) has recently produced accounts, and the following are extracts:

Statement of profit or loss (extract)

	£	£
Sales		800,000
less cost of sales:		
opening inventory	140,000	
purchases	500,000	
	640,000	
less closing inventory	(160,000)	
		480,000
Gross Profit		320,000

Statement of financial position (extract)

	£	£
Current Assets:		
Inventory	160,000	
Receivables	230,000	
Cash	25,000	
		415,000
Current Liabilities:		
Payables	145,000	

All sales are made on credit.

Required:

(a) Calculate the total working capital.

(b) Calculate the average period in days of inventory, receivables and payables, and use these amounts to calculate the cash cycle. Carry out all these calculations to the nearest whole day.

1.8 Cash receipts and payments take many different forms but they can be broadly categorised into regular, capital, exceptional and drawings.

Complete the table below by selecting and inserting the number of the correct description from the list of options below to match the type of cash receipt or cash payment.

Type of receipt or payment	**Description**
Capital payments	
Regular revenue receipts	
Drawings	
Exceptional payments	

Options:

1 Payments that relate to the proceeds from the disposal of non-current assets.

2 Payments that relate to the acquisition of non-current assets.

3 Payments made to the owners of the business.

4 Payments received from the owners of the business.

5 Income received from HM Revenue & Customs.

6 Income received from the operating activities of the business that are expected to occur frequently.

7 Income received from the operating activities of the business that are not expected to occur frequently.

8. Payments arising from the operating activities of the business that are expected to occur frequently.
9. Payments arising from the operating activities of the business that are not expected to occur frequently.
10. Payments that do not arise from the operating activities of the business but that are expected to occur frequently.
11. Payments that do not arise from the operating activities of the business and that are not expected to occur frequently.

2 Forecasting data for cash budgets

this chapter covers...

In this chapter we will explain various methods of forecasting data that can then go on to be used in a cash budget.

We will start with a review of the terms 'mark-up' and 'margin' since calculations involving these can be used to help forecast data (for example selling prices).

A large part of the chapter is then taken up with a thorough examination of time series – the use of data that relates to points in time. This includes using moving averages to determine trends as well as incorporating additive or multiplicative seasonal variations into forecasts.

We then move on to incorporating allowances for inflation into cash budgets, including the creation and use of index numbers.

The next section involves the manipulation of formulae to forecast data that moves consistently in one direction. This is part of the topic of linear regression.

The chapter concludes with a brief section on the practical problems of using the various techniques to estimate future data reliably.

FORECASTING TECHNIQUES – INTRODUCTION

Forecasting is often carried out at the start of the budgeting cycle. Forecasting is concerned with using data (from internal or external sources) to estimate what will happen in the future. Budgeting (including cash budgeting) involves committing to plans of how the business will be managed in the future. The budgets will take into account information from various forecasts.

We need to be able to use a range of techniques to forecast both income and expenditure, and use these forecasts to determine future cash receipts and payments.

We will start by looking at the use of mark-up and margin to help forecast sales or purchase values. Later on we will examine other techniques.

MARK-UP AND MARGIN

You are probably familiar with the use of mark-up and margin from your other studies, but we will recap the main points and ensure that you could answer any tasks on this topic that could occur in this unit.

Both mark-up and margin are ways of expressing profit (forecast or actual).

- Mark-up expresses the profit as a percentage of the cost
- Margin expresses the profit as a percentage of the sales value

Usually the profit being referred to is the gross profit (the difference between the values of 'sales' and 'cost of sales'. It can apply to a trading situation (the difference between buying price and selling price), or to a manufacturing situation where manufacturing cost is used instead of buying price.

The following diagram shows how both terms are expressed using the same sample data of an item that has a cost of £200 and a selling price of £250.

Mark-up		**Margin**
Cost is treated as 100%		Selling price is treated as 100%
Mark-up is 25%	Profit £50	Margin is 20%
Cost is treated as 100%	Cost £200	Cost is treated as 80% of selling price
Mark-up profit is calculated as a % of cost		Margin profit is calculated as a % of selling price
Mark-up is £50 / £200 %		Margin is £50 / £250 %
= 25%		**= 20%**

Example 1

Suppose a business requires a margin of 22% on all sales.

If items are manufactured by the business for £60 each this would represent (100 – 22 = 78)% of the selling price.

The selling price would be £60 x 100/78 = £76.92 (to nearest penny)

The profit would be £60 x 22/78 = £16.92

The mark-up would be £16.92 / £60 x 100 = £28.20% (to 2 decimal places).

Example 2

Suppose a trading business requires a mark-up of 30% on all purchases.

If items are to be sold for £90 each, the cost must represent 100 / 130 of this amount.

Cost would be 100 / 130 x £90 = £69.23 (to nearest penny)

Profit would be 30 / 130 x £90 = £20.77

The margin would be £20.77 / £90 x 100 = 23.08% (to 2 decimal places).

TIME SERIES ANALYSIS

Time series analysis is concerned with numerical ways that the past can be used to forecast the future. The term **trend analysis** is also used to describe the technique that we will now examine. It is useful as a tool to help us to forecast future sales units, but it can also be used in other circumstances, as we will see later on in this section.

At its simplest, the idea is based on the assumption that data will continue to move in the same direction in the future as it has in the past.

For example, suppose the following are the number of pairs of shoes that were sold by a shoe manufacturer, Comfy Feet, over the last few months:

Month 1	10,000
Month 2	11,000
Month 3	12,000
Month 4	13,000
Month 5	14,000
Month 6	15,000
Month 7	16,000

It does not require a great deal of arithmetic to calculate that if the trend continues to increase at a rate of 1,000 pairs a month, then shoe sales could be forecast at 17,000 pairs in Month 8 and 18,000 pairs in Month 9. Of course this is a very simple example, and life is rarely this straightforward.

Before we move on, we will examine the techniques available to forecast simple data. They will become very useful later.

when each monthly change is identical . . .

You saw that in the case of Comfy Feet shoes that in each month the sales were 1,000 pairs of shoes more than the previous month. Using the last known figure of 16,000 pairs of shoes in Month 7, we can then add 1,000 to arrive at a forecast of 17,000 pairs in Month 8, and so on.

calculating the average monthly change . . .

A slightly more complicated technique could have been used to arrive at the same answer. If we compare the number of sales in Month 7 with the number in Month 1, we can see that it has risen by 6,000 pairs. By dividing that figure by the number of times the month changed in our data we can arrive at an average change per month. The number of times that the month changes is 6, which is the same as the number of 'spaces' between the months, or the total number of months minus 1. Shown as an equation this becomes:

$$\textit{Average Monthly Sales Change} = \frac{\textit{(Sales in Final Month – Sales in First Month)}}{\textit{(Number of Months – 1)}}$$

$$= \frac{(16{,}000 - 10{,}000)}{(7 - 1)}$$

$$= +\ 1{,}000$$ . . . which is what we would expect.

The + 1,000 would then be added to the sales data in Month 7 of 16,000 (the last actual data) to arrive at a forecast of 17,000 for Month 8.

This technique is useful when all the increases are not identical, but we want to work out an average increase in order to forecast the trend.

constructing a graph

The same result can be produced graphically. Using the same shoe shop example we can extend the graph in a straight line based on the actual data to provide a forecast line.

The graph below shows an extra two months (8 and 9) added and the straight line extended to forecast sales of 17,000 and 18,000, which is again what you would expect.

If in another situation the actual data does not produce exactly equal increases, the graph will produce the same answer as the average annual change, provided that the straight line runs through the first and last data points.

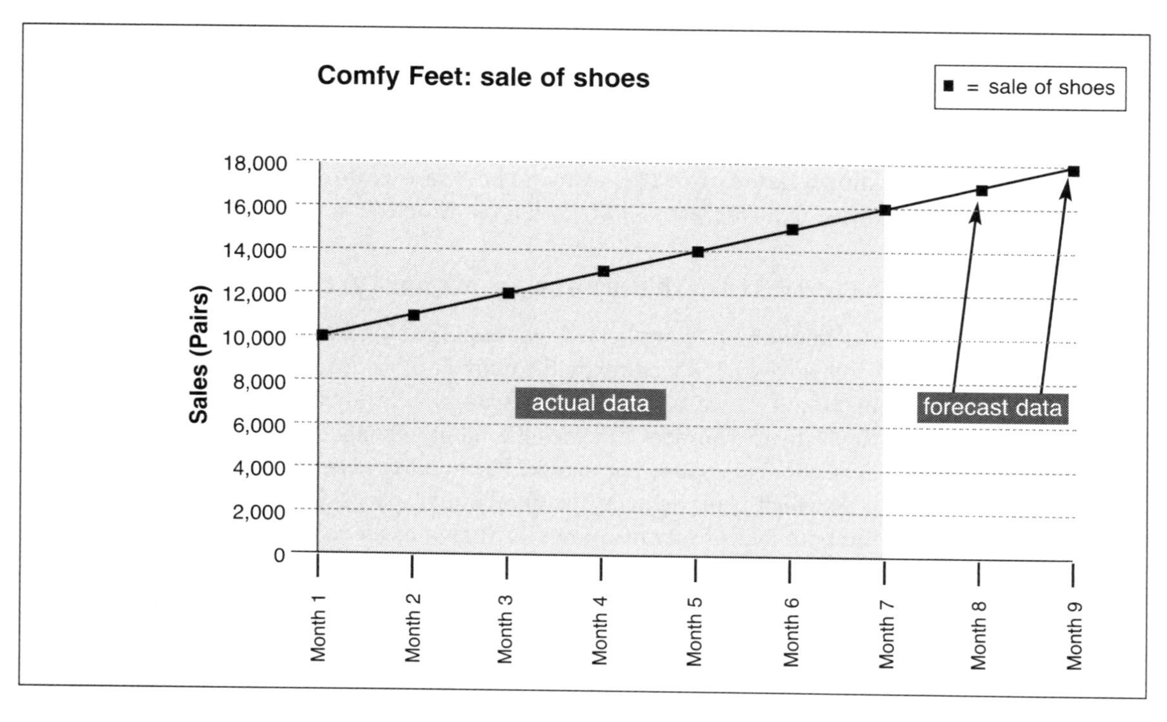

using a formula

The data in the example could have been expressed in the following formula:

$$y = mx + c$$

where

y is the forecast amount

m is 1,000 (the amount by which the data increases each year)

x is the number of years since the start year (20-1)

c is 10,000 (which is the sales figure in the start year of 20-1)

If we wanted a forecast for the year 20-9, we could calculate it as:

Forecast = (1,000 x number of years since 20-1) + 10,000

y (the forecast) = (1,000 x 8) + 10,000

= 18,000, which is what we would expect.

This formula works because the formula is based on the equation of a straight line.

We will examine the use of formulas and other methods of forecasting later in the chapter in the section on 'linear regression'.

using percentage increases or decreases

In the last few pages, we have used examples where the change in each period was either an identical amount (measured in whatever the data relates to – for example pairs of shoes) or similar amounts that we want to average. These situations provide us with a straight line on a graph as we have just seen.

An alternative regular change in the data could arise if each period the data is based on a percentage change in the data from the previous period. Even if the percentage is always the same, this will result in data that could follow a curve, not a straight line. This would make it difficult to forecast using just a graph, but it is still easy to calculate from the data.

We will use an example to demonstrate how this works.

worked example

The number of holidays booked per year to a developing resort is as follows:

Year 1	10,000
Year 2	12,000
Year 3	14,400
Year 4	17,280

We can quickly see that the increase each year is not the same in numbers of holidays, but the increase is getting larger each year.

We can calculate the percentage rise each year, and see if it is always the same. If it is we could use this percentage increase to forecast what we expect year 5 and year 6 to be, assuming the figures continue to follow this pattern.

The increase from year 1 to year 2 is 12,000 – 10,000 = 2,000 holidays. This increase as a percentage of year 1 is (2,000 ÷ 10,000) x 100 = 20%.

Looking at the increase from year 2 to year 3, calculate the percentage as:

(14,400 – 12,000) ÷ 12,000 x 100 = 20%. Notice that we always work out the percentage increase based on the first of the two figures that we are comparing.

We can also see that from year 3 to year 4 the increase is 2,880 which is also 20% of 14,400.

To use this 20% increase to forecast year 5, we simply work out 20% of the year 4 figure and add it to the year 4 data:

17,280 x 20% = 3,456

17,280 + 3,456 = 20,736

We could also use this method to forecast year 6:

20,736 x 20% = 4,147 (approximately)

20,736 + 4,147 = 24,883 (which can be approximated to 25,000)

We would have to be careful not to go too far into the future using this (and any other) forecasting method, as it will become less reliable the further it gets from the historical data.

This data (including the forecast) would look like this on a graph. As you can see it shows a curve as the figures get larger with a bigger increase each time.

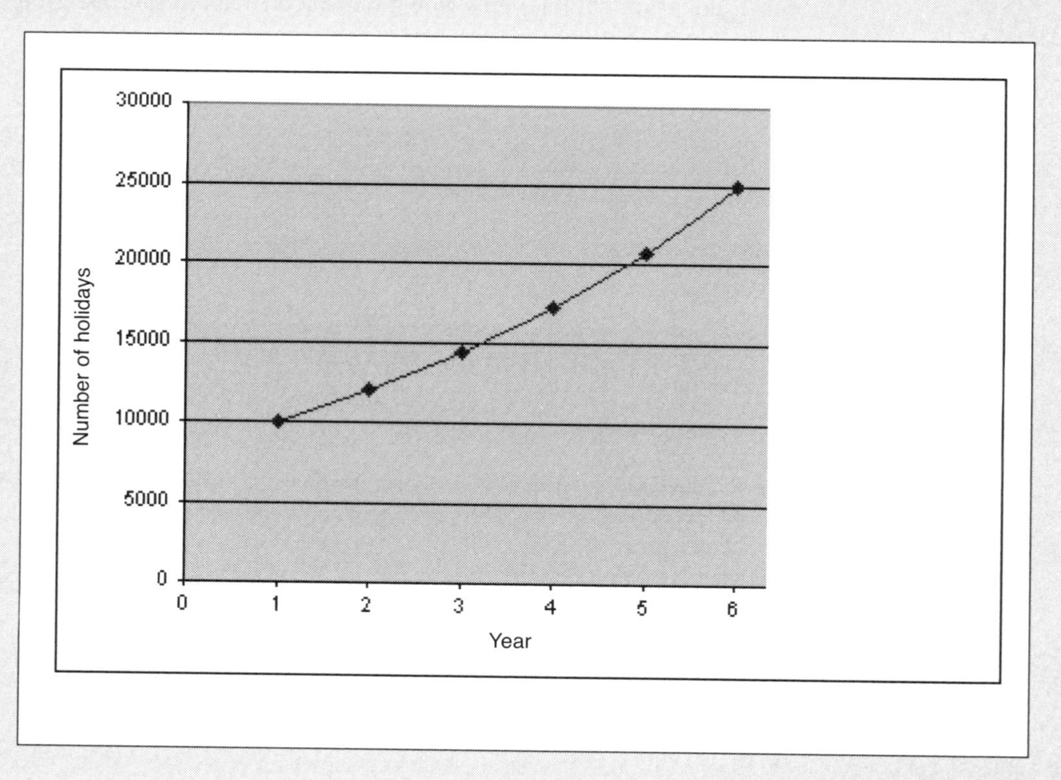

We can also use the same idea for percentage decreases. The following example will illustrate this.

worked example

The price of a certain type of laptop computer was as follows:

Year 1	£600.00
Year 2	£510.00
Year 3	£433.50

This represents a 15% price reduction each year, as follows:

Year 2 reduction (£90 ÷ £600) x 100 = 15%

Year 3 reduction (£76.50 ÷ £510) x 100 = 15%

If we expect this to continue, then the year 4 price will be calculated as

15% x £433.50 = £65.02 (rounded)

£433.50 – £65.02 = £368.48

When plotted, the graph would show a downwards curve as the price decreases.

TIME SERIES AND MOVING AVERAGES

In the last section we saw how simple historical data can be used to forecast future data in the following circumstances:

- when the historical data increases or decreases in regular, equal amounts
- when the historical data increases or decreases in similar amounts that can be averaged
- when the changes in historical data are a consistent percentage change (increase or decrease)

We also saw how these data patterns would look on graphs so that we could use these as a source for our calculations in some circumstances.

We are now going to see how historical data that has a more complicated pattern can be analysed and used to forecast future data. We will be using moving averages **to analyse the historical data. This can provide us with data** on:

- the **trend** – the general direction that the data is moving, and we will use this to forecast the future direction of the trend, and
- **seasonal variations** – the predictable movements in that data that occur in regular cycles. Because the pattern of seasonal variations repeats over time we can combine forecast seasonal variations with our forecast trend to establish a comprehensive forecast

The technique of establishing the trend by using moving averages is useful if we want to isolate the effect of seasonal variations (and smooth out random movements) from our data. We will now see how the technique operates in detail.

how do moving averages work?

A **moving average** is the term used for a series of averages calculated from a series of data (eg sales per month, labour costs per month) so that

- every average is based on the same number of pieces of data, (eg three pieces of data in a 'three point moving average'), and
- each subsequent average moves along that series of data by one piece of data so that compared to the previous average it
  - uses one new piece of data and
  - abandons one old piece of data

For example, suppose a factory used a manufacturing process that operated on a three-week cycle for technological reasons. At the end of each three-week period the production machinery is cleaned and the process starts again. Meanwhile as the operatives become more competent at controlling the process, output is gradually rising. The production figures for the last few weeks are as follows:

Week number	Production output (units):
1	20
2	46
3	27
4	23
5	49
6	30
7	26
8	52
9	33

As the three-week cycle will influence the output, we can calculate a three-point moving average, with workings as follows:

First moving average	(20 + 46 + 27) ÷ 3	= 31
Second moving average	(46 + 27 + 23) ÷ 3	= 32
Third moving average	(27 + 23 + 49) ÷ 3	= 33
Fourth moving average	(23 + 49 + 30) ÷ 3	= 34
Fifth moving average	(49 + 30 + 26) ÷ 3	= 35
Sixth moving average	(30 + 26 + 52) ÷ 3	= 36
Seventh moving average	(26 + 52 + 33) ÷ 3	= 37

Notice how we move along the list of data. In this simple example with nine pieces of data we can't work out any more three point averages since we have arrived at the end of the numbers after seven calculations.

Here we chose the number of pieces of data to average each time so that it corresponded with the number of points in a full cycle (in this case the three week production cycle of the manufacturing business). By choosing three points that correspond with the number of weeks in the production cycle we always had one example of the output of every type of week in our average. This means that any influence on the average by including a first week is cancelled out by also including data from a second week and a third week in the production cycle.

We must therefore always be careful to work out moving averages so that exactly one complete cycle is included in every average.

working out the trend line

By using moving averages we have worked out what is called the **trend line**, and we can use this to help with our forecast. A trend line is essentially a line showing a trend that can be plotted on a graph. When determining a trend line, each average relates to the data from its mid point, as is shown in the layout of the figures we have just calculated:

Week number	Production *(units)*	Moving average (trend) *(units)*
1	20	
2	46	31
3	27	32
4	23	33
5	49	34
6	30	35
7	26	36
8	52	37
9	33	

This means that the first average that we calculated (31 units) can be used as the trend point of week 2, with the second point (32 units) forming the trend point of week 3 (see dotted lines). The result is that we

- know exactly where the trend line is for each period of time, and
- have a basis from which we can calculate 'seasonal variations'
- can use the average movement of the trend to forecast the trend in future

calculating seasonal variations

Even using our limited data in this example we can see how **seasonal variations** can be calculated. They are **the difference between the actual data at a point and the trend at the same point**. These seasonal variations are shown in the right-hand column of the table on the next page. The data used are the figures already calculated above. All the data are in units.

Week number	Production	Trend	Seasonal variation
1	20		
2	46	31	+15
3	27	32	–5
4	23	33	–10
5	49	34	+15
6	30	35	–5
7	26	36	–10
8	52	37	+15
9	33		

We can see in this example that the seasonal variations repeat as follows:

- the first week in the production cycle always has an output of 10 units less than the trend
- the second week in the production cycle has an output of 15 units more than the trend, and
- the third week in the cycle regularly has a production output of 5 units less than the trend

Note the way that plus and minus signs are used to denote the seasonal variations, and be careful to calculate them accurately:

- a plus sign in this case means that the actual production figure is higher than the trend (see week 2)
- a minus sign in this case means that the actual production figure is less than the trend (see week 3)

Using the same data we can now go on to forecast the production for future weeks by:

- estimating where the trend will be by the chosen week, and
- incorporating the seasonal variation based on the appropriate week in the cycle

The forecast production for weeks 10 – 12 is carried out as follows:

Week number	Forecast trend	Seasonal variation	Forecast
10	39	–10	29
11	40	+15	55
12	41	–5	36

Here we can calculate the forecast trend easily, since it is consistently increasing by 1 unit of output each week.

using forecast data in the cash budget

We can now see how this forecast data can be used in a cash budget. Using the data from the example on the previous page, we will assume:

- all output is sold immediately as it is produced
- the selling price is £2,000 per unit
- sales are made on four weeks' credit

The following receipts would appear in the cash budget for weeks 12 – 16.

	Week 12	Week 13	Week 14	Week 15	Week 16
Receipts from sales	£104,000	£66,000	£58,000	£110,000	£72,000

Note that due to lagging, the receipts in weeks 12 and 13 relate to the actual production in weeks 8 and 9. The forecast data for weeks 10 – 12 is used to calculate the receipts in weeks 14 – 16.

We will now use a Case Study to demonstrate how the same technique could be used to forecast price data for a cash budget.

Case Study

THE KNAWBERRY: FORECASTING SEASONAL PRICES

situation

A supermarket obtains its supplies of the knawberry (a popular soft fruit) from three sources, depending on the time of year.

- In January – April it is bought from UK growers who raise the plants in glasshouses so that they will crop earlier than plants grown outdoors.
- In May – August it is obtained from UK farmers who grow the fruit outdoors.
- In September – December it is bought from overseas growers whose climate allows production at this time of the year.

Prices paid by the supermarket to the suppliers have been as follows over the last three years.

Year	Source	Price (per kilo)
1	UK glasshouse	£7
	UK outside	£4
	Overseas	£16
2	UK glasshouse	£10
	UK outside	£7
	Overseas	£19
3	UK glasshouse	£13
	UK outside	£10
	Overseas	£22

The monthly demand for the fruit (which will form the basis of the purchasing requirements) has already been calculated for the months of April – October of year 4, as follows:

April	1,600 kilos
May	1,900 kilos
June	2,500 kilos
July	2,600 kilos
August	2,400 kilos
September	2,000 kilos
October	1,200 kilos

All growers are paid on two months' credit.

required

- Using a three point moving average and seasonal variations, forecast the buying prices that will be payable in year 4.
- Show an extract from the payments section of the cash budget for June – November year 4 relating to the knawberry.

solution

Year	Source	Price	Trend	Seasonal variation
		£	£	£
1	UK glasshouse	7		
	UK outside	4	9	–5
	Overseas	16	10	+6
2	UK glasshouse	10	11	–1
	UK outside	7	12	–5
	Overseas	19	13	+6
3	UK glasshouse	13	14	–1
	UK outside	10	15	–5
	Overseas	22		

The trend in the prices is rising by £1 each 'season'. We can use this with the seasonal variations to forecast the prices in year 4.

Source	Forecast trend	Seasonal variation	Forecast
	£	£	£
UK glasshouse	17	–1	16
UK outside	18	–5	13
Overseas	19	+6	25

We can now use the demand data, together with the forecast prices and credit period to calculate our payments extract from the cash budget.

June	July	Aug	Sept	Oct	Nov
£	£	£	£	£	£
25,600	24,700	32,500	33,800	31,200	50,000

Note that the amounts paid in June relate to April purchases (due to the credit period), and are therefore based on 1,600 kilos at £16. Similarly, the July – October payments are based on the UK outside prices and quantities in May to August. The November payment is for overseas goods bought in September at £25 per kilo.

USING CENTRED MOVING AVERAGES

In the examples and Case Study that we have just examined we have assumed that cycle is based on an odd number of 'seasons'. For example, we used a three point moving average to calculate the trend because in the production example a three week cycle was in operation. In the 'Knawberry' Case Study we also used a three point moving average, this time because the year was divided into three sections.

If the number of 'seasons' is an even number (eg 4, 6, 8 etc) then establishing the trend will involve a slightly more complex calculation. If we just used the same technique that we have seen each moving average would fall between data points. This is because an average gives us information about the middle point from which the data is derived. For example, if four point moving averages are calculated from the following quarterly sales figures the first one would fall between the data for 'spring' and 'summer' and subsequent ones would also fall between data points like this:

Year	Season	Data	4 point moving average
1	Winter	2,400	
1	Spring	3,400	
			3,150
1	Summer	3,800	
			3,300
1	Autumn	3,000	
			3,450
2	Winter	3,000	
2	Spring	4,000	

This would mean that we would have no way of calculating seasonal variations as the averages would not fall alongside actual figures. To avoid this problem the initial moving averages are re-averaged in pairs and the results (the 'centred averages') form a trend that can be used both for forecasting and to calculate seasonal variations. Our example would then appear as shown in the table at the top of the opposite page.

Notice that each pair of 4 point moving averages is re-averaged and the result placed between them. For example the average of 3,150 and 3,300 is 3,225. As this now falls alongside 'summer' in year 1 it can be used to calculate the seasonal variation as normal.

Year	Season	Data	4 point moving average	Centred average (trend)	Seasonal variation
1	Winter	2,400			
1	Spring	3,400			
			3,150		
1	Summer	3,800		3,225	+575
			3,300		
1	Autumn	3,000		3,375	–375
			3,450		
2	Winter	3,000			
2	Spring	4,000			

We will now use a comprehensive Case Study to illustrate this technique. It also shows how to deal with a situation where the seasonal variations themselves also need averaging because they do not repeat exactly.

Case Study

THE CENTRED COMPANY: FORECASTING USING CENTRED AVERAGES

The Centred Company sells various products, including umbrellas. The quarterly management accounts for recent quarters have revealed that the following numbers of umbrellas were sold.

	Quarter 1	Quarter 2	Quarter 3	Quarter 4
20-0	4,000	1,600	2,200	4,800
20-1	4,400	2,000	2,500	5,200
20-2	4,800	2,400	3,100	5,600
20-3	5,200	2,800	3,400	6,000

required

1 Use moving averages to analyse the historical data into the trend and the seasonal variations.

2 Use the data from (1) to forecast the sales for each quarter of 20-4.

solution

1 Calculating the trend and seasonal variations

Step 1 The first thing to do is to rearrange the historical data into a single column with spaces in between each of the figures – this is to the right of the date column:

Year	Quarter	Step 1 Historical sales data	Step 2 4-point moving average	Step 3 Averaged pairs (trend)	Step 4 Seasonal variation
20-0	1	4,000			
	2	1,600			
			3,150		
	3	2,200		3,200	–1,000
			3,250		
	4	4,800		3,300	+1,500
			3,350		
20-1	1	4,400		3,387.5	+1,012.5
			3,425		
	2	2,000		3,475	–1,475
			3,525		
	3	2,500		3,575	–1,075
			3,625		
	4	5,200		3,675	+1,525
			3,725		
20-2	1	4,800		3,800	+1,000
			3,875		
	2	2,400		3,925	–1,525
			3,975		
	3	3,100		4,025	–925
			4,075		
	4	5,600		4,125	+1,475
			4,175		
20-3	1	5,200		4,212.5	+987.5
			4,250		
	2	2,800		4,300	–1,500
			4,350		
	3	3,400			
	4	6,000			

Step 2 Calculate the 4-point moving averages. This is the average of each group of four figures, starting with 20-0 quarters 1 to 4, followed by 20-0 quarter 2 to 20-1 quarter 1, and so on. Place each moving average in the appropriate column, alongside the centre point of the figures from which it was calculated. We are using a 4-point average because there are 4 quarters in our data. This also means that the average will fall alongside gaps between our original data. Note that the shaded lines and arrows are drawn here for illustration only – to show where the figures come from.

Step 3 Calculate the average of each adjacent pair of moving averages. These are also known as 'centred moving averages'. This is carried out so that these figures can be placed alongside the centre of each pair, and will therefore fall in line with the original quarterly data (see shaded arrow). If there was an odd number of 'seasons' in a cycle (for example 13 four-weekly periods) then this stage would not be required. We have now calculated the trend figures. Notice that the first trend calculated is in quarter 3 of the first year, and the last one is in quarter 2 of the last year. This is inevitable when calculating a trend from quarterly data using moving averages.

Step 4 Calculate the seasonal variations, and insert them into the last column. These are the amounts by which the actual figures (left hand column) are greater or smaller than the trend figures. Be careful to use the correct + or – sign. The shaded arrows show the figures that are used.

2 forecast the sales for each quarter of 20-4

In order to use the data that we have calculated for a forecast we will need to work out some average figures. This is because in this Case Study you will notice that:

- the trend is not increasing by exactly the same amount every quarter
- the seasonal variations are similar, but not quite identical for each of the same quarters

We can use the technique for calculating the average increase in the trend that we looked at earlier:

Average Trend Change =

$$\frac{\text{(Last known trend – First known trend)}}{\text{(Number of Quarterly trends – 1)}} = \frac{(4{,}300 - 3{,}200)}{11} = +100$$

We can also average the seasonal variations by grouping them together in quarters:

	Quarter 1	Quarter 2	Quarter 3	Quarter 4
20-0			–1,000	+1,500
20-1	+1,012.5	–1,475	–1,075	+1,525
20-2	+1,000	–1,525	– 925	+1,475
20-3	+987.5	–1,500		
Totals	+3,000	–4,500	–3,000	+4,500
Averages	+1,000	–1,500	–1,000	+1,500

At this stage we should check that the average seasonal variations total zero. Here they do, but if they do not then minor adjustments will need to be made to the figures.

We can now use the average trend movements and the average seasonal variations to create a forecast. We start with the trend at the last point when it was calculated, and work out where it will be at future points by using the average movements. For example quarter 1 of 20-4 is 3 quarters past quarter 2 of 20-3, which is when we last knew the trend. We then incorporate the average seasonal variations to complete the forecast.

Forecast Workings:

		Forecast Trend		Seasonal variations	Forecast
20-4	Qtr 1	4,300 + (3 x 100)	= 4,600	+1,000	5,600
	Qtr 2	4,300 + (4 x 100)	= 4,700	–1,500	3,200
	Qtr 3	4,300 + (5 x 100)	= 4,800	–1,000	3,800
	Qtr 4	4,300 + (6 x 100)	= 4,900	+1,500	6,400

MULTIPLICATIVE SEASONAL VARIATIONS

So far in our study of forecasting using trends we have always expressed the seasonal variations as simply positive or negative numbers which are added to or deducted from the trend data. These are called 'additive' seasonal variations and assume that each individual seasonal variation will be the same – no matter what happens to the trend. For example an additive seasonal variation of +20 will still be added to the trend to arrive at the forecast – whether the relevant trend point is 100 or 500.

In some situations this could provide an inaccurate forecast because in reality the seasonal variations could get bigger if the trend figures became greater. An alternative to assuming that seasonal variations are additive, is to use 'multiplicative' seasonal variations. These would normally be calculated as a percentage of the trend, and so would increase if the trend line increased.

A simple example of a forecast using multiplicative seasonal variations is as follows:

Period	**Trend**	**S.V.**	**Forecast**
1	150	+20%	180
2	160	–30%	112
3	170	–20%	136
4	180	+30%	234
5	190	+20%	228
6	200	–30%	140
7	210	–20%	168
8	220	+30%	286

In this example the seasonal variations repeat after four periods. Note the way that the seasonal variations become larger as the trend increases. For example, the seasonal variation in period 1 is 150 x 20% = 30, but the seasonal variation in the next equivalent season (period 5) is 190 x 20% = 38.

Whether additive or multiplicative seasonal variations would give the best forecast will depend on the type of data that is being analysed and how it acts in reality. A situation where multiplicative seasonal variations might be appropriate is the cost of heating – winter costs are always more than the general trend, but as costs tend to rise generally the winter seasonal variations would increase in proportion to the trend. This is illustrated in the following Case Study.

FACTORY HEATING COSTS: MULTIPLICATIVE SEASONAL VARIATIONS

A company uses trend analysis incorporating multiplicative seasonal variations to forecast the heating costs for its factory.

The trend figures for 20-5 quarterly costs were as follows:

Quarter 1	£15,000
Quarter 2	£15,300
Quarter 3	£15,600
Quarter 4	£15,900

The seasonal variations have been analysed and average the following percentages of the trend:

Quarter 1	+45%
Quarter 2	–30%
Quarter 3	–40%
Quarter 4	+25%

required

Forecast the cost of heating the factory in 20-6.

solution

The trend figures are increasing by £300 per quarter, giving the following trend for 20-6, and the seasonal variations are then calculated and incorporated.

Quarter	Trend	Seasonal variation	Forecast
	£	£	£
1	16,200	+7,290	23,490
2	16,500	–4,950	11,550
3	16,800	–6,720	10,080
4	17,100	+4,275	21,375

ALLOWING FOR INFLATION

Because prices and costs change over time it is important to make sure that budgets take account of the most accurate estimates of the amounts that will apply in the budget period. Inflation will have a particular impact on:

- selling prices
- purchase prices
- expenses
- cost of non-current assets
- labour costs

selling prices

Because selling prices are set within an organisation it is possible to obtain information about future prices from the relevant personnel, as discussed in Chapter 1. However it is important to be aware that selling prices are subject to market forces as well as inflation, and it is vital to check that data that has been provided has been based on valid assumptions.

prices for purchases, expenses and non-current assets

Depending on the number of different suppliers that the organisation has, it may be possible to obtain information about expected price rises of individual inputs. For example, car manufacturers will be able to obtain market reports about likely movements in the price of pressed steel. Where substantial non-current assets are to be purchased the cost should be ascertained accurately in advance.

Where changes in costs cannot be investigated individually, index numbers (as described below) can be used to calculate the impact of expected price changes in different categories of cost. It should be remembered that an organisation may have a range of different supplies and expenses, and it probably will not be sufficient to apply the same allowance for inflation to all costs. For example, business rates may well be increasing by a different percentage than raw materials.

labour costs

Like selling prices, wage rates are controlled by the organisation, although they are subject to external pressures such as the legal requirements of the Minimum Wage in the UK. Although wage cost indices are available for all industrial sectors, it is better to use information about the specific organisation – for example taking account of the timing and percentage of any anticipated wage rise.

HOW TO ALLOW FOR INFLATION

There are two basic ways that we can make calculations to allow for inflation. These are:

- **applying percentage increases** (or decreases for the opposite – deflation) to the prices and/or costs; we saw in detail earlier in this chapter how to carry out these calculations
- **using index numbers** – we will describe what index numbers are and how we can use them to carry out the calculations that we need for cash budgets

USING INDEX NUMBERS

Index numbers are used to assist in the comparison of various numerical data over time. The traditional index that measures inflation by comparing the cost of a group of expenses typically incurred by households in the UK is the Retail Price Index (RPI). This has more recently been supplemented by the Consumer Prices Index (CPI). There are many other types of index numbers that have been created for specific purposes. For the measurement of cost changes some of the following types of index may be useful:

- the price of specific items, either based on the retail price or the cost to specific industries (eg the price of unleaded petrol)
- the average price of a group of items, usually using a weighted price (ie taking relative quantities into account) for example the average price per litre of all types of motor fuel
- the average wage rate for a particular job, or for all employment
- the currency exchange rates between specific currencies

Whatever type of index we need to use, the principle is the same. The index numbers represent a convenient way of comparing figures. For example, the Retail Price Index (RPI) was 82.61 in January 1983, and 245.8 in January 2013. This means that average household costs had increased by nearly 3 times in the 30 years between. We could also calculate that if something that cost £5.00 in January 1983 had risen exactly in line with inflation, it would have cost £14.88 in January 2013. This calculation is carried out using the formula:

$$\textit{Historical price} \quad \times \quad \frac{\textit{Index of time converting to}}{\textit{Index of time converting from}}$$

For example, the item that cost £5.00 in January 1983 would in January 2013 cost:

$$£5.00 \times \frac{245.8 \text{ (RPI in January 2013)}}{82.61 \text{ (RPI in January 1983)}} = £14.88$$

An organisation will clearly not be dealing with a 30 year time span when constructing a cash budget, but the principle of the use of index numbers remains the same.

base year

The Retail Price Index that we have just examined has a base point (or 'base year') of January 1987. This is the point in time when the index had a value of exactly 100. You will notice that the index for January 1983 was below 100 (as average prices were cheaper than in 1987), and the current index is much higher than 100. While the choice of the base point obviously affects the numerical data in the index, there usually is little other significance in its position. An index with a different base point could be calculated which would provide all the same information, as we will see in the next section.

creation of an index

You may be required to create an index from given historical data, and we will now see how this is carried out.

Suppose that you are provided with the following prices for one unit of a certain material over a period of time:

Month	Jan	Feb	March	April	May	June
Price	£29.70	£30.00	£28.30	£30.09	£31.00	£31.25

The first thing to do is to decide which point in time is to be the base point – the price at this point will be 100 in our new index. In this example we will first use January as our base point, but later we will see how another date could have been chosen.

Next, the price of another date (we'll use February) is divided by the price at the base point. The result is then multiplied by 100 to give the index at that point (ie February):

(£30.00 / £29.70) x 100 = 101.01

Note that the index number is not an amount in £s, it is just a number used for comparison purposes. In this example we've rounded to 2 decimal places – and we will need to be consistent for the other figures.

If we carry out the same calculation for the March price we get the following:

(£28.30 / £29.70) x 100 = 95.29

Notice that here the answer is less than 100, which makes sense because the price in March is lower than the price in January. Checking that each index number is the expected side of 100 (ie higher or lower) is a good idea and will help you to detect some arithmetical errors.

The full list of index numbers is as follows – make sure that you can arrive at the same figures.

Month	Jan	Feb	March	April	May	June
Price	£29.70	£30.00	£28.30	£30.09	£31.00	£31.25
Index	100.00	101.01	95.29	101.31	104.38	105.22

We could have chosen a different date to act as our base point – if we chose March, then the calculation for January would have been:

(£29.70 / £28.30) x 100 = 104.95

Then the full list of index numbers would have been as follows:

Month	Jan	Feb	March	April	May	June
Price	£29.70	£30.00	£28.30	£30.09	£31.00	£31.25
Index	104.95	106.01	100.00	106.33	109.54	110.42

Again, make sure that you could arrive at the same figures.

Don't forget that although we have used the creation of a price index in the above example, you could also be asked to create an index from any suitable historical data. Whatever the type of data, the arithmetic required is the same.

use a specific index if possible

Index numbers referring to costs or prices are commonly used in the cash management process. If we want to use cost index numbers to monitor past costs or forecast future ones, then it is best and more accurate to use as specific an index as possible. For example, if we were operating in the food industry, and wanted to monitor or forecast the cost of coffee, we should use an index that analyses coffee costs in the food industry. This would be much more accurate than the RPI, CPI or even a general cost index for the food industry.

a reminder about lagging

When incorporating an allowance for inflation, we must be careful to remember that price changes that occur in one month will only impact when the receipt or payment occurs. For example if we increase our selling prices by 5% in January, but sell our goods on two months' credit, it will not affect the cash budget until March.

HIGH-RISE SUPPLIES: ALLOWING FOR INFLATION IN THE CASH BUDGET

High-Rise Supplies, a trading company, has produced the following extract from its initial draft cash budget for the months of July - October, based on prices and costs at June levels.

Sales are made on two months' credit, purchases on one month's credit.

Expenses and labour costs are paid in the month they are incurred.

Rent is payable half yearly in advance.

High-Rise Supplies: Draft Cash Budget (extract) for the period July - October

	July	August	September	October
	£	£	£	£
Receipts				
Sales	60,000	63,000	55,000	68,000
Payments				
Purchases	25,000	28,000	26,000	24,000
Labour	19,000	17,000	18,000	20,000
Rent	18,000	–	–	–
Expenses	12,000	12,000	12,000	12,000

The following information about price and cost changes is now available:

- Selling prices are due to increase by 3% from 1 July.
- Purchase prices are forecast to rise by 4% from 1 September.
- A pay rise of 2.5% has been agreed to take effect from 1 July.
- Rent is to rise to £40,000 per year with effect from 1 July.
- Expenses are expected to follow the following forecast cost index:

June	291.0
July	291.8
August	292.3
September	293.0
October	293.7

required

Revise the cash budget extract to incorporate appropriate allowances for price and cost changes.

solution

Revised Cash Budget (extract) for the period July - October

	July	August	September	October
	£	£	£	£
Receipts				
Sales (1)	60,000	63,000	56,650	70,040
Payments				
Purchases (2)	25,000	28,000	26,000	24,960
Labour (3)	19,475	17,425	18,450	20,500
Rent (4)	20,000	–	–	–
Expenses (5)	12,033	12,054	12,082	12,111

Notes:

(1) The sales price change impacts after 2 months.

(2) The purchase price change impacts one month after 1 September.

(3) The labour pay rise takes effect immediately.

(4) The rent rise to £40,000 per year = £20,000 per half year.

(5) Expenses rise each month in line with the forecast index. For example, August expenses are calculated as

$$£12,000 \times \frac{292.3 \text{ (August index)}}{291.0 \text{ (June index)}}$$

= £12,054

the overall impact of inflation

If inflation is higher than anticipated then the following generalisations can be made about its impact.

- selling prices can be increased
- buying prices, labour costs and expenses may increase

Depending on the structure of the business and the amount and timing of these increases, profit may well also increase. However each £1 of increased profit will not be worth as much as previously!

One other impact of inflation is that interest rates tend to move in the same direction as inflation. This means that when inflation is high interest rates are normally high. If the organisation has borrowed a substantial amount of money, this will add to its costs, whereas if the organisation has surplus funds it will generate more revenue from this source.

LINEAR REGRESSION

Earlier in this chapter we saw that when data moves over time with consistent increases (or decreases) it can be illustrated by

- a straight line on a graph, and / or
- a formula in the form 'y = mx + c'

Linear regression (or 'regression analysis') is the term used for the process of identifying the straight line that best matches the historical data. Once the information about the straight line has been established it can be used to generate a forecast, either alone or in conjunction with seasonal variations.

In this section we are going to examine in outline the main ways that linear regression can be carried out, and then see how forecast calculations can be carried out using the formula for a straight line.

Where data exactly matches a straight line (as with the 'Comfy Feet' data earlier in this chapter) there is no need to use any special techniques. In other situations the following could be used:

- **Average annual change**. This method was described earlier, and is useful if we are confident that the first and last points (taken chronologically since we are looking at data over time) are both representative. It will smooth out any minor fluctuations of the data in between. We used this method in the 'Centred Company' Case Study earlier in this chapter.
- **Line of best fit**. Where the data falls only roughly into a straight line, but the first and last points do not appear to be very representative the

average annual change method would give a distorted solution. Here a line of best fit can be drawn onto the data points on a graph that will form a better estimate of the movement of the data. The following graph illustrates a situation where the line of best fit may provide a better solution than the average annual change method.

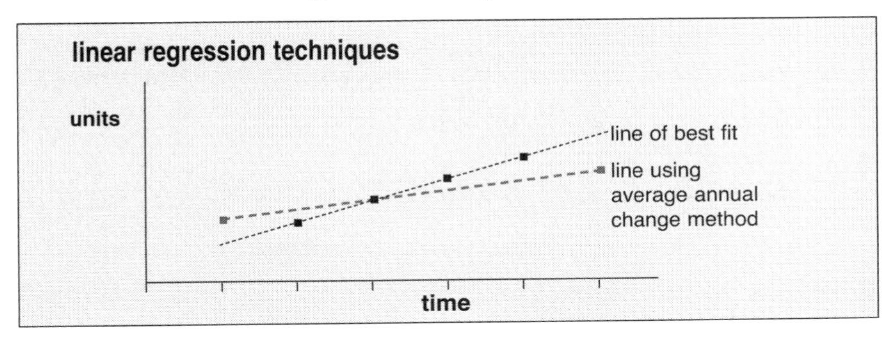

- **Least squares method**. This is a mathematical technique for developing the equation of the most appropriate line. It is more accurate than drawing a line of best fit onto a graph by eye, but the calculations involved are outside the scope of this book.

All linear regression techniques assume that a straight line is an appropriate representation of the data. When looking at time series this means that we are assuming that the changes in the data that we are considering (known as the dependent variable) are in proportion to the movement of time (the independent variable). This would mean that we are expecting (for example) the sales level to continually rise over time. When we use time series analysis we must remember that sometimes data do not travel forever in a straight line, even though they may do so for a short time.

using a formula for forecast calculations

The formula of a straight line ($y = mx + c$) always has the following components:

- a fixed value ('c' in the formula $y = mx + c$); this is the point where the straight line starts from
- a gradient value ('m' in the formula); this determines how steep the line is, and whether it is going up (when 'm' is positive) or going down (when 'm' is negative)

The formula can be used (for example) to predict prices, costs or demand. Sometimes the formula is shown in a slightly different style (for example $y = a + bx$), but the components are still the same.

We will now use the formula to demonstrate how different elements can be calculated.

practical example

For example, suppose we are told that the price of a component over time is believed to increase based on the formula $Y = a + bX$, where

- Y is the price in £, and
- X is the year number

We are told that in year number 4 the price was £68, and in year number 8 the price was £76.

We would like to calculate '*a*' and '*b*' in the formula, and then use this information to predict the price in year 11.

We can use a calculation to determine how much the price is moving by each year:

	Price		Year	
	£76		8	
	£68		4	
Differences	£8	divided by	4	= £2 per year

This is the 'gradient' amount '*b*', and we can use it to calculate the amount '*a*' by using price information from either of the years that we know. For example, using year 4 data and putting it into the formula gives:

£68 = a + (£2 x 4 [the year number])

£68 = a + £8 So a must be £60

Now we have the full formula that we can use for any year:

Y = £60 + £2 x X

In year 11, this would give a price of:

Y = £60 + (£2 x 11) = £82

We will now use an example to illustrate the use of the formula to predict demand.

Sales of a national daily newspaper have been declining steadily for several years. The demand level is believed to follow the formula Y = a + bX, where Y is the demand in numbers of newspapers, and X is the year number. Calculations have already been carried out to establish the values of 'a' and 'b', which are:

- a is 200,000
- b is –2,500

Note that 'b' is a negative figure, so each year the demand decreases.

You are asked to calculate the expected sales in year 14.

If we insert the known data into the formula, we can calculate the demand for year 14 as follows:

Y = 200,000 – (2,500 x 14) Y = 165,000

PROBLEMS WITH FORECASTING

When using the forecasting techniques that we have examined in this chapter it is very important to appreciate that the results of our calculations will not always provide accurate forecasts.

We often make the assumption that the future direction of a trend, percentage change or index will be based on what has happened in the past. For example, the technique of using moving averages to determine the trend and then to assume that it will continue to increase or decrease by the same amount each period is based entirely on this assumption. Of course while that may be a reasonable assumption to make, it is not a guaranteed way to forecast. If all data kept moving in the same direction as it always has then there would be no economic cycles, no 'booms or busts' and everyone would be able to make perfect forecasts about everything.

We know that many issues can impact on a business and its cash flow, and must always remember that a forecast (just like a weather forecast) will not always give an accurate picture of the future. Some of the influences on a business forecast include:

- changes in general economic conditions
- the product life cycle of items traded (how long they are popular products)
- increased or decreased competition
- changes in the businesses of suppliers and customers
- changes in world commodity prices (eg oil prices)
- changes in interest rates and inflation
- changes in currency exchange rates

Many of these changes could arise unexpectedly and have a large impact on our budgets. However, we should not abandon the idea of creating a forecast or cash budget on the grounds that it is simply 'too difficult to get right'. Instead we should acknowledge the assumptions that we have incorporated into our calculations and appreciate the impact that incorrect assumptions would have.

Chapter Summary

- There are several statistical techniques that can be used to help with forecasting data that can be used in cash budgets. These include using identical or average changes in data, using percentage changes, using moving averages to establish trends and using index numbers. Regression analysis can also be used to identify the attributes of a straight line trend.

- The simplest technique is to examine past data to establish whether the movement is regular increases or decreases and to assume that these movements will continue into the future. If the movements are similar but not identical an average movement can be calculated and used.

- Some data tends to move based on percentage increases or decreases from the previous piece of data. If this is the case then this percentage can be applied to estimate future data.

- Moving averages can be used to establish trends in historical data. This involves calculating averages based on the length of known cycles so that cyclical movements (seasonal variations) are eliminated from the trend. The trend can be used to develop a simple forecast, and forecast seasonal variations can then be incorporated to develop a comprehensive forecast.

- Index numbers (as well as percentage movements) can be used to forecast data, and are especially useful for allowing for inflation in prices and costs. Historical data can be used to create an index.

- The formula for a straight line that has been developed through regression analysis can be used to forecast data.

- There are problems with relying too heavily on any statistical forecasting techniques. Many techniques make the assumption that the past can be used to predict the future, and there are many other real-life issues that may affect the validity of that assumption.

Key Terms

trend analysis	a numerical technique for analysing historical data so that it can be used for forecasting future data – it involves identifying and separating seasonal and other variations so that the underlying trend can be ascertained
trend	data that has been produced from historical data, after the effects of cyclical movements and minor random changes have been stripped away; it enables the general movement in the underlying data to be identified and used for forecasting
index numbers	a sequence of numbers that are used to compare data (for example quantities or prices), usually over a time period
seasonal variations	regular variations in data that occur in a repeating pattern; these can be additive or multiplicative
linear regression	the process of identifying the attributes of a straight line that matches historical data

Activities

2.1 A company has a forecast cost of £73.50 for a new product that it will manufacture. Complete the following table to show the range of forecast selling prices and gross profits.

Round each selling price to the nearest penny.

	Selling Price *£.p*	**Gross Profit** *£.p*
Mark-up of 20%		
Mark-up of 22%		
Margin of 15%		
Margin of 17%		

2.2 The following is a graph of selling prices (in units) made by Wye Limited. The selling prices are from £100 in Year 1 to approximately £21 in Year 8.

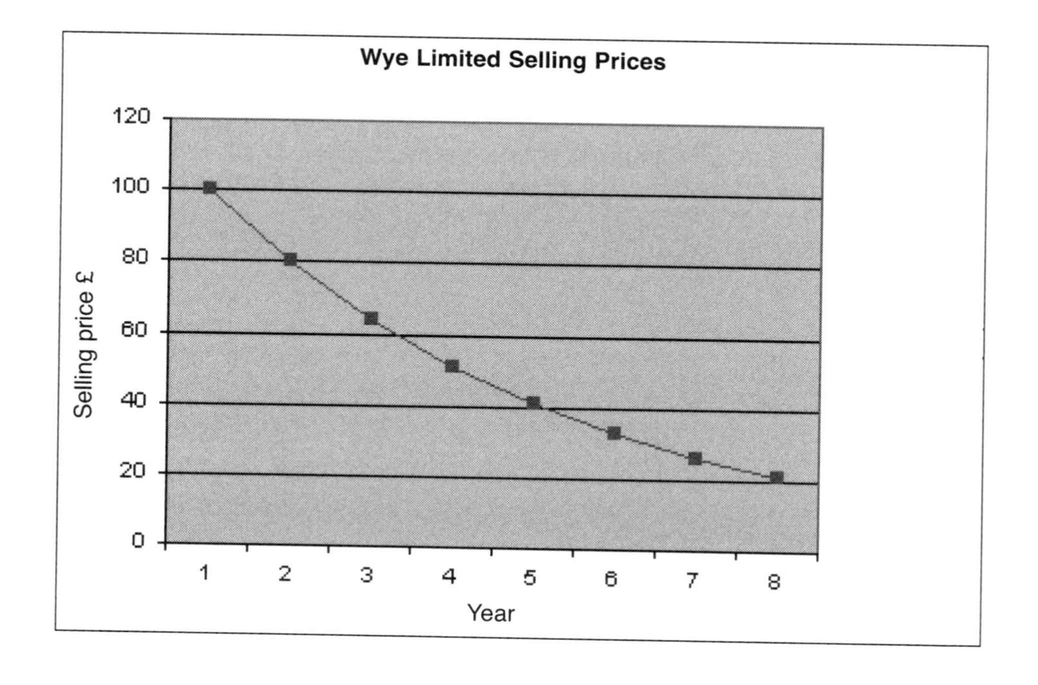

Required:

(a) Examine the graph and the following statements, and select the statement that is true.

(a) Selling prices are increasing each year by a fixed percentage	
(b) Selling prices are decreasing each year by a fixed percentage	
(c) Selling prices are increasing each year by equal amounts	
(d) Selling prices are decreasing each year by equal amounts	

(b) Estimate the Selling price in year 10, and select the answer from the following:

(a) £20	
(b) £16	
(c) £13	
(d) £32	

2.3 The Shackshop is open 5 days a week (Tuesday to Saturday) and records the following cash sales over a three week period:

	Tues	**Wed**	**Thurs**	**Fri**	**Sat**
Week 1	£915	£960	£1040	£1080	£1080
Week 2	£940	£985	£1065	£1105	£1105
Week 3	£965	£1010	£1090	£1130	£1130

Required:

(a) Using a five point moving average, analyse this data into the trend and seasonal variations. (**Note**: a five point moving average works on the same principle as a three point moving average, but takes a series of averages of five numbers instead of three).

(b) Use the data from (a) to forecast the cash sales for each day of week 4.

2.4 A company has analysed its sales in units over the last two years, and produced the following information:

Year	**Quarter**	**Trend** *(no. units)*	**Seasonal variation** *(no. units)*
1	1	5,800	–430
	2	5,870	–350
	3	5,935	+880
	4	6,010	–100
2	1	6,090	–430
	2	6,165	–350
	3	6,220	+880
	4	6,290	–100

Required:

(a) Calculate the average trend movement per quarter over the last two years.

(b) Use the average trend movement to forecast the expected sales (in units) in quarters 3 and 4 of year 3.

2.5 Jazza Limited is preparing its forecast sales and purchase information for January of next year.

The sales volume trend is to be identified using a three point moving average based on the actual monthly sales volumes for the current year.

(a) Complete the table below to calculate the monthly sales volume trend and identify any monthly variations.

	Sales volume *(units)*	**Trend**	**Monthly variation** *(volume less trend)*
August	18,720		
September	11,880		
October	10,440		
November	19,800		
December	12,960		

The monthly sales volume trend is [ ] units.

(b) **Additional information**

The selling price per unit has been set at £4.

Monthly purchases are estimated to be 40% of the value of the forecast sales.

The seasonal variations operate on a 3 month repeating cycle.

Required:

Using the trend and the monthly variations identified in Part (a), complete the table below to forecast the sales volume, sales value and purchase value for January of the next financial year.

	Forecast trend	**Variation**	**Forecast sales volume**	**Forecast sales** £	**Forecast purchases** £
January					

(c) Additional information

The company uses an industry wage rate index to forecast future monthly wage costs. Employees receive a pay increase in March each year, based on the index for that month. The current monthly wage cost of £6,220 was calculated when the wage index was 326. The forecast wage rate index for the next three months is:

January	358
February	372
March	386

Required:

If the company uses the forecast wage rate index, what will the wage cost for March be, to the nearest £?

Select the correct option:

(a)	£7,365	
(b)	£5,253	
(c)	£6,454	
(d)	£5,994	

2.6 A company uses a specific price index to forecast the buying prices of its raw materials. It cost £240,000 to buy 20,000 kilograms when the index was 196. The index is forecast to be 221 in June, and in that month 22,500 kilograms of the raw material need to be purchased.

Required:

Calculate:

(a) The estimated cost per kilogram of the raw materials to be bought in June (calculate to 2 decimal places).

(b) The estimated total cost of the raw materials to be purchased in June.

2.7 A computer program has used linear regression to analyse the sales data of a garden furniture manufacturer. Using quarter numbers (quarter 20 is the first quarter of year 20-0) the sales trend has been determined as:

Sales Trend (in £) = (Quarter Number x £1,500) + £62,000.

The Seasonal Variations have been determined as the following percentages of the trend.

Quarter 1 –10%

Quarter 2 +70%

Quarter 3 +25%

Quarter 4 –85%

Required:

Use the above data to calculate the forecast of sales in £ for each quarter of 20-2.

2.8 The following historical data relates to sales in units of the Elgar Company.

	Quarter 1	**Quarter 2**	**Quarter 3**	**Quarter 4**
Year 1	1,000	860	660	560
Year 2	920	780	580	480
Year 3	840	700	500	400
Year 4	760	620	420	320

Required:

(a) Using centred moving averages, analyse this data into the trend and additive seasonal variations.

(b) Use the data to forecast the unit sales for each quarter of year 5.

2.9 The following historical data has been extracted from company records. The data relates to the purchase price per litre on an oil-based raw material.

Month	Jan	Feb	March	April	May	June
Price £	1.45	1.48	1.41	1.52	1.55	1.57

Required:

Create an index based on these prices, using April as the base point. Calculate your index numbers to 2 decimal places.

3 Preparing cash budgets

this chapter covers...

In this chapter we will examine in detail how a cash budget is prepared. This is an important part of your studies, and you will need to be able to prepare a cash budget (or extracts) accurately.

We will start by summarising the source of the main data for a cash budget, and illustrating how a simple cash budget can be prepared for a new business. We will see how this document links with other financial documents, in particular the budgeted statement of financial position. We will also revise how to prepare a statement that reconciles profit with cash movement.

From there we will move on to examining the specific issues that can cause difficulty when preparing a cash budget, and which will need to be mastered. Specifically we will learn how to deal with units and prices, split receipts, discounts, irrecoverable debts, bank account interest, accruals, prepayments and depreciation.

We will then see how our techniques can be applied to an existing business as well as a new business, and illustrate this with more complex Case Study.

We will also deal with the calculation of closing trade receivables and trade payables and also show how amounts paid or received in connection with non-current assets can be worked out. Finally, we will examine the calculation of tax payments, and the impact of inventory levels on payments for materials.

The activities at the end of the chapter are particularly important because the techniques covered can only be perfected with thorough practice.

PREPARING A CASH BUDGET FOR A NEW BUSINESS

In this chapter we will build up a cash budget using the format that we looked at at the end of Chapter 1.

We will start by looking at the cash budget for a new trading organisation, so that we can get a clear idea of the main principles. We will also see how the cash budget fits in with the budgeted statement of profit or loss and statement of financial position. Later on we will see how we can build on our technique to develop cash budgets for existing businesses by incorporating data from the opening statement of financial position.

Note: your assessment could ask you to prepare a statement of profit or loss from cash and other data – ie the above procedure in reverse. This is the 'incomplete records' procedure covered in your Level 3 studies.

rounding

Throughout the calculations for figures in our cash budgets in this book we will be rounding amounts to the nearest £ where necessary. It would never make sense to use figures in a cash budget that were any more accurate than this. Some organisations may prepare cash budgets rounded to larger amounts (for example the nearest thousand pounds) if this suits their needs better.

the basic process – linking with other budgets

The data that we use to create all our budgets must be consistent so that all our budgets are based on the same assumptions. We will find that much of the data for a cash budget can be found in a **budgeted statement of profit or loss**, if this has already been prepared. However, the key to accurate cash budgets is to remember that receipts and payments are based on **when the receipts and payments occur**, and therefore most of the figures in this statement will need analysing or modifying.

When we receive or pay cash at a different time to the recording of the sale, purchase or expense, this is known as **lagging**. It is these lagged figures – based on the time of receipt or payment – that we will use in our cash budget. For example, if credit sales of £10,000 were made in January, on two months' credit, then the money would be received in March. Although the sale would be recorded in the statement of profit or loss in January, it must appear in the March column in the cash budget.

A cash budget will not show any non-cash items that appear in the budgeted statement of profit or loss – the most common example of this is **depreciation**. There are also items that will appear in the cash budget, but are not shown in the budgeted statement of profit or loss. These are capital items (purchase or disposal of non-current (fixed) assets), disbursements like drawings and tax, and exceptional items like financing (funds from equity or loans). These were discussed in Chapter 1.

The diagram below shows how the data in a simple cash budget links with the data used in other budgets.

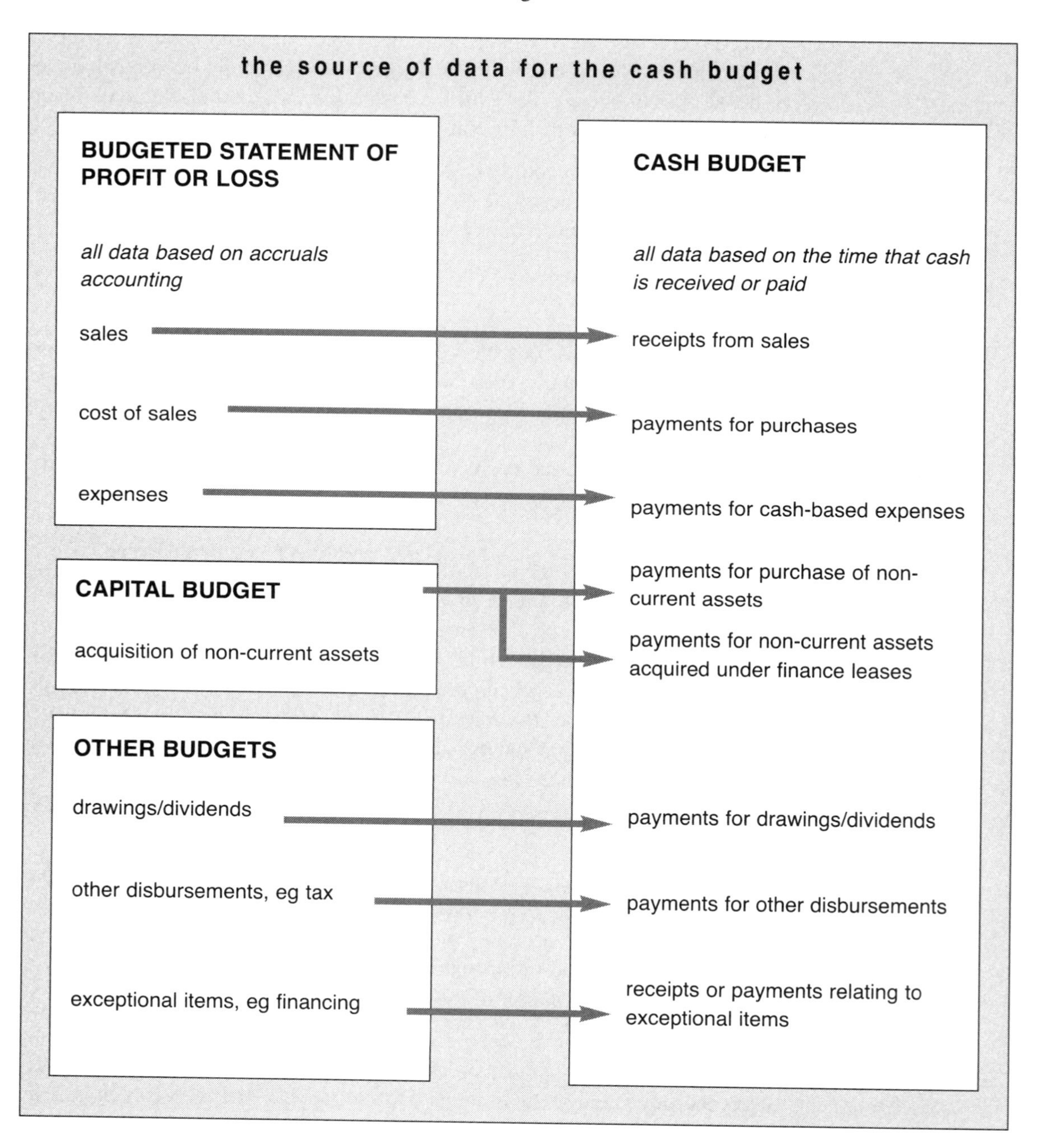

We will now use a Case Study to show how a simple cash budget can be produced for a new business, using the sources of data shown in the diagram on the previous page. We will also demonstrate how a budgeted statement of financial position can be prepared for the end of the period.

Case Study

FIRST TRADE: SIMPLE CASH BUDGET

Jim First is planning to start a trading business. He has prepared the following budgeted statement of profit or loss for the initial four months' trading.

Jim First: Budgeted statement of profit or loss

	£	£
Sales		22,000
less cost of sales:		
Opening inventory	0	
Purchases	21,000	
less closing inventory	(7,000)	
		14,000
Gross profit		8,000
less:		
Cash expenses	4,000	
Depreciation	1,000	
		5,000
Net profit		3,000

Jim also provides you with the following information regarding his plans:

- **Sales** are to be made on two months' credit. The sales figures in the budgeted statement of profit or loss are based on monthly sales as follows:

	£
Month 1	4,000
Month 2	6,000
Month 3	5,000
Month 4	7,000
Total sales	22,000

- **Purchases** made in the first month must be paid for immediately. Subsequent purchases will be on one month's credit. The purchases figure in the budgeted statement of profit or loss is made up as follows:

	£
Month 1	6,000
Month 2	6,000
Month 3	4,000
Month 4	5,000
Total purchases	21,000

- Cash expenses are based on paying out £1,000 in each of the first four months of the business.
- Equipment is to be bought for £15,000 in the first month of the business. The depreciation shown in the budgeted statement of profit or loss is based on depreciating these non-current assets at 20% per year on a straight-line basis.
- Jim has £25,000 to invest in the business in month 1. The business has no opening cash balance.
- Jim wishes to withdraw £2,000 from the business in month 4.

required

- Prepare a cash budget in receipts and payments format for the first four months' trading of First Trade.
- Prepare a budgeted statement of financial position as at the end of the four month period.

solution

The cash budget is prepared in the following way.

- The capital invested is entered as a receipt in month 1.
- The receipts from sales are entered on the appropriate line, taking account of the two months' credit by lagging the receipts by two months, ie sales for months 1 and 2 are received in months 3 and 4. Note that the sales made in months 3 and 4 do not appear on this cash budget as the money will not be received until months 5 and 6.
- The payments for purchases and expenses are entered into the appropriate lines, using the data on payment terms. Remember that the first month's purchases are paid for in month 1 and subsequent purchases are given one month's credit.
- The payments for non-current assets and drawings are entered as appropriate.
- The receipts and payments totals are completed, and each month's cash flow is calculated (ie total receipts minus total payments).
- The bank balance brought forward for month 1 is inserted (here it is zero).
- The carried forward bank balance for each month is calculated in turn. This is based on the calculation for each month using the formula:

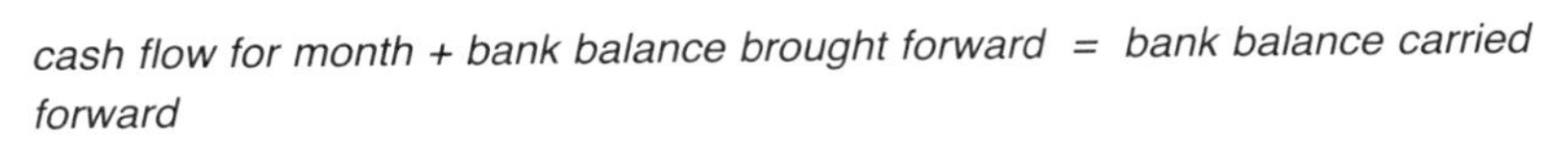

cash flow for month + bank balance brought forward = bank balance carried forward

The closing bank balance (bank balance carried forward) for one month is then entered as the opening bank balance for the following month (bank balance brought forward). Negative figures are shown in brackets.

FIRST TRADE – CASH BUDGET FOR MONTHS 1 TO 4

	Month 1 *£000*	Month 2 *£000*	Month 3 *£000*	Month 4 *£000*
Receipts:				
Initial Investment	25			
Receipts from Sales	–	–	4	6
Total Receipts	25	–	4	6
Payments:				
Purchases	6	–	6	4
Expenses	1	1	1	1
Non-current Assets	15	–	–	–
Drawings	–	–	–	2
Total Payments	22	1	7	7
Cash Flow for Month	3	(1)	(3)	(1)
Bank Balance brought forward	0	3	2	(1)
Bank Balance carried forward	3	2	(1)	(2)

We can see from the cash budget that if everything goes according to plan, Jim's business bank balance will be £3,000 in credit at the end of month 1, but will fall to an overdrawn balance of £2,000 by the end of month 4.

Jim would therefore need to arrange suitable finance if he wishes to follow this budget.

He should also consider the impact of things not going according to plan. For example sales may be lower than forecast and expenses may be higher. This 'what-if' planning process is called sensitivity analysis, and in Chapter 4 we will see how to deal with this issue.

The budgeted statement of financial position as at the end of the four month period is prepared as follows:

- The non-current assets are inserted based on their carrying value (cost less accumulated depreciation). This is £15,000 minus £1,000 equals £14,000.
- The inventory value of £7,000 is taken from the closing inventory in the budgeted statement of profit or loss.
- The trade receivables amount is equal to the sales for months 3 and 4, since these will not have been received in the four month period (remember these were not shown in the cash budget).
- The bank overdraft is taken straight from the closing balance in the cash budget.
- The trade payables amount relates to the purchases made in month 4 which are unpaid (and were not shown in the cash budget).
- The capital account figure is made up as shown using the initial investment, budgeted profit and budgeted drawings.

FIRST TRADE – BUDGETED STATEMENT OF FINANCIAL POSITION AS AT THE END OF MONTH 4

	£	£	£
Non-current Assets:	**Cost**	**Dep'n**	**Net**
Equipment	15,000	1,000	14,000
Current Assets:			
Inventory		7,000	
Trade receivables		12,000	
		19,000	
Less Current Liabilities:			
Bank Overdraft	2,000		
Trade payables	5,000		
		7,000	
			12,000
Total Net Assets			26,000
Capital Account:			
Initial investment			25,000
Add budgeted profit			3,000
Less budgeted drawings			(2,000)
			26,000

LINKS WITH OTHER BUDGETS

cash budget and master budget

A full set of budgets for an organisation will normally include:

- a **budgeted statement of financial position** (as at the end of the budget period)
- a **budgeted statement of profit or loss**
- a **cash budget**

The budgeted statement of financial position is based on the same format as the historical statement of financial position produced for financial accounting purposes, but is based in the future. It is a statement of the **expected assets**, **liabilities** and **capital** at the end of the budgeting period.

Because this document will tie in with the other two main budgets, it will incorporate the profit generated in the budgeted statement of profit or loss, and the final cash or bank balance as predicted in the cash budget.

The budgeted statement of profit or loss and the budgeted statement of financial position are together known as the **master budget**.

subsidiary budgets

There are also a number of other **subsidiary budgets** that often have to be created in more complex businesses in order to build up sufficient information to create the master budget and the budgeted cash flow statement. You may need to extract information from a sales budget or a production budget and use the information in a cash budget.

PRACTICAL ISSUES RELATING TO CASH BUDGETS

dealing with units and prices

The source data that we have available to produce our cash budget may be in a form of units (numbers of items) that are to be purchased or sold. These units may be bought and/or sold at varying prices at different times. When compiling data for our cash budget we must take a logical approach, multiplying the relevant number of units by the appropriate price, but taking care to use the data correctly.

Let us see what we mean by using an example.

worked example: price changes

A business trades in a single product, and the following numbers of units for purchase and sale have been planned for the next few months:

Month	**Purchases** *(no. units)*	**Sales** *(no. units)*
January	60	55
February	70	63
March	68	65
April	75	71
May	80	85

Purchases are paid for on two months' credit, whilst all sales are made on one month's credit.

Items bought in January, February and March will cost £118 per unit, and those bought in April and May will cost £125 per unit. Sales invoiced in January and February will be charged at £140 per unit and those sold in March, April and May will be charged at £150 per unit.

We are asked to calculate the receipts from sales and the payments for purchases in the months of March, April, and May.

We need to note that:

- the prices relate to the months when the items are bought and sold (not to the months when the cash is received or paid)
- the price change for sales is at a different time to the one for purchases
- there is a time lag of one month for sales receipts and two months for payments for purchases

We can then calculate the receipts and payments as follows:

	March £	**April** £	**May** £
Receipts from Sales:			
February Sales (63 x £140)	8,820		
March Sales (65 x £150)		9,750	
April Sales (71 x £150)			10,650
Payments for Purchases:			
January Purchases (60 x £118)	7,080		
February Purchases (70 x £118)		8,260	
March Purchases (68 x £118)			8,024

dealing with 'split' receipts

Sometimes receipts from a month's sales may not all be received at the same time. This may be because either

- some sales are made on a cash basis, and
- some customers are allowed different credit terms to others, or
- the budget is to take account of a percentage of sales being paid for late

The principle of dealing with this situation in both the cash budget and the statement of financial position is identical to that already used, but more calculation will be required. The best way to deal with the cash budget is to use additional line(s) to account for the different assumed credit terms. If this is not possible due to the layout that is imposed, a separate working will serve the same purpose.

We will use a worked example to demonstrate the principle.

worked example: 'split receipts'

A new company has projected sales (all credit sales) as follows:

Month 1 £200,000; Month 2 £250,000; Month 3 £320,000

It is assumed that 80% of each month's sales will be received one month later, and the remaining 20% in the following month (ie two months after the sale).

An extract from the cash budget can be drawn up as follows:

	Month 1	Month 2	Month 3
	£000	*£000*	*£000*
Receipts from sales:			
(1 month's credit)	–	160 (1)	200 (2)
(2 months' credit)	–	–	40 (3)
Total receipts from sales	–	160	240

Workings:
(1) £200,000 x 80%
(2) £250,000 x 80%
(3) £200,000 x 20%

The trade receivables figure in the budgeted statement of financial position as at the end of month 3 would be made up as follows:

Part of month 2 sales	£50,000	(£250,000 x 20%)
All of month 3 sales	£320,000	
Total trade receivables	£370,000	

The same principle would apply if purchases were to be paid using varying credit terms, although this situation is less common.

dealing with discounts

If businesses offer discounts to trade receivables for prompt payment (or take advantage of those offered by trade payables) this will have an impact on the cash budget. The key to remember is that the amount of any discount will reduce the amount received or paid, and the receipts or payments must therefore be adjusted accordingly.

worked example: dealing with discounts

For example, suppose a business offers a 3% discount if its customers pay in the month of sale, but no discount if they pay on two months' credit. If the business estimates that 50% of its customers will take advantage of this discount, then it would have the following receipts relating to June sales of £100,000, and July sales of £120,000:

	June	July	Aug	Sept
	£	£	£	£
Receipts – Current month's sales	48,500	58,200	–	–
Receipts – Two months' credit	–	–	50,000	60,000

Note that the sales receipts for June and July are calculated by working out half of the month's sales and deducting 3%.

dealing with irrecoverable debts

If a business anticipates that it will incur some irrecoverable debts (customers who fail to pay) then it makes sense to incorporate this into a cash budget. Although it would be impossible to accurately predict exactly when and how much would be lost in this way, it would be prudent to make an estimate based on previous experience and current trading conditions.

When adjusting a cash budget for irrecoverable debts it is important to remember that we are assuming that these amounts will not be paid to the business, and that the anticipated receipts will be lower as a result. It would be normal practice in the cash budget to spread such an allowance for non-payment over all months' credit sales, even though it may not actually occur in that way. The amount of irrecoverable debts anticipated would probably be estimated in the form of a percentage of sales, and that is the approach that we will use in the following example, which also incorporates other issues that we have just examined.

worked example – allowing for irrecoverable debts

A business offers its customers a 2% discount for payment in the month of sale.

It is expected that customers of 40% of each month's sales will take advantage of this discount.

30% of each month's sales will be paid for during the month following the sale, and 29% of each month's sales will be paid for two months after the sale. The remaining 1% of each month's sales will be assumed to be uncollectable and will be treated as irrecoverable debts in the cash budget.

Sales are budgeted to be:

January	£400,000
February	£430,000
March	£420,000

The receipts from these sales would be calculated as follows:

	January	February	March	April	May
	£	£	£	£	£
Receipts:					
Current month's sales (after discount)	156,800	168,560	164,640		
One month's credit		120,000	129,000	126,000	
Two months' credit			116,000	124,700	121,800

Note that the whole month's sales amount is not collected.

In this example it is reduced by the discount, amounting to (40% x 2% = 0.8%), and the irrecoverable debt allowance of 1%, leaving 98.2% to be received in cash.

So receipts from January sales, for example, are:

£156,800 + £120,000 + £116,000 = £392,800 (which equals 98.2% of the sales of £400,000)

This calculation to reconcile your figures is a useful way to check your method of working and arithmetic.

Remember that while prompt payment discounts can apply to sales and/or purchases, there is no equivalent to irrecoverable debts that we would apply to the payments that our organisation makes. We cannot plan not to pay any of the amounts that we owe!

dealing with bank account interest

In the previous examples given we have ignored any bank interest, ie

- interest received from positive cash balances
- interest payable on a bank overdraft

Although interest calculations in practice would probably be based on daily bank balances, using monthly balances will usually provide a satisfactory estimate of the interest payments involved.

In the next worked example we assume that bank interest is received or paid monthly, based on the closing bank balance at the end of the previous month.

One issue to be careful about is to check whether the interest quoted is based on monthly or annual rates. If the percentage rate is monthly, this can be applied directly to the balance, but where the rate is annual (the normal situation) it must first be divided by 12 to arrive at a monthly rate before the interest is calculated.

Because interest amounts are likely to be relatively small some rounding may be required. It is certainly never worth estimating interest amounts in less than whole pounds.

It is also worth double-checking that your decimal point is correct when calculating the interest!

worked example – dealing with bank interest

Suppose the following cash budget figures had been calculated before taking account of bank interest.

The bank will pay interest at 0.5% per month on a closing credit balance of the previous month, and charge interest at 1.0% per month on overdrawn balances.

The bank balance at the end of the previous December is £10,000.

	January £	February £	March £
Total receipts (before any interest)	6,500	4,500	6,000
Total payments (before any interest)	15,000	6,500	7,000

The bank interest would be accounted for in the cash budget as follows (see next page):

	January	February	March
	£	£	£
Receipts (before any interest)	6,500	4,500	6,000
Interest received	50	8	–
Total receipts	6,550	4,508	6,000
Payments (before any interest)	15,000	6,500	7,000
Interest paid	–	–	4
Total payments	15,000	6,500	7,004
Cash flow for month	(8,450)	(1,992)	(1,004)
Balance brought forward	10,000	1,550	(442)
Balance carried forward	1,550	(442)	(1,446)

The order of calculation is clearly important since the interest on each balance has an impact on the next month's balance, which in turn affects the next interest amount. Each month's cash balance must therefore be finalised before the next month's figures are finalised.

If you are using a budgeted statement of profit or loss for the same period, it will also be necessary to treat any interest as income or expenditure. This of course will have an impact on net profit, and if a draft figure has been calculated it will need revising.

Note that banks may credit or debit the bank account with interest on a quarterly basis. The calculation of the interest would be carried out in the same way.

a note on debenture interest

Some businesses are financed by fixed interest loans known as debentures. You may be told, for example, that a business has raised finance by issuing £10,000 of 5% Debenture Stock. It will need to account in the statement of profit or loss for paying 5% x £10,000 = £500 interest. This will also need to be accounted for as a payment on the relevant date(s) in the cash budget.

dealing with a range of adjustments

One of the source documents that we may use to prepare our cash budget is a budgeted statement of profit or loss that has already been prepared. If this is the case then we will need to convert data that was prepared on an accruals basis into cash-based figures. This could apply to the sales and purchases that are shown in a statement of profit or loss as well as the expenses.

If you have learned how to produce accounts from incomplete records you will be familiar with the logic of the calculations that we are going to use, but note that here we are going to be carrying out the calculations in the opposite direction.

trade receivables amounts

We have already seen how receipts from sales can be calculated if we are provided with information about the proportions of sales that are to be received at various points in time. An alternative approach that you may need to take would be if you are provided with an amount for the budgeted sales for the period, together with the budgeted trade receivables amount at the end of the budget period. To calculate the expected receipts from sales in the budget period we need to deduct the amount which is still to be receivable at the end of the period from the budgeted sales.

For example, if budgeted sales were £150,000 for the first period of a new business, and trade receivables at the end of the period were budgeted at £35,000, then the amount expected to be received in cash must be £150,000 – £35,000 = £115,000. Logically, if the £35,000 is still receivable at the end of the period then it won't be received in cash during the period.

If we are dealing with an existing business with a trade receivables figure at the start of the budgeted period as well, then this figure is added into the calculation of receipts from sales.

For example, suppose budgeted sales for a period are £200,000, and the trade receivables amount at the start is £60,000, with the trade receivables at the end of the period budgeted at £75,000. The budgeted cash receipts will be calculated as £60,000 + £200,000 – £75,000 = £185,000.

trade payables amounts

Just like the calculation of receipts from sales that we have just examined, a similar calculation of the payments for purchases can be carried out if information on trade payables at the start and end of the period is provided. To calculate the amount to be paid in cash during the budget period, the amount payable at the start of the period is added, and the budgeted payable amount at the end is deducted.

For example, suppose budgeted purchases for a period are £120,000, and the trade payables amount at the start that relates to purchases is £40,000, with the trade payables at the end of the period budgeted at £35,000. The budgeted cash payments for purchases will be calculated as £40,000 + £120,000 – £35,000 = £125,000.

accruals

Where we have a budgeted expense figure that incorporates an accrual at the end of the period the accrual will have increased the expense since it relates to an amount related to the period but not to be paid until later. We therefore need to deduct any period-end accrual to get back to the cash-based expense.

For example, if electricity expense was budgeted at £1,500 for the period, and this incorporated an accrual at the end of the period of £300, then the cash-based amount would be £1,500 – £300 = £1,200.

If an accrual at the start of the period had been incorporated into the budgeted expense (ie an amount accrued at the end of the previous period) then the procedure is the opposite. This means that any opening accrual must be added to arrive at the cash-based amount.

For example, suppose general expenses were budgeted at £3,000 for the period. If this incorporated an opening accrual of £200 (brought forward from the previous period) and an accrual at the end of the period of £350 then the cash-based amount would be £3,000 + £200 – £350 = £2,850. This is because the £200 will need to be paid in this period, but the £350 will not be paid until the following period.

prepayments

Prepayments are the opposite of accruals. As the name suggests they are amounts that are paid in the period before the period that the expense relates to. It follows that the treatment for converting data from a budgeted statement of profit or loss into a cash-based form is the opposite to that for accruals.

Where they have been incorporated into expenses, prepayments at the end of a period should be added and those at the beginning deducted to arrive at the cash-based amount.

For example, suppose insurance for the period was budgeted at £5,000 as an expense. If this was after incorporating prepayments at the start of the period of £1,000 and the end of the period of £1,250, then the cash-based amount would be £5,000 – £1,000 + £1,250 = £5,250.

depreciation

As illustrated in earlier Case Studies, depreciation is not a cash-based expense, and should therefore never appear in cash budgets. Instead the amount paid for the asset is recorded as a payment at the time when the asset is bought. If a particular expense includes some depreciation then the depreciation element should be deducted from the total expense before being used in the cash budget.

For example, factory overheads are budgeted at £80,000 for the period, but this includes depreciation of machinery amounting to £15,000. Assuming there were no accruals or prepayments incorporated into the factory overheads, the amount to be recorded in the cash budget would be £80,000 – £15,000 = £65,000.

Other non-cash items related to non-current assets are profits or losses on disposal of such assets. As these are non-cash amounts that are based on the depreciation that has been charged they will not appear in the cash budget. Instead the actual amount received as proceeds will appear as a cash receipt at the appropriate time.

Case Study

TRICKEY TRADING: WORKING FROM A BUDGETED STATEMENT OF PROFIT OR LOSS

situation

John and Janet Trickey plan to start a new trading business as a partnership, and have already drawn up a budgeted statement of profit or loss for the first three months of the new business. This has been produced using accruals accounting, and is as follows:

Budgeted statement of profit or loss for months 1-3

	£	£
Sales		120,000
less cost of sales		72,000
Gross Profit		48,000
less expenses:		
Power, light & heat	4,800	
Telephone & postage	1,600	
Rent & rates	2,200	
Insurance	1,200	
Staff salaries	9,000	
General expenses	1,500	
Irrecoverable debts	960	
Depreciation of equipment	1,000	
		22,260
Net Profit		25,740

You have also established the following information from talking to John and Janet and examining their plans:

- The couple will be investing £60,000 cash into the business. Of this amount, £20,000 will be spent immediately on equipment (the depreciation of which is shown in the budget on the previous page).
- Sales are made up of £30,000 in month 1, £40,000 in month 2, and £50,000 in month 3. 20% of sales are made for cash, with the remainder on 2 months' credit. An allowance of 1% of credit sales is made for irrecoverable debts.
- Purchases of goods for resale are planned to be £36,000 in month 1, £28,000 in month 2, and £32,000 in month 3. Unsold goods will remain in stock as inventory. All purchases are made on one month's credit.
- Accruals at the end of the three month period have been incorporated into the expense of Power, Light and Heat of £800.
- The following prepayments at the end of the three month period have been incorporated into the expenses of Rent & Rates – £1,000, and Insurance – £3,600.
- All Power, Light & Heat, and Telephone & Postage payments take place in month 3.
- All Rent & Rates and Insurance Payments take place in month 1.
- Payments for Staff Salaries and General Expenses are spread evenly over the three months.
- John and Janet each plan to take £2,500 from the business in drawings each month.

required

(a) Prepare a cash budget for the first three months of John and Janet's business.

(b) Prepare a reconciliation of profit with cash movement for the period.

solution

(a) The completed cash budget is shown on the next page. The notes that follow explain and show workings for the more complex parts.

Trickey Trading: Cash Budget for Months 1-3

	Month 1 £	Month 2 £	Month 3 £
Receipts			
Initial Investment	60,000	–	–
Receipts from sales:			
Cash Sales	6,000	8,000	10,000
Credit Sales	–	–	23,760
Total Receipts	66,000	8,000	33,760
Payments			
Purchases	–	36,000	28,000
Power, Light & Heat	–	–	4,000
Telephone & Postage	–	–	1,600
Rent & Rates	3,200	–	–
Insurance	4,800	–	–
Staff Salaries	3,000	3,000	3,000
General Expenses	500	500	500
Drawings	5,000	5,000	5,000
Payment for Equipment	20,000	–	–
Total Payments	36,500	44,500	42,100
Net Cash Flow for Month	29,500	(36,500)	(8,340)
Bank Balance brought forward	0	29,500	(7,000)
Bank Balance carried forward	29,500	(7,000)	(15,340)

Notes:

(1) Receipts from Cash Sales: these are based on 20% of the respective month's sales figures. The allowance for irrecoverable debts does not apply to cash sales.

(2) Receipts from Credit Sales: since the credit sales are made on 2 months' credit, the first month's credit sales are received in month 3. This figure is calculated as £30,000 x 80% x 99% = £23,760. The 99% part of the calculation allows for the irrecoverable debts of 1%. In the statement of profit or loss this allowance is shown as an expense item, but in the cash budget it simply reduces the receipts.

(3) Payments for Purchases: the figures are based on lagging the purchase amounts by one month.

(4) Power, Light & Heat: the amount of £4,800 – £800 accrual = £4,000 is paid in month 3.

(5) Telephone & Postage: the amount (without any adjustments) is paid in month 3.

(6) Rent & Rates: the prepayment of £1,000 is added to the amount of £2,200 that is shown in the statement of profit or loss, and the total of £3,200 is shown in month 1.

(7) Insurance: here the prepayment is three times the amount shown in the statement of profit or loss. This probably means that the payment in month 1 covers a whole year's insurance of £1,200 + £3,600 = £4,800.

(8) Staff Salaries and General Expenses: the amounts (without any adjustments) are spread over three months.

(9) Drawings: the drawings for the two partners are added together and shown as cash payments. They are not shown in the statement of profit or loss as they are an appropriation of profit, not an expense.

(10) Payment for Equipment: this is shown in month 1 as a cash payment. Note that depreciation is not recorded in the cash budget.

(b) The completed reconciliation statement is shown below. It follows the same logic as previously, but has to take account of various complexities. The notes that follow explain the more complicated calculations.

	£
Budgeted Profit for Period	25,740
Add non-cash expenditure used in calculation of profit:	
Depreciation	1,000
Accruals of Power, Light and Heat	800
Add cash receipts not used in calculation of profit:	
Capital Invested	60,000
Deduct cash payments not used in the calculation of profit:	
Purchase of Equipment	(20,000)
Payment of Drawings	(15,000)
Prepayment of Rent and Rates	(1,000)
Prepayment of Insurance	(3,600)
Adjust for changes in inventory:	
Deduct increase in inventory (1)	(24,000)
Adjust for changes in trade receivables:	
Deduct increase in trade receivables (2)	(71,280)
Adjust for changes in trade payables:	
Add increase in trade payables (3)	32,000
(Decrease) in cash	(15,340)

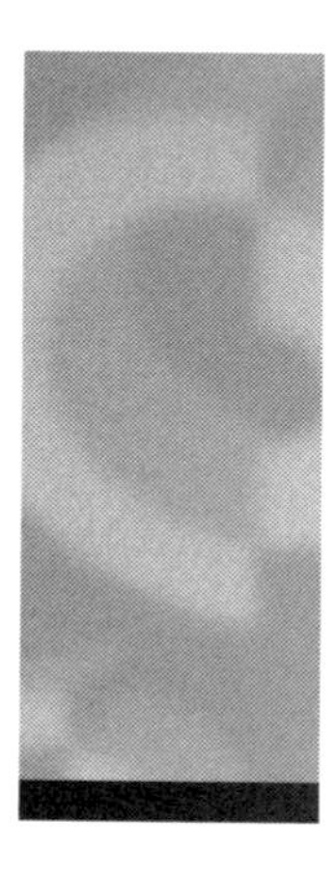

Notes:

(1) Inventory at the end of the period is calculated as the difference between the purchases of £36,000 + £28,000 + £32,000 = £96,000, and the cost of sales of £72,000. There is no opening inventory. The increase in inventory is therefore £24,000.

(2) The trade receivables at the end of the period is made up of credit sales for months 2 and 3, after allowing for irrecoverable debts. The trade receivables is therefore (£40,000 + £50,000) x 80% x 99% = £71,280. As there are no opening receivables this figure also represents the increase in receivables.

(3) Trade payables at the end of the period consist of month 3 purchases of £32,000. As there are no opening trade payables this figure also represents the increase in trade payables.

DEALING WITH ESTABLISHED BUSINESSES

In this chapter so far we have seen how a cash budget and budgeted statement of financial position can be prepared for a new business. If we need to prepare these documents for a business that is already trading the main principles are identical. The only extra factor to account for is the cash impact in this budget period of transactions that occurred in the previous budget period. These will typically be:

- receipts in this period from sales made in the last period, and
- payments in this period related to purchases incurred in the last period
- accruals and prepayments at the end of the last period (and therefore also at the start of the current period) that affect the current period

We have already seen how to deal with accruals and prepayments at the start of the period. Any opening accruals are added to the current period expense, and any opening prepayments are deducted from the current period expense.

The amounts relating to delayed receipts from sales and delayed payments for purchases will show up as trade receivables and trade payables at the end of the previous period, and we can often pick up the data from this source. We will then just need to check when the cash receipt or payment is expected to occur to be able to insert the right figures into our cash budget.

For example, if we are producing a cash budget for January to March, we will need information about the trade receivables and trade payables at the end of the previous December.

Suppose the December trade receivables figure is £20,000, made up of November sales of £12,000 and December sales of £8,000. If the credit customers pay on two months' credit, we will need to include in our cash budget:

- £12,000 receipt in January (in respect of November sales), and
- £8,000 receipt in February (in respect of December sales)

If we are provided with a statement of financial position or balance sheet at the end of the preceding period, then the cash / bank figure shown there will form the opening cash balance figure for our cash budget. We will now use a Case Study to see how this approach fits alongside the techniques that we used earlier. The Case Study will also demonstrate how the reconciliation of profit and cash is prepared for an existing business.

Case Study

MOORE TRADING: BUDGETS FOR AN ESTABLISHED BUSINESS

situation

Jane Moore has been trading for several years. She has prepared the following budgeted Satement of Profit or Loss for the first four months' trading of her year 10. Jane sells goods on two months' credit, and pays for purchases on one month's credit.

Budgeted statement of profit or loss, January - April Year 10

	£	£
Sales		30,000
less cost of sales:		
opening inventory	5,000	
purchases	21,000	
less closing inventory	(6,000)	
		20,000
Gross profit		10,000
less:		
expenses	4,300	
depreciation	2,000	
		6,300
Profit for the period		3,700

Jane also provides you with the following information regarding her plans for the part of year 10 covered by her budgets:

- The sales figures in the budgeted statement are based on monthly sales as follows:

	£
January	6,000
February	7,000
March	8,000
April	9,000
Total sales	30,000

- The purchases figure in the budgeted statement is made up as follows:

	£
January	4,000
February	6,000
March	6,000
April	5,000
Total purchases	21,000

- There is an expense accrual at the end of year 9 of £500 (as shown in the statement of financial position below), and an anticipated expense accrual of £800 at the end of month 4 of year 10. The cash paid out for expenses in months 1 to 4 of year 10 will be spread evenly over the 4 months.
- The depreciation shown in the budgeted statement of profit or loss is based on depreciating equipment at 20% per year on a straight-line basis. Equipment that cost £20,000 was purchased in January of year 9. Further equipment is to be bought for £10,000 in January year 10.
- Jane wishes to withdraw £1,500 from the business in each of the months of February and April in year 10.
- Bank interest is to be ignored.

The draft statement of financial position has already been prepared as at the end of year 9, and an extract is shown here. Notes on the statement of financial position follow on the next page.

Moore Trading

Statement of financial position Extract as at 31 December Year 9

	£	£	£
Non-current Assets			
	Cost	**Dep'n**	**Net**
Equipment	20,000	4,000	16,000
Current Assets:			
Inventory		5,000	
Trade Receivables		11,000	
Bank		10,000	
		26,000	
Less Current Liabilities:			
Trade Payables	4,000		
Accruals	500		
		4,500	
			21,500
Total Net Assets			37,500

Notes on the statement of financial position:

- The trade receivables relates to sales of £6,500 in November and £4,500 in December. These sales are on two months' credit.
- The trade payables relate to December purchases. Payment is due to be made in January.
- The business is financed entirely by the capital account.

required

(a) Prepare a cash budget for the first four months of year 10.

(b) Prepare a reconciliation of profit with cash movement for the period.

solution

(a) Moore Trading: Cash Budget for January to April of Year 10.

	January £	February £	March £	April £
Receipts				
Receipts from year 9 sales	6,500	4,500	–	–
Receipts from year 10 sales	–	–	6,000	7,000
Total receipts	6,500	4,500	6,000	7,000
Payments				
Purchases made in year 9	4,000	–	–	–
Purchases made in year 10	–	4,000	6,000	6,000
Expenses	1,000	1,000	1,000	1,000
Non-current assets	10,000	–	–	–
Drawings	–	1,500	–	1,500
Total payments	15,000	6,500	7,000	8,500
Cash flow for month	(8,500)	(2,000)	(1,000)	(1,500)
Bank balance brought forward	10,000	1,500	(500)	(1,500)
Bank balance carried forward	1,500	(500)	(1,500)	(3,000)

Notes:

The **expense payments** are calculated as follows:

Expenses from budgeted statement of profit or loss £4,300 + Opening Accrual £500 – Closing Accrual £800 = £4,000. This is spread evenly over the four months.

The **receipts and payments figures** arising from each year have been shown here as separate lines for clarity, but this is not always required. The opening bank balance in January of £10,000 is taken from the statement of financial position extract.

Make sure that you can see where each figure in the cash budget comes from.

(b) The completed reconciliation statement is shown below. Since we are now examining an existing business we need to ensure that we take account of data from the opening statement of financial position when calculating certain changes. The notes that follow explain the more complicated calculations.

	£
Budgeted Profit for Period	3,700
Add non-cash expenditure used in calculation of profit:	
Depreciation	2,000
Increase in Expense Accruals (1)	300
Deduct cash payments not used in the calculation of profit:	
Purchase of Equipment	(10,000)
Payment of Drawings	(3,000)
Adjust for changes in inventory:	
Deduct increase in inventory (2)	(1,000)
Adjust for changes in trade receivables:	
Deduct increase in trade receivables (3)	(6,000)
Adjust for changes in trade payables:	
Add increase in trade payables (4)	1,000
(Decrease) in cash (5)	(13,000)
Opening cash balance	10,000
Closing cash balance (overdrawn)	(3,000)

Notes:

(1) The adjustment for accruals is based on the increase in accruals of £800 – £500 = £300. It follows a similar logic to changes in trade payables. This could alternatively be shown as two adjustments.

(2) The increase in inventory is calculated from the two figures shown in the budgeted statement of profit or loss.

(3) The opening trade receivables (shown on the opening statement of financial position) are £11,000. The closing trade receivables are made up of March and April sales (£8,000 + £9,000 = £17,000). The increase in trade receivables is therefore £6,000.

(4) The opening trade payables figure is £4,000 as shown on the statement of financial position. The closing trade payables figure represents the April purchases of £5,000. The increase is therefore £1,000.

(5) The cash balance has reduced from an opening balance of £10,000 (positive) to an overdrawn £3,000. This is a decrease of £13,000.

CALCULATION OF CLOSING RECEIVABLES AND PAYABLES

We saw earlier in this chapter that there are links between the 'trade receivables' and 'trade payables' figures shown in the statement of financial position and the cash budget. In the Case Study for 'Moore Trading' on pages 95 - 98 we used data from statements of financial position to help us establish the figures to use in the cash budget and to reconcile profit with cash.

We are now going to ensure that we can also calculate the closing trade receivables and trade payables figures that would appear in a budgeted statement of financial position for a date immediately following a cash budget. We saw a simple example of this in the Case Study 'First Trade'.

These figures that we need will be ones that are not used as receipts or payments in the cash budget because they would arise after the period – instead they are amounts owing to or by the organisation at the period end. You may like to think of these figures as the ones that 'fall off' the end of the cash budget.

We will use the following Case Study to demonstrate how the figures work.

Case Study

CASCADE LIMITED

situation

Credit sales and purchases in the first three months of the year is estimated as follows:

	January	February	March
	£	£	£
Credit sales	18,400	19,600	17,900
Credit purchases	14,500	15,100	15,600

The expected pattern for receipts from credit sales and payments for purchases is as follows:

	Month after transaction	Following month
Receipts from credit sales	60%	40%
Payments for purchases	70%	30%

required

(a) Calculate the receipts and payments arising from these figures that would appear in a cash budget for February and March.

(b) Calculate the trade receivables and trade payables amounts as at 31 March.

solution

(a) The months when the sales should be received can be calculated using a table:

	February £	March £	April £	May £
January sales 60%	11,040			
January sales 40%		7,360		
February sales 60%		11,760		
February sales 40%			7,840	
March sales 60%			10,740	
March sales 40%				7,160
Total receipts	11,040	19,120	18,580	7,160
	Use in cash budget for February and March		Total equals trade receivables at end of March	

The totals relating to February and March would be used directly in a cash budget for the first quarter of the year.

The amounts shown as being received in April and May arise entirely from the sales in the first quarter, and therefore when added together give the trade receivables figure for 31 March (£18,580 + £7,160 = £25,740).

(b) We can take the same approach to calculate the payments and trade payables figures:

	February £	March £	April £	May £
January purchases 70%	10,150			
January purchases 30%		4,350		
February purchases 70%		10,570		
February purchases 30%			4,530	
March purchases 70%			10,920	
March purchases 30%				4,680
Total payments	10,150	14,920	15,450	4,680
	Use in cash budget for February and March		Total equals trade payables at end of March	

The trade payables amount at 31 March is therefore (£15,450 + £4,680 = £20,130).

Earlier in the chapter we used formulas to calculate cash receipts and payments. These formulas can often be used to calculate closing trade receivables or trade payables balances, depending on the data provided:

Receipts from credit sales
= opening trade receivables + credit sales – closing trade receivables

Payments for credit purchases
= opening trade payables + credit purchases – closing trade payables

By manipulating these formulas you will be able to calculate the closing figures if you have all the other data.

For example, suppose we have the following figures:

- receipts from credit sales £140,600
- opening trade receivables £42,350
- credit sales £138,400

We can see that by using the formula:

£140,600 = £42,350 + £138,400 – closing trade receivables

This becomes:

£140,600 = £180,750 – closing trade receivables

We can then see that closing trade receivables must be the difference between £180,750 and £140,600. This gives us the answer of £40,150.

CALCULATIONS INVOLVING NON-CURRENT ASSETS

We have seen that **depreciation** is a non-cash item, and therefore does not appear in cash budgets. The same applies to the **profit or loss** on the sale of a non-current asset; these are not cash items either.

The cash items related to non-current assets are:

- cash paid for the purchase of additions to non-current assets
- cash paid to lease additions to non-current assets under a finance lease
- cash received for the proceeds of non-current assets that are sold

These can appear in cash budgets, and we may need to calculate the figures.

Non-current assets that are acquired through finance leases are capitalised through the statement of financial position in the same way as purchased non-current assets. The cash payments are then normally made in instalments over the duration of the lease.

calculation of amounts paid for non-current assets

To carry out these calculations we need to remember how the carrying amounts for non-current assets are calculated. Carrying amounts are calculated as cost minus accumulated depreciation. You may have learned about this topic in your financial accounting studies.

Opening carrying amount

+ cost of additions in period

– depreciation for period

– carrying amount of disposals in period

= closing carrying amount

We can use this formula to calculate the cost of additions, provided we have all the other data referred to.

For example, suppose we are told that:

- opening carrying amount of non-current assets is £750,000
- closing carrying amount of non-current assets is £980,000
- depreciation in the period was £63,000
- there were no disposals of non-current assets during the period

Using the formula we can insert the given figures:

£750,000 + additions – £63,000 – £0 = £980,000

We can deduct the £63,000 from the £750,000, to give:

£687,000 + additions = £980,000

The additions therefore must be £293,000. Provided the additions are all paid in cash this figure would appear in a cash budget or statement.

If, alternatively, we were told that additions valued at £100,000 were acquired through a finance lease, we could calculate that the additions purchased for cash must be £293,000 – £100,000 = £193,000. The £193,000 would then appear in the cash budget, along with the cash amounts paid to the finance lease company. We would need to be informed of how much these lease payments were.

calculation of amounts received on disposal of non-current assets

If we know how the profit or loss on the disposal of non-current assets is calculated we can use this information to work out the proceeds of disposal.

Disposal proceeds – carrying amount of asset disposed of = profit on disposal

Remember that carrying amount is usually cost minus accumulated depreciation. If the disposal proceeds are lower than the carrying value the result is a loss on disposal.

For example, suppose we are told that:

- an item disposed of had a cost of £35,000
- the item had accumulated depreciation of £23,480
- the disposal resulted in a loss of £3,100

We can calculate the carrying amount by deducting the accumulated depreciation from the cost (£35,000 – £23,480 = £11,520). Since a loss is incurred we know that the proceeds are lower than the carrying amount. The proceeds will be the carrying amount minus the loss.

The proceeds must be £11,520 – £3,100 = £8,420.

Assuming this amount is received in cash it would appear in a cash statement or budget.

calculations involving revaluations of non-current assets

So far in our calculations relating to non-current assets we have assumed that the carrying amount has been based on cost minus accumulated depreciation.

You may also be asked to carry out similar calculations involving assets that have been revalued. Depending on when the revaluation was carried out, the carrying value could be:

- the revaluation amount, or
- the revaluation amount less subsequent depreciation, or
- the revaluation amount, less subsequent impairment amount(s)

For our calculations in this unit we can treat both depreciation after revaluation and impairment amounts in the same way – as non-cash adjustments.

For example, supposing we are told that:

- some land was purchased for £1.5m in 20-5
- the land was revalued to £1.8m on 31/12/20-7
- the land was sold on 31/6/20-8, generating a profit of £150,000

The carrying amount at the date of sale will be the revaluation carried out six months earlier (there is normally no depreciation charged on land). The proceeds of disposal can therefore be calculated as £1,800,000 + £150,000 = £1,950,000. Note that we ignore the original cost in this calculation.

We could also calculate the original cost of a revalued asset, as the following example shows:

- an asset was purchased on 1/1/20-3
- an asset was originally depreciated by £25,000 per year

- on 31/12/20-6 the asset was revalued to £170,000, and this reduced the carrying value by £30,000

The cost minus depreciation at the revaluation date must have been £170,000 + £30,000 = £200,000.

The original cost must have been higher than that figure by four year's depreciation:

Original cost = £200,000 + (4 x £25,000) = £300,000.

Once an asset is revalued we can ignore any cost or depreciation that occurred prior to the revaluation if we are trying to calculate the disposal proceeds.

For example, if we are asked to calculate the disposal proceeds based on:

- The original cost of a building was £1.4m on 1/1/20-1
- The depreciation for 20-1 and 20-2 was £56,000 per year
- On 31/12/20-2 the building was revalued to £1.9m
- The depreciation after revaluation was calculated at £100,000 per year
- The building was sold on 31/12/-4 and incurred a net loss of £40,000

The carrying value at disposal would have been £1,900,000 – (2 x £100,000) = £1,700,000.

The proceeds on disposal would therefore be £1,700,000 – £40,000 = £1,660,000.

Notice that the data prior to revaluation has been ignored.

CALCULATION OF CORPORATION TAX PAYMENTS

You may be presented with data relating to a limited company and be required to calculate the amount of Corporation Tax that will be paid during a period. This could be so that the appropriate payment could be inserted into a cash budget, or it could be as part of a reconciliation of profit with cash.

Corporation Tax payments are often made after the period that the tax relates to. The amount shown in the statement of profit or loss will be the tax charge for the period, and will probably not be the same as the amount paid during the period.

The technique that we will use to establish the payment is the same one that we used to calculate payments for purchases or expenses when using opening and closing balances.

A Corporation Tax account in the books of a limited company will typically look like the following example:

Corporation Tax Account

Bank	£100,300	Balance b/f	£80,500
Balance c/f	£71,450	Statement of profit or loss	£91,250
	£171,750		£171,750

The opening and closing balances relate to the amounts of Corporation Tax owing (to HMRC) at the start and end of the period. The amount shown in the statement of profit or loss will be credited to the Corporation Tax account, and the payment of tax will be debited.

It should therefore be straight forward to calculate the tax payment from the other figures.

For example if the tax amount shown in the statement of profit or loss for 20-4 is £21,000, and the tax amounts payable shown in the statement of financial position are £20,000 at 1 January 20-4 and £22,000 at 31 December 20-4, the tax paid can be calculated as:

£21,000 + £20,000 – £22,000 = £19,000

There is one particular issue to be careful of when using tax data in a statement reconciling profit and cash. If the profit figure at the start of the statement is the operating profit this will be profit before tax is deducted. In this case we need to show the whole amount of tax payment, instead of just the movement in payables as we would (for example) when showing the impact of purchases.

CALCULATION OF VAT PAYMENTS

You will probably be familiar with the operation of Value Added Tax (VAT) from your other studies. In this unit you may be required to calculate the amount of VAT that will need to be paid (or possibly received) from fairly simple data.

The standard rate of VAT is currently 20%, and this tax will be charged by a VAT registered business on its standard rate sales. The tax will therefore add 20% to the amount that is received from customers, and is known as output tax. This must be paid over to HM Revenue & Customs (HMRC), after VAT that the business has been charged by its suppliers (input VAT) has been deducted.

For example, suppose a business has made standard rated sales of £300,000 (excluding VAT) over a period. The business has been charged £255,000 (including standard rate VAT) by its suppliers over the same period.

The amount of VAT payable to HMRC can be calculated as follows:

	£
Output tax (£300,000 x 20%)	60,000
Input tax (£255,000 x 20/120)	42,500
VAT payable to HMRC	17,500

If the amount of input tax exceeded the output tax, then the difference would be paid by HMRC to the business.

PAYMENTS FOR RAW MATERIALS

When we examined the cash cycle in Chapter 1 we saw that inventory is part of the working capital of an organisation. If inventory levels increase but all the other elements of working capital remain unchanged then there will be less cash available.

In a manufacturing business purchases of raw materials (which of course require cash) are affected by raw material inventory. The following illustration assumes that the raw materials used in each period remains constant, but the inventory level changes. All figures shown are in units of raw materials.

	Period 1	Period 2	Period 3	Period 4
Raw materials usage	20,000	20,000	20,000	20,000
– opening inventory	2,000	4,000	7,000	8,000
+ closing inventory	4,000	7,000	8,000	2,000
= raw materials purchases	22,000	23,000	21,000	14,000

Notice that as the inventory level increases in periods 1 to 3 the amount of purchases is higher than the usage by the difference between the opening and closing inventory levels. As the inventory level falls in period 4 the purchases figure is lower than the usage quantity. Since cash payments will always be based on purchases (lagged to take account of credit terms) when raw material inventory levels increase the payments are larger and cash balances will fall.

The following Case Study will illustrate how the payments for purchases of raw materials can be calculated.

Case Study

STOCKER LIMITED: IMPACT OF INVENTORY LEVELS ON PAYMENTS

Stocker Limited has budgeted for the following levels of raw material inventory over the next few periods:

Inventory valuation at start of following periods:

1	2	3	4	5
£25,300	£28,250	£26,400	£30,000	£29,100

The raw materials usage budget shows the following figures for the same periods:

1	2	3	4	5
£89,400	£77,500	£86,100	£90,000	£96,100

Payments for purchases are made as follows:

- 60% of raw material purchases are paid in the period after delivery
- 40% of raw material purchases are paid 2 periods after delivery

required

Calculate the amounts to be paid for raw materials in each of periods 3 and 4.

solution

The first stage of the calculation is to work out the purchases to be made in each period, using the inventory levels and the usage data.

	Period 1 £	Period 2 £	Period 3 £	Period 4 £	Period 5 £
Raw materials usage	89,400	77,500	86,100	90,000	96,100
– opening inventory	25,300	28,250	26,400	30,000	29,100
+ closing inventory	28,250	26,400	30,000	29,100	Not known
= raw materials purchases	92,350	75,650	89,700	89,100	

Now the purchase amounts can be lagged to provide the information for the payments.

Payments in following periods:					
	Period 1 £	**Period 2** £	**Period 3** £	**Period 4** £	**Period 5** £
Period 1 purchases		55,410	36,940		
Period 2 purchases			45,390	30,260	
Period 3 purchases				53,820	35,880
Total purchase payments			82,330	84,080	

Lastly we include a Case Study which demonstrates the calculation of receipts and payments from various data sources. These tasks will consolidate the principles and techniques you will have learnt in this chapter.

Case Study

CROSSROADS CATERING:USING DATA FROM STATEMENTS OF FINANCIAL POSITION

situation

Robert Johnson owns Crossroads Catering and prepares quarterly statements of profit or loss and statements of financial position. These are prepared on an accruals basis.

Food for meals is purchased fresh when required and therefore very little inventory is maintained. The main customers of the restaurant are local businesses and organisations. All sales and purchases are made on credit terms.

The **statement of profit or loss** for Crossroads Catering for the quarter ended 30 June is as follows:

	£	£
Sales		46,200
Less: Food Purchases		(9,140)
Gross profit		37,060
Less: Expenses		
Wages	14,400	
Rent	3,000	
Catering expenses	2,600	
Insurance	1,550	
Depreciation of Equipment	1,000	
		22,550
		14,510

Extracts from the statements of financial position at 1 April and 30 June show the following:

Statement of financial position (extracts)

	1 April	**30 June**
	£	£
Trade receivables	18,020	16,950
Trade payables	915	1,034
Accruals – catering expenses	480	290
Prepayments – insurance	550	400
Prepayments – rent	1,000	1,260

required

Calculate the actual business cash receipts and cash payments for the quarter to 30 June, using the following table:

	£
Sales receipts	
Purchases (food) payments	
Wages payments	
Rent payments	
Catering expense payments	
Insurance payments	
Equipment depreciation	

solution

	£
Sales receipts	47,270
Purchases (food) payments	9,021
Wages payments	14,400
Rent payments	3,260
Catering expense payments	2,790
Insurance payments	1,400
Equipment depreciation	0

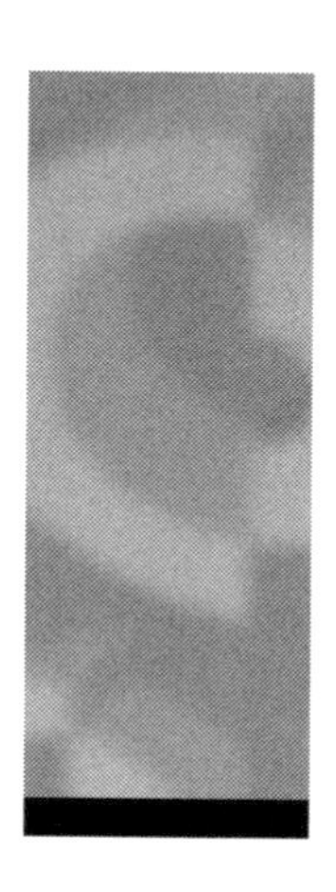

Workings:

	£
Sales receipts	46,200 + 18,020 – 16,950
Purchases (food) payments	9,140 + 915 – 1,034
Wages payments	No adjustments
Rent payments	3,000 – 1,000 + 1,260
Catering expense payments	2,600 + 480 – 290
Insurance payments	1,550 – 550 + 400
Equipment depreciation	Non-cash item

Chapter Summary

- Most of the data that is used to prepare a cash budget is also used to prepare a budgeted statement of profit or loss. In a cash budget the receipts and payments are accounted for on the basis of the time at which the cash flows, rather than on an accruals basis. Data from other sources is also used in a cash budget.

- When sales or purchases that are made on credit are inserted into a cash budget the entries are lagged based on the credit terms to be applied. For example, receipts from sales made on two months' credit would be lagged by two months, and entered in the cash budget two months after the sale was made.

- When preparing a cash budget for an existing business, the opening cash balance will often be taken from the statement of financial position of the same date. Trade receivables and trade payables shown on the same document will also need to be accounted for in the cash budget based on the expected dates of the receipt or the payment.

- A reconciliation of profit with cash movement can be prepared by commencing with the profit figure and adjusting for items that are treated differently in the budgeted statement of profit or loss and cash budget. This will produce a statement that concludes with the budgeted cash movement over the period.

- Cash receipts and payments can be calculated from a range of information, including sales and receivables figures, purchases and payables figures and also from data on non-current asset movements.

- Payments for materials can be calculated from a combination of material usage data and information on planned inventory levels.

cash budget	a budget that sets out the inflows and outflows of cash in a budget period – the receipts and payments format is the most suitable form of cash budget for monitoring and controlling cash in a business
lagging	accounting for the time difference between a credit sale or purchase and the cash receipt or payment
budgeted statement of profit or loss	one of the main summary budgets that can be prepared for the budget period, in the same format as a historical statement of profit or loss
master budget	the combination of the budgeted statement of profit or loss and the budgeted statement of financial position

Activities

3.1 Sonita is planning to open a retail shop. The following is her budgeted statement of profit or loss for the first four months of the business.

	£	£
Sales		40,000
less cost of sales:		
opening inventory	0	
purchases	30,000	
less closing inventory	(5,000)	
		25,000
Gross profit		15,000
less:		
cash expenses	8,000	
depreciation	2,000	
		10,000
Net profit		5,000

Sonita also provides you with the following information regarding her plans:

- Sales are to be made only for cash (not on credit). The figure in the statement of profit or loss represents £10,000 sales for each of the four months.
- Purchases made in the first month must be paid for immediately. Subsequent purchases will be on one month's credit. The purchases figure in the budgeted statement of profit or loss is made up as follows:

	£
Month 1	9,000
Month 2	8,000
Month 3	7,000
Month 4	6,000
Total purchases	30,000

- Cash expenses are based on paying out £2,000 in each of the first four months of the business.
- Equipment is to be bought for £30,000 in the first month of the business. The depreciation shown in the budgeted statement of profit or loss is based on depreciating these assets at 20% per year on a straight-line basis.

- Sonita has £35,000 to invest in the business in month one. The business has no opening cash balance.
- Sonita wishes to withdraw £1,000 from the business in each of the first four months of trading (a total of £4,000).
- Bank interest can be ignored.

Required:

(a) Prepare a cash budget for the first four months' trading of Sonita's business.

(b) Prepare a reconciliation of budgeted profit with budgeted cash movement.

3.2 Jim Smith has recently been made redundant; he has received a redundancy payment and this, together with his accumulated savings, amounts to £10,000.

He has decided to set up his own business selling computer stationery and will start trading with an initial capital of £10,000 on 1 January. On this date he will buy a van for business use at a cost of £6,000.

He has estimated his purchases, sales, and expenses for the next six months as follows:

	Purchases £	Sales £	Expenses £
January	4,500	1,250	750
February	4,500	3,000	600
March	3,500	4,000	600
April	3,500	4,000	650
May	3,500	4,500	650
June	4,000	6,000	700

Jim will pay for purchases in the month after purchase and expects his customers to pay for sales in the month after sale.

All expenses will be paid for in the month in which they are incurred.

Jim realises that he may need bank overdraft facilities before his business becomes established. He asks you to help him with information for the bank and, in particular, he asks you to prepare the following:

Required:

A month-by-month cash budget for the first six months of trading.

3.3 Sarah is planning to start a trading business. The following is her budgeted statement of profit or loss for the first three months of the business (before overdraft interest).

	£	£
Sales		50,000
less cost of sales:		
opening inventory	0	
purchases	40,000	
less closing inventory	(10,000)	
		30,000
Gross profit		20,000
less:		
rent	1,000	
cash expenses	6,000	
depreciation	2,000	
		9,000
Net profit		11,000

Sarah also provides you with the following information regarding her plans:

- Sales are to be made on credit. Although she will formally offer one month's credit, she wishes the budgets to assume that only 75% of the sales will be paid in this time, and 25% of the sales will take two months before the cash is received. The sales figure in the statement of profit or loss represents the following monthly sales:

Month 1	£10,000
Month 2	£16,000
Month 3	£24,000
	£50,000

- All purchases will be on one month's credit. The purchases figure in the budgeted statement of profit or loss is made up as follows:

Month 1	£10,000
Month 2	£14,000
Month 3	£16,000
Total purchases	£40,000

- The annual rent of £4,000 is payable at the start of month 1.
- Cash expenses are based on paying out £2,000 in each of the first three months of the business.
- Equipment is to be bought for £32,000 in the first month of the business. The depreciation shown in the budgeted statement of profit or loss is based on depreciating these non-current assets at 25% per year on a straight-line basis.
- Sarah has £40,000 to invest in the business in month one. The business has no opening cash balance.

- Sarah wishes to withdraw £2,000 from the business in each of the first three months of trading.
- Overdraft interest for each month is calculated at 1% of the month's overdrawn balance at the beginning of the month, and is paid during the month.

Required:

(a) Prepare a cash budget for the first three months' trading of Sarah's business.

(b) Calculate the revised budgeted profit after accounting for the bank overdraft interest shown in the cash budget.

(c) Reconcile the revised budgeted profit with the budgeted movement in cash for the period.

3.4 The statement of financial position of Antonio's Speciality Food Shop at 31 August 20-5 was:

	£	£	£
	Cost	**Dep'n**	**Net**
Non-current assets	15,000	3,000	12,000
Current assets			
Inventories		5,000	
Receivables		800	
		5,800	
Less current liabilities			
Payables	3,000		
Bank overdraft	1,050		
		4,050	
Working capital			1,750
NET ASSETS			13,750
FINANCED BY			
Antonio's capital			13,750

On the basis of past performance, Antonio expects that his sales during the coming six months will be:

September	October	November	December	January	February
£8,000	£8,000	£10,000	£20,000	£6,000	£6,000

Antonio allows credit to some of his regular customers, and the proportions of cash and credit sales are usually:

	Cash sales	Credit sales
November	80%	20%
December	60%	40%
All other months	90%	10%

Customers who buy on credit normally pay in the following month. Antonio's gross profit margin is consistently 25 per cent of his selling price. He normally maintains his inventories at a constant level by purchasing goods in the month in which they are sold: the only exception to this is that in November he purchases in advance 50 per cent of the goods he expects to sell in December.

Half of the purchases each month are made from suppliers who give a 2 per cent prompt payment discount for immediate payment and he takes advantage of the discount. He pays for the remainder (without discount) in the month after purchase.

Expenditure on wages, rent and other running expenses of the shop are consistently £2,000 per month, paid in the month in which they are incurred.

Non-current assets are depreciated at 10 per cent per annum on cost price.

Required:

(a) Prepare a cash budget showing Antonio's bank balance or overdraft for each month in the half-year ending 28 February 20-6.

(b) If Antonio's bank manager considered it necessary to fix the overdraft limit at £3,500, explain what Antonio should do in order to observe the limit.

3.5 Roman Sowski owns a domestic cleaning business and prepares quarterly statements of profit or loss and statements of financial position. These are prepared on an accruals basis.

Cleaning materials are purchased when required and therefore very little inventory is maintained.

All sales and purchases are made on credit terms.

The statement of profit or loss for Roman Sowski's business for the quarter ended 30 June is as follows:

	£	£
Sales		165,200
Less: Purchases		(13,140)
Gross profit		152,060
Less: Expenses		
Wages	60,400	
Rent of office	12,000	
Office expenses	17,600	
Van expenses	7,550	
Van depreciation	1,000	
		98,550
		53,510

Extracts from the statements of financial position at 1 April and 30 June show the following:

Statement of financial position at	**1 April**	**30 June**
	£	£
Trade receivables	18,620	16,100
Trade payables	715	1,124
Accruals – office expenses	180	240
Prepayments – van expenses	501	523
Prepayments – rent of office	1,200	1,860

Required:

Calculate the actual business cash receipts and cash payments for the quarter to 30 June.

	£
Sales receipts	
Purchases payments	
Wages paid	
Rent paid	
Office expenses	
Van expenses	
Van depreciation	

3.6 Major Enterprises Limited has been trading for a number of years. The business has requested assistance with calculating sales receipts for entry into a cash budget.

Actual sales values achieved are available for January and February and forecast sales values have been produced for March to June.

Major Enterprises Limited estimates that cash sales account for 15% of the total sales. The remaining 85% of sales are made on a credit basis.

(a) Complete the table below to show the split of total sales between cash sales and credit sales.

	ACTUAL		**FORECAST**			
	January	**February**	**March**	**April**	**May**	**June**
Total sales	37,000	42,600	45,800	50,000	55,600	61,700
Cash sales						
Credit sales						

(b) Major Enterprises estimates that 70% of credit sales are received in the month after sale with the balance being received two months after sale. For example, 70% of January's credit sales are received in February with the balance being received in March.

Using the table below and your figures from (a) calculate the timing of sales receipts from credit sales that would be included in a cash budget for Major Enterprises Limited for the period February to June.

	CREDIT SALES £	**CASH RECEIVED**				
		February £	**March** £	**April** £	**May** £	**June** £
January						
February						
March						
April						
May						
Monthly credit sales receipts						

3.7 Mason Ltd is preparing cash payment figures ready for inclusion in a cash budget. The following information is relevant to the payment patterns for purchases, wages and expenses.

Purchases are calculated as 60% of the next month's forecast sales and are paid two months after the date of purchase. For example, purchases in July are based on the estimated sales for August and paid for in September.

	July £	**August** £	**September** £	**October** £	**November** £	**December** £
Total sales (actual)	86,000	87,700	86,200			
Total sales (forecast)				88,000	90,000	93,200

Wages are paid in the month that they are incurred and expenses are paid in the month after they are incurred. The actual and forecast figures for wages and expenses are:

	July £	**August** £	**September** £	**October** £	**November** £	**December** £
Wages (actual)	11,750	11,750	12,000			
Wages (forecast)				12,300	12,300	12,750
Expenses* (actual)	5,829	6,179	7,490			
Expenses* (forecast)				8,830	7,656	7,495

*Expenses exclude depreciation

A new machine is to be purchased in October at a total cost of £36,000. Payment for the machine is to be made in three equal monthly instalments, beginning in October.

The machine is to be depreciated monthly on a straight-line basis at 20% per annum.

Required:

Prepare an extract of the payments section of the cash budget for Mason Ltd for the three months ended December. Use the table on the next page.

PAYMENTS	October £	November £	December £
Purchases			
Wages			
Expenses			
New machine			
Total payments			

3.8 Pete Still has been trading for several years. He has prepared the following budgeted statement of profit or loss for the first four months' trading of 20-6.

Still Trading Budgeted statement of profit or loss January – April 20-6		
	£	£
Sales		60,000
less cost of sales:		
Opening inventory	9,000	
Purchases	38,000	
less Closing inventory	(6,000)	
		41,000
Gross profit		19,000
add discounts received		456
		19,456
less:		
Power, light & heat	1,850	
Insurance	1,030	
Telephone & postage	1,890	
General expenses	1,200	
Depreciation	5,000	
Irrecoverable debt allowance	630	
		11,600
Net profit		7,856

Pete also provides you with the following information regarding his plans for the first four months of 20-6.

- The sales figures in the budgeted statement of profit or loss are based on monthly sales as follows:

	£
January	16,000
February	12,000
March	15,000
April	17,000
Total sales	60,000

  30% of sales are made for cash and 70% are on credit. Of the credit sales, half is received in the month after sale, and the remainder (less an irrecoverable debt allowance) is received in the month after that. Pete wishes to make an allowance of 1.5% of credit sales for irrecoverable debts.

- The purchases figure in the budgeted statement of profit or loss is made up as follows:

	£
January	8,000
February	9,000
March	10,000
April	11,000
Total purchases	38,000

- A discount for payment in the month of purchase of 2% is offered by suppliers of 60% of purchases. This will be taken up by Pete, and he will pay for the remaining purchases in the month after they are bought.

- Power, light & heat expense shown in the budgeted statement of profit or loss incorporates an accrual at 1 January of £300 and an accrual at 30 April of £550. The cash amount paid is the same for each of the four months in this period.

- Insurance expense shown in the budgeted statement of profit or loss incorporates a prepayment at 1 January of £250, and a prepayment of £2,340 at 30 April. All insurance is paid in February.

- Telephone and Postage expense shown in the budgeted statement of profit or loss incorporates no accrual at 1 January, but an accrual at 30 April of £90. The cash amount paid is the same for each of the four months in this period.

- General Expenses are spread evenly over the first four months of 20-6.

- The depreciation shown in the budgeted statement of profit or loss is based on depreciating equipment at 25% per year on a straight-line basis. Equipment that cost £30,000 was purchased in January of 20-4. Further equipment is to be bought for £30,000 in January 20-6.

- Pete wishes to withdraw £2,000 from the business in each of the months of February and April 20-6.

- Bank interest can be ignored.

The draft statement of financial position has already been prepared as at the end of December 20-5, and an extract is shown below.

Still Trading

Extract from statement of financial position as at 31 December 20-5

	£	£	£
Non-Current Assets			
	Cost	Dep'n	Net
Equipment	30,000	15,000	15,000
Current Assets:			
Inventory		9,000	
Trade receivables			21,000
Prepayments		250	
Bank		10,000	
		40,250	
Less **Current Liabilities:**			
Trade payables	4,000		
Accruals	300		
		4,300	
			35,950
Total net assets			50,950

Notes regarding the statement of financial position:

- The trade receivables are due to be received as follows: £12,000 will be received in January and £9,000 in February. The allowance for irrecoverable debts has already been deducted in the calculation of these figures.
- The trade payables relate to December purchases. Payment is due to be made in January.
- Accruals and prepayments relate to the earlier notes.
- The business is financed entirely by the capital account.

Required:

Prepare a cash budget for the first four months of 20-6.

3.9 The following planned information is provided regarding the next year for Freeman Enterprises Limited.

Budgeted statement of profit or loss for year ended 31 December 20-5

	£	£
Sales revenue		780,000
Less: cost of sales:		
Opening inventory	84,500	
Purchases	395,000	
Closing inventory	(95,000)	
		384,500
Gross profit		395,500
Expenses		232,500
Operating profit		163,000
Corporation Tax		79,000
Profit after Tax		84,000

- Trade receivables are budgeted at £115,000 at the start of 20-5 and £112,300 at the end of 20-5.
- Trade payables are budgeted to rise from £91,000 at the start of 20-5 to £104,200 at the end of 20-5.
- Non-current assets will be disposed of during 20-5, incurring a budgeted loss of £4,500 which is included in 'expenses'.
- Non-current assets at the start of 20-5 are budgeted at £180,000, and at the end of 20-5 at £130,500. There are no planned acquisitions of non-current assets.
- Depreciation included in 'expenses' is £33,500.
- Corporation Tax owing to HMRC is budgeted at £55,000 at the start of 20-5 and £68,000 at the end of 20-5.
- The budgeted cash position at 1 January 20-5 is £44,000 overdrawn.

Required:

Complete the following table to arrive at the expected cash balance at 31 December 20-5. Use + or – signs as appropriate.

	£
Operating profit	163,000
Change in inventory	
Change in trade receivables	
Change in trade payables	
Adjustment for non-cash items	
Proceeds from disposal of non-current assets	
Payment of Corporation Tax	
Net change in cash position	
Budgeted cash position 1 Jan 20-5	–44,000
Budgeted cash position 31 Dec 20-5	

3.10 Invent Limited has budgeted for the following levels of raw material inventory (in units) over the next few periods:

Inventory (in units) at start of following periods:

1	2	3	4	5
555	603	701	489	600

The raw materials usage budget shows the following figures (in units) for the same periods:

1	2	3	4	5
1,960	2,202	2,300	2,150	2,200

Each unit of raw material costs £70 to purchase.

Payments for purchases are made as follows from Period 1 onwards:

- 50% of raw material purchases are paid in the period after delivery
- 40% of raw material purchases are paid 2 periods after delivery
- 10% of raw material purchases are paid 3 periods after delivery

Required:

Calculate the amounts to be paid for raw materials in each of periods 3 and 4.

4 Using cash budgets

this chapter covers...

The earlier chapters in this book mainly concentrated on the preparation of accurate cash budgets. In this chapter we are going to see how we can tackle the next logical stages and make good use of the budgets.

We will start by illustrating how cash budgets can be modified to take account of changes in the assumptions about the data used to draw them up in the first place. This data includes, for example, estimates of sales levels and credit terms given to customers.

This process will tell us how sensitive the original cash budget is to changes in data, and for that reason the process is known as 'sensitivity analysis'. Even if the initial budget is thought to be based on the best estimates, it is important to know whether any possible changes in circumstances would have a significant impact on the cash position.

We will then look at specific situations to see how the impact of decisions can be quantified.

The next part of the chapter deals with using the cash budget to monitor the actual data as it becomes available. By making comparisons between the budget and what actually happens we can see whether any action needs to be taken to keep the business on track.

To carry out these comparisons we will have to understand the possible reasons for differences (variances) between the budget and actual data, and be able to make sensible suggestions about what (if any) action is required.

We will also see how a simple reconciliation statement – ie a summary of the variances and the reasons for them – can provide an instant view of the situation that will be useful to the managers.

SENSITIVITY ANALYSIS

In the last two chapters we have seen how cash budgets can be developed for various organisations. In this chapter we are going to see how we can make effective use of cash budgets, firstly to see how changes in cash flow would impact on them, and then by using the budgets to monitor and control actual results.

assumptions made in cash budgeting

In each Case Study and example we have used various assumptions that are reflected in the final budget. These assumptions are about issues like:

- forecast sales levels
- selling prices charged
- credit terms offered, and whether receipts would be in line with them
- prices paid for purchases, expenses and non-current assets
- labour rates and the number of labour hours required
- how quickly payments need to be made

If any one of these assumptions turns out to be incorrect it would make a difference to the cash budget, and could even invalidate all the planning that has taken place.

the importance of sensitivity analysis

The problem that arises therefore is to determine how sensitive the cash budget is to possible changes in the initial assumptions. If a change in one assumption produced a cash difference of only a small amount we would not be too concerned. However sometimes a change in one assumption can lead to severe changes in the cash position.

Sensitivity analysis helps us to determine which assumptions are critical and which have less impact.

Sensitivity analysis is a technique that investigates the impact that changes will have on the budget, so that the organisation can be made aware of how the situation can vary from the projected position.

Sensitivity analysis is sometimes called 'what-if' analysis, and that really sums up what it does. The technique simply shows us what will happen to the budget if changes occur.

Sensitivity analysis involves 'trying out' various alterations from our original assumptions to assess the impact. This can be done by changing one category of receipt or payment, for example:

- what if our purchase prices go up by 5%?
- or, using two changes, what if our purchase prices go up by 5% and we have to pay for them after one month instead of two months?

You may be asked to carry out some sensitivity analysis in a given task, and we will look at the numerical techniques shortly. Before we do that it is worth examining an important practical tool for carrying out sensitivity analysis – the computer spreadsheet.

using a spreadsheet for sensitivity analysis

The format of a cash budget that we have been using in the last two chapters is very easy to reproduce on a computer spreadsheet, using formulas to carry out the arithmetic.

Once a spreadsheet is set up it is a simple matter to change any of the data, or to add lines for additional receipts or payments. The totals of receipts and payments will automatically adjust when changes are made, together with the bank/cash balances at the bottom of the budget.

carrying out sensitivity analysis manually

The type of change to data that can be carried out in sensitivity analysis generally falls into one of three categories:

- **changes in underlying volumes**

  Here we mean changes in the sales units, or the production or purchase units. It could also apply to some extent to overheads or non-current assets (eg hiring or buying additional equipment not included in the original budget).

- **changes in prices**

  We will initially deal with some straightforward price changes, and then in the next section examine the impact of inflation and how to deal with it.

- **timing changes**

  We also need to see the impact when the receipts and payments are the same amounts as the original cash budget, but they occur at different times. Examples would be allowing longer (or shorter) credit terms on sales, or paying for purchases or other outgoings at a different time than was originally planned.

changing the data – the process

There are two approaches to changing the cash budget data:

1 The whole cash budget could be redrafted. While this would be a simple matter when using a spreadsheet model, it would be very time-consuming manually, especially if there were several alternative options to consider.

2 The impact on the cash movements for each month could be calculated from just examining the changes proposed. This approach requires the application of some logic to the problem, but is a quicker technique than redrafting the whole budget if a spreadsheet is not available.

The second technique is often useful, and we will now look in more detail at how this is carried out. The key is to look at each month separately, and calculate for that month

- any change in receipts, and
- any change in payments, that together result in
- a change in cash movement

The revised closing cash balance for that month can then be calculated, and carried forward to the next month. The exercise can be carried out in the form of a table. We will use a straightforward example to demonstrate the process.

The following cash budget is taken from the Moore Trading Case Study used in Chapter 3, pages 95-98. It is based on all sales being made on two months' credit. March sales are estimated at £8,000.

Moore Trading: Cash Budget for January to April of Year 10.

	January £	February £	March £	April £
Receipts				
Receipts from year 9 sales	6,500	4,500	–	–
Receipts from year 10 sales	–	–	6,000	7,000
Total receipts	6,500	4,500	6,000	7,000
Payments				
Purchases made in year 9	4,000	–	–	–
Purchases made in year 10	–	4,000	6,000	6,000
Expenses	1,000	1,000	1,000	1,000
Non-current assets	10,000	–	–	–
Drawings	–	1,500	–	1,500
Total payments	15,000	6,500	7,000	8,500
Cash flow for month	(8,500)	(2,000)	(1,000)	(1,500)
Bank balance brought forward	10,000	1,500	(500)	(1,500)
Bank balance carried forward	1,500	(500)	(1,500)	(3,000)

Suppose that we wanted to see the impact of changing our terms of sale to one month's credit, with effect from January sales. For simplicity we will assume that all our customers comply with the revised terms. By following the procedure outlined above we would get the following results:

	January	February	March	April
	£	£	£	£
'Old' receipts from sales	6,500	4,500	6,000	7,000
'New' receipts from sales	6,500	10,500	7,000	8,000
Changes to receipts	–	+6,000	+1,000	+1,000

Revised cash flow figures

	January	February	March	April
	£	£	£	£
Cash flow for month	(8,500)	4,000	0	(500)
Bank balance brought forward	10,000	1,500	5,500	5,500
Bank balance carried forward	1,500	5,500	5,500	5,000

In this example two months' sales receipts would arise in February, increasing the receipts for that month by £6,000. The changes in receipts for March and April result from receiving different months' sales than originally planned. The overall result is a new bank balance at the end of April of £5,000 instead of the original £3,000 overdrawn figure.

Note that using this technique it is only necessary to examine those lines in the cash budget that are subject to change. Here there was no impact on payments so there was no need to revisit those figures.

We will now present a Case Study incorporating more than one change to the cash budget data.

Case Study

THE SENSITIVE COMPANY: ASSESSING THE IMPACT OF BUDGET CHANGES

A cash budget has been prepared (see next page), based on various assumptions, including the following:

- Completed units sell for £200 each, on two months' credit.
- Raw materials purchases are made on one month's credit.
- Dividends paid are based on 50 pence per share.

	January £	February £	March £	April £
Receipts				
Receipts from year 20-6 sales	6,500	3,500	–	–
Receipts from year 20-7 sales	–	–	4,000	4,400
Total receipts	6,500	3,500	4,000	4,400
Payments				
Raw material purchases	1,000	840	960	1,000
Labour	1,320	1,260	1,320	1,440
Fixed overheads	800	800	800	800
Debenture interest	1,200	–	–	–
Dividends	–	–	–	10,000
Total payments	4,320	2,900	3,080	13,240
Cash flow for month	2,180	600	920	(8,840)
Bank balance brought forward	12,000	14,180	14,780	15,700
Bank balance carried forward	14,180	14,780	15,700	6,860

possible changes

The impact of a number of possible changes all occurring together needs to be assessed:

- The unit selling price is reduced to £195 each with effect from January, a £5 reduction from the current selling price of £200.
- Purchases of raw materials are to be paid for in the month of purchase (instead of one month later), and are subject to a 4% settlement discount. This takes effect from the January purchases. April purchases are to be £880 before discount.
- Dividends to be paid in April are based on 60 pence per share, instead of 50 pence per share.

required

Calculate the impact of **all** the possible changes on each month's closing bank balance.

solution

	January £	February £	March £	April £
Changes to Receipts	–	–	(100)	(110)
Changes to Payments				
'Old' purchase payments	1,000	840	960	1,000
'New' purchase payments	1,806	922	960	845
Changes to purchase payments	806	82	0	(155)
Change to dividend	–	–	–	2,000
Total changes to payments	806	82	0	1,845
Revised cash flow position				
Cash flow for month	1,374	518	820	(10,795)
Bank balance brought forward	12,000	13,374	13,892	14,712
Bank balance carried forward	13,374	13,892	14,712	3,917

In these calculations increases in receipts or payments have been shown as positive figures and reductions as negative figures (in brackets).

It is important to remember that a lower receipts figure has the same impact as a higher payments figure – ie a reduction in cash flow!

The detail recorded in the workings is a matter of personal preference, but you should show enough detail in your calculations to enable your working method to be checked.

QUANTIFYING SPECIFIC DECISIONS

There are some specific operational decisions that can impact on both profitability and cash flow. In this section we will examine how we can use our skills to help make the decisions and quantify their impact. We will look at decisions regarding:

- early settlement discounts
- special offers and substitute materials or labour

early settlement discounts

Early settlement discounts are offered by some businesses to customers that pay more quickly than normal. These are also known as prompt payment discounts. We need to understand the impact of both:

- accepting or rejecting an offer of an early settlement discount by a supplier, and
- offering early settlement discounts to our customers

Both of these decisions have implications for cash flow and profitability. The cash flow impact can be quantified using the techniques that we have already used based on sensitivity analysis.

deciding whether to pay a supplier early to obtain a discount

Where we are considering paying a supplier early to obtain a discount the first issue to consider is whether we have access to sufficient cash to do so. We can establish this by carrying out sensitivity analysis on our cash budget using the techniques that we have already seen. We must ensure that before we consider the issue further that we either have:

- sufficient cash, or
- sufficient access to cash through (for example) an overdraft limit

If we don't have enough cash then there is no point in considering whether taking a discount is profitable.

To determine whether taking an early settlement discount is profitable we need to establish the annual equivalent interest rate of the discount, and then compare it with the normal cost of money to our business. The cost of money could be (for example):

- the interest rate on an overdraft facility that we are using, or
- the interest rate on a deposit account that we are using – this would measure the interest that we wouldn't be able to receive because we were using the cash for paying early (the 'opportunity cost' of the money)

If the annual equivalent interest rate of the discount is higher than the cost of money to our business then it would be profitable to accept the discount and make payment early.

The annual equivalent simple interest rate of the discount can be calculated by using the following formula:

$$[d / (100 - d)] \times [365 / (N - D)] \times 100\%$$

where d = settlement discount percentage

N = normal settlement period in days

D = settlement period for early payment in days

worked example

A company is continually using its overdraft facility which charges 20% pa. A decision needs to be made whether to accept an offer from a supplier for a 2% discount for payment within 15 days. The normal payment terms are 45 days. If payments are made early the company will remain comfortably within its overdraft limit.

The first issue to note is that the company could make the payments early from a cash point of view – since they will remain within the overdraft limit. Having established that, we can move on to see whether accepting the discount is profitable.

The annual equivalent simple interest rate of the discount offered is

[2 / (100 – 2)] x [365 / (45 – 15)] x 100%

= [2/98] x [365 / 30] x 100%

= 24.83%

As this rate of 'income' is greater than the current cost of money of 20% the discount should be accepted and the payments made early.

deciding whether to offer early settlement discounts to customers

When deciding whether to offer discounts to customers the same two issues of cash flow and profitability should be considered. Since any customers that accept the discount offered will pay early this will improve the cash flow. Unless the organisation already has more cash than it really needs (for example if it is overcapitalised) receiving cash early is usually an advantage. The remaining issue to consider therefore is the cost of offering a discount since this will impact on profit.

The annual equivalent interest rate of the discount needs to be calculated and compared with the interest that could be generated by the organisation. The annual equivalent interest rate of the discount is calculated using the same formula that was explained above. The interest that the organisation could generate could relate to (for example):

- the interest rate that the organisation could earn from a deposit account
- the reduction in bank overdraft interest resulting from lower overdraft balances

Notice that we are carrying out a similar comparison to the one described when we were concerned with accepting discounts. This time though we are comparing the cost of the discount with the income that it could generate.

worked example

A company is considering offering a prompt payment discount to customers of 1% for payment within 10 days. Customers usually pay in an average of 50 days. The company normally maintains its current account in credit when it earns 2.5% interest pa. The company sometimes needs to use its overdraft facility, and when this occurs it is charged 14% pa.

The annual equivalent interest of the discount is:

[1 / (100 – 1)] x [365 / (50 – 10)] x 100%

= [1/99] x [365 / 40] x 100%

= 9.22%

The cost of offering the discount is in between the income that could be generated when in credit (2.5% pa) and the rate of overdraft interest that would be saved when overdrawn (14% pa). Offering the discount would therefore only be profitable during periods when the company was using its overdraft facility.

One consideration when deciding how much discount to offer is that customers may well be carrying out similar calculations. Discounts that are pitched at a level that is profitable for the seller may be uneconomic for the buyer and therefore not be taken up.

special offers and substitute materials or labour

We may need to quantify the impact of decisions such as:

- purchasing materials early in order to take advantage of a reduced price
- purchasing substitute materials at a different price and / or on different terms from the normal materials
- employing substitute labour or contractors at a different rate and / or on different terms from the normal labour

Just like decisions about settlement discounts, there are two issues to consider – whether there is sufficient cash available, and whether the decision is profitable

Any decision that involves making payments early will only be feasible if there is sufficient cash available. The cash impact can be assessed by using techniques that we illustrated earlier in this chapter under the section on 'sensitivity analysis'.

If sufficient cash is available then the question of profitability can be examined by examining the savings compared to the additional costs to be incurred.

The following Case Study will illustrate how the impact of a decision on purchasing materials early at a special price can be quantified.

Case Study

OPPORTUNE LIMITED: PURCHASING EARLY

Opportune Limited is a manufacturing company that normally purchases 120 tonnes of raw material each month at a price of £380 per tonne. The company has the opportunity to purchase 400 tonnes at a special price of £365 per tonne in January. If less than 400 tonnes are purchased in January the normal price would apply. The supplier will continue with the normal terms of 30 days credit.

Opportune Limited is currently using its overdraft facility which has a limit of £120,000, and has budgeted for the following closing net cash flows based on the normal monthly purchase of materials.

	Jan £	Feb £	March £	April £	May £	June £
Overdraft Interest	(100)	(160)	(180)	(126)	(150)	(185)
Cash flow for month	(6,000)	(2,000)	5,400	(2,400)	(3,500)	(1,500)
Bank balance b/f	(10,000)	(16,000)	(18,000)	(12,600)	(15,000)	(18,500)
Bank balance c/f	(16,000)	(18,000)	(12,600)	(15,000)	(18,500)	(20,000)

The overdraft interest charge of 1% per month is based on the closing balance of each month and has been incorporated into the cash flow and balances, and is shown for information.

required

(a) Calculate the revised cash flow and bank balances for each of the six months if the option to purchase early at the special price is taken up.

(b) Comment briefly on the opportunity in terms of both cash availability and profitability.

solution

(a) If the materials are purchased early then the quantities to be purchased would be as follows, based on using 120 tonnes per month:

	Jan	Feb	March	April	May	June
Purchase (tonnes)	400	0	0	80	120	120

These purchases would all be on 30 days credit.

The following table shows the impact on the bank balances of purchasing early at the special price.

	Jan £	Feb £	March £	April £	May £	June £
'Old' purchase payments	45,600	45,600	45,600	45,600	45,600	45,600
'New' purchase payments	45,600	146,000	0	0	30,400	45,600
'Old' o/d interest	(100)	(160)	(180)	(126)	(150)	(185)
'New' o/d interest	(100)	(160)	(1,184)	(684)	(258)	(142)
Revised monthly cash flow	(6,000)	(102,400)	49,996	42,642	11,592	(1,457)
Bank balance b/f	(10,000)	(16,000)	(118,400)	(68,404)	(25,762)	(14,170)
Bank balance c/f	(16,000)	(118,400)	(68,404)	(25,762)	(14,170)	(15,627)

(b) The revised cash balances in (a) above show that the company should remain within its £120,000 overdraft facility – but only by a small margin.

The profitability of the option can be approximately calculated as:

Savings in material costs (400 tonnes x £15)	£6,000
Less additional overdraft interest (£2,528 – £901)	£1,627
Net savings	£4,373

In addition there would be some minor savings in overdraft interest in future periods based on the revised cash flows.

COMPARING THE CASH BUDGET WITH THE ACTUAL FIGURES

The cash budget, like any other budget, has a major advantage in that it can be used for monitoring and control. It would make no sense if the completed budget were simply locked away after completion and the organisation carried on regardless!

When making comparisons between the cash budget and the actual cash flow it is important to identify the reasons for any differences, but it should be possible to identify possible or likely reasons from the three categories listed above. It should also be possible to investigate the differences (or variances) further and obtain information about the causes.

It will be necessary to ask:

- which variances should be investigated?
- which variances require that action should be taken?
- which variances just need to be monitored?

We can use a similar approach to that used when monitoring other budgets. This is based on a few key questions:

- **is the difference significant?**

  If the difference between the budget and the actual cash flow is small it is unlikely to be worth investigating fully, unless there is a danger that it is the beginning of a trend that will become significant.

- **do we know the cause of the difference?**

  If we know the cause then we are in a strong position, even if action is subsequently needed. If the difference is significant and we do not yet know the cause, then we should find out more.

- **will the difference right itself anyway?**

  If the difference will automatically right itself – for example a late receipt from a major customer – then we may just need to monitor the situation.

- **will the difference recur?**

  A one-off variance can probably be managed, but if it is expected to recur, it may need different treatment. For example, if a late receipt from a customer is a warning sign of the customer's inability to pay then it should lead to a re-examination of the trading relationship with that customer.

- **is the cause controllable?**

  Some situations are outside the control of the organisation, and time should not be wasted trying to achieve the impossible. If interest rate rises or a change in currency exchange rates have had an impact on cash flow, then a strategy will have to be developed to manage the situation. This may also involve amending the original budget.

reconciling differences (variances)

It is often useful to reconcile the effect of the differences to the overall difference in the cash position. This will show how much impact each issue has created and illustrate clearly how the overall situation has developed. The reconciliation is normally easy to prepare and also gives a useful check on our logic and arithmetic. The terminology 'adverse' and 'favourable' variances is commonly used to distinguish between variances that show a position worse than expected (adverse) or better than expected (favourable).

worked example

Suppose a company had prepared a cash budget for March, but the actual figures were significantly different, as follows:

	Cash budget	Actual cash
	£	£
Receipts from sales	235,000	203,500
Receipt from share issue	500,000	0
Total receipts	735,000	203,500
Payments for materials	130,500	125,000
Payments for labour	85,000	87,000
Payments for operating expenses	42,800	43,000
Repayment of loan	300,000	0
Purchase of non-current assets	200,000	30,000
Payment of Corporation Tax	53,000	53,000
Total payments	811,300	338,000
Cash flow for month	(76,300)	(134,500)
Bank balance b/f	100,000	100,000
Bank balance c/f	23,700	(34,500)

We can see from the figures that the actual cash flow for the month differs from the cash budget by minus £58,200 (an 'adverse' variance). The expected negative cash flow of £76,300 is an actual negative flow of £134,500. We need to reconcile the differences and their causes back to the variance of £58,200 adverse.

Suppose that we establish the following facts about the cash flows:

- Receipts from sales are lower due to worse sales in February than budgeted.
- The budgeted share issue (which was to be used to buy new non-current assets and to pay off an outstanding loan) has been delayed until April. Only a minimum of non-current assets were purchased, and the remainder, together with the loan repayment has been delayed.
- Payments for materials are lower due to a new policy to reduce inventory levels.
- The labour force payment includes overtime payments to carry out an additional inventory check as part of the implementation of the new inventory policy.

We can now prepare a reconciliation, using the variances for each category. Adverse variances are shown in brackets, and favourable ones without.

Category	Variance		Reason for variance
	£		
Receipts from Sales	(31,500)	Adverse	Sales below budget
Receipts from Share Issue	(500,000)	Adverse	Issue delayed
Payment for Materials	5,500	Favourable	New inventory policy
Payment for Labour	(2,000)	Adverse	New inventory policy
Payment for Operating Expenses	(200)	Adverse	Not known
Repayment of Loan	300,000	Favourable	Delayed
Payment for Non-current Assets	170,000	Favourable	Delayed
Net cash flow variance	(58,200)	Adverse	

We could summarise the reconciliation further by listing just the reasons, so that we can see clearly the impact.

Reason	Net variance	
	£	
Sales below budget	(31,500)	Adverse
Delay of Shares issue etc	(30,000)	Adverse
New Inventory Policy	3,500	Favourable
Reason Not Known	(200)	Adverse
Net cash flow variance	(58,200)	Adverse

Check carefully that you can follow the logic and arithmetic of the above statements. It is easy to become confused with positive and negative amounts and variances.

The Case Study that follows demonstrates how to analyse possible causes of differences.

CASH-GONE LIMITED: EXAMINING CASH DIFFERENCES

Cash-Gone Limited is a trading company selling to the UK manufacturing industry.

The following figures compare the company's cash budget – as initially prepared for the period Oct-Dec – with the actual figures for the same period.

	Cash Budget			Actual Cash		
	Oct	Nov	Dec	Oct	Nov	Dec
	£000	£000	£000	£000	£000	£000
Receipts						
Cash sales	20	20	20	20	19	15
Trade receivables	50	40	50	45	45	35
Total receipts	70	60	70	65	64	50
Payments						
Purchases	10	11	10	10	12	10
Wages	20	20	20	20	23	20
Rent	5	5	5	5	5	5
Administration	10	10	10	10	10	9
Non-current assets	0	30	0	38	2	0
Total payments	45	76	45	83	52	44
Monthly cash flow	25	(16)	25	(18)	12	6
Bank balance brought fwd	10	35	19	10	(8)	4
Bank balance carried fwd	35	19	44	(8)	4	10

required

- Summarise the differences for each category of receipt and payment between the forecast and the actual data, and suggest possible causes for each difference.
- Prepare a reconciliation using categories of receipts and payments.

solution

- **Receipts from Cash Sales: £6,000 less than budgeted**

  The actual receipts are down by £1,000 in November and by £5,000 in December. Since these are cash sales the cause cannot be a timing difference, but must result from a difference in cash sales volume. Since the major difference is in December this could be the result of the original forecast not estimating accurately the sales in this month where many businesses shut down for long periods.

- **Receipts from Receivables: £15,000 less than budgeted**

  The actual receipts are down by £5,000 in October, but greater by the same amount in November – this could be a possible timing difference only due to delayed receipts. In December the receipts are £15,000 fewer than budgeted. This could be a timing difference, or could be due to lower sales in the relevant period.

- **Payments for Purchases: £1,000 more than budgeted**

  Since only November payments differ from the budget, a timing difference seems unlikely. It could be due to increased inventories, or to a price rise. Since sales are not higher than in the budget it cannot be due to demand.

- **Payment for Wages: £3,000 more than budgeted**

  Since this occurs only in November it appears to be a one-off difference rather than a pay increase or more employees. It could relate to overtime working or possibly a bonus that was not originally planned.

- **Payment for Administration: £1,000 less than budgeted**

  The payment is lower only in December. This could be a timing difference to be caught up with in January, or maybe a saving that will be repeated in future months.

- **Payment for Non-current Assets: £10,000 more than budgeted**

  The total cost is £10,000 higher than budgeted, and the larger part of this payment is made one month earlier than planned. This could point to an earlier acquisition, or less available credit than planned. In addition, the price could be higher than planned, or more assets or higher specification assets could have been purchased.

The overall net difference is a reduction in cash of £34,000. This accounts for the difference between the budgeted and actual closing December cash balances, as shown in the following reconciliation:

Reconciliation

	£	
Receipts from cash sales	(6,000)	Adverse
Receipts from receivables	(15,000)	Adverse
Payments for purchases	(1,000)	Adverse
Payment for wages	(3,000)	Adverse
Payment for administration	1,000	Favourable
Payment for non-current assets	(10,000)	Adverse
Net cash flow variance	(34,000)	Adverse

TAKING CORRECTIVE ACTION

The types of action that can be taken when cash budget variances have been identified will depend on the causes of those differences. It is also worth remembering that some issues may involve major decisions in the organisation at a high level – for example altering credit control policies.

As already discussed, only significant variances should be a cause for action. What is a significant variance could be an issue for company policy, and could be measured in amounts of cash, or percentages of the budget figures. Unless small variances are thought to be indicative of a future trend, or are the result of two significant but opposite variances then action should not be required.

In the table below are some examples of typical causes of cash budget variances, and possible actions that could be followed to remedy the situation. The table concentrates on adverse causes, but action could also be taken to maximise the benefit from favourable situations.

Causes of cash variances	**Possible actions**
Receipts from credit sales delayed	Improve credit control Offer discounts for prompt payment
Sales volumes reduced	Improve product Improve marketing Reduce selling price
Purchase volumes increased	Improve inventory control Reduce wastage
Purchase prices increased	Negotiate better prices Change suppliers
Payments made prematurely	Negotiate longer credit terms Ensure available credit is taken
Labour costs increased	Increase labour efficiency Reduce absenteeism Reduce overtime working Negotiate flexible contracts

Chapter Summary

- Sensitivity analysis involves examining what happens to a budget when changes are made in the assumptions on which it is based. It is also known as 'what-if' analysis, and can be carried out using a spreadsheet or with manual calculations. Manual calculations are easier if they focus only on the parts of the budget that are subject to change.

- Decisions about whether to offer or accept prompt payment discounts should be based on the impact on both cash and profit. The same logic applies to decisions about special offers or substitutions of materials or labour.

- Cash budgets can be monitored and controlled by comparing the actual cash figures with the budget and then calculating any differences (or variances). Once the causes of significant variances have been established, corrective action can be taken as appropriate.

Key Terms

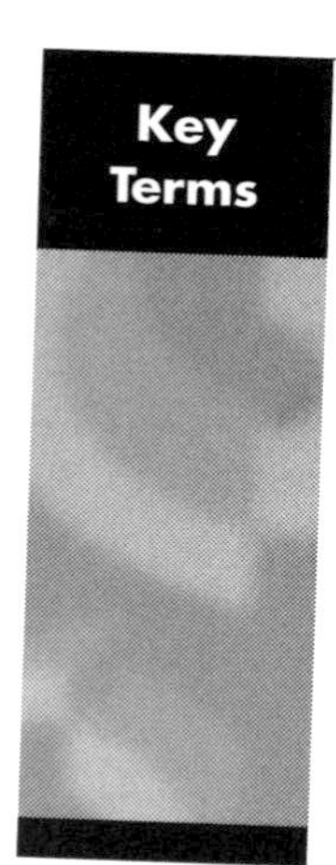

early settlement discount	the discount offered by some businesses to customers that pay more quickly than normal – they are also known as 'prompt payment discounts'
sensitivity analysis	examining the budget to determine how sensitive it is to the various assumptions on which it has been prepared
variance	the financial difference between the budgeted data and the actual data – in a cash budget the variances relate to differences in receipts or payments

4.1 The following cash budget has been prepared, based on various assumptions, including the following:

- Completed units sell on two months' credit.
- Raw materials purchases are made on one month's credit.

	January £	February £	March £	April £
Receipts				
Receipts from sales	8,500	7,500	5,000	9,000
Receipt of loan		20,000		
Total receipts	8,500	27,500	5,000	9,000
Payments				
Raw material purchases	3,000	2,800	3,960	3,000
Labour	1,320	1,260	1,320	1,440
Fixed overheads	1,800	1,800	1,800	1,800
Debenture interest	1,200	–	–	–
Non-current assets	–	24,000	–	–
Total payments	7,320	29,860	7,080	6,240
Cash flow for month	1,180	(2,360)	(2,080)	2,760
Balance b/f	10,000	11,180	8,820	6,740
Balance c/f	11,180	8,820	6,740	9,500

The impact of both the following possible changes occurring now needs to be assessed:

- Three months' credit offered on sales with effect from January sales.
- The non-current assets to cost £26,000, and to be paid for in January.

Required:

Calculate the impact on each month's closing bank balance of these two changes.

4.2 Sun-Rise Supplies, a trading company, has produced the following extract from its initial draft cash budget for the months of July to October, based on prices and costs at June levels.

Purchases are made on one month's credit.

Expenses and labour costs are paid in the month they are incurred.

Rent is payable half yearly in advance.

Draft cash budget (extract) for the period July to October				
	July	**August**	**September**	**October**
	£	£	£	£
Payments				
Purchases	25,000	28,000	26,000	24,000
Labour	19,000	17,000	18,000	20,000
Rent	18,000	–	–	–
Expenses	10,000	10,000	10,000	10,000

The following information is now available regarding price and cost changes:

- Purchase prices will rise by 2.5% from 1 August.
- A pay rise of 3.5% has been agreed to take effect from 1 October.
- Rent is to rise to £42,000 per year with effect from 1 July.
- Expenses are expected to follow the following forecast cost index:

June	150.0
July	151.2
August	151.4
September	152.0
October	152.1

Required:

Revise the cash budget extract to incorporate appropriate allowances for price and cost changes.

4.3 The cash budget set out below has been based on various assumptions, including the following:

- Completed units sell on two months' credit.
- Raw materials purchases are made on one month's credit.

	January £	February £	March £	April £
Receipts				
Receipts from sales	8,500	7,500	5,000	9,000
Total receipts	8,500	7,500	5,000	9,000
Payments				
Raw material purchases	3,000	2,800	3,960	3,000
Labour	1,320	1,260	1,320	1,440
Fixed overheads	1,800	1,800	1,800	1,800
Total payments	6,120	5,860	7,080	6,240
Cash flow for month	2,380	1,640	(2,080)	2,760
Bank balance brought forward	10,000	12,380	14,020	11,940
Bank balance carried forward	12,380	14,020	11,940	14,700

The impact of both the following possible changes occurring now needs to be assessed:

1. A discount of 5% is to be offered to customers who pay in the month of sale. 50% of sales will be received on this basis. The remainder will continue to pay in two months. This is to come into effect from January. March sales are expected to be £10,000, and April sales £12,000.
2. Raw material costs are due to rise by 7% with effect from those purchased in March.

Required:

Calculate the impact on each month's closing bank balance of the two possible changes.

4.4 Cash-Change Limited is a trading company selling to the UK manufacturing industry. The following figures are an extract from a cash budget as initially prepared for the period April to June, together with the actual figures for the same period.

	Cash budget			Actual cash		
	April *£000*	**May** *£000*	**June** *£000*	**April** *£000*	**May** *£000*	**June** *£000*
Receipts						
Cash sales	10	20	25	12	19	24
Trade receivables	50	50	50	45	45	60
Payments						
Purchases	10	13	10	10	10	10
Wages	20	20	20	20	20	20
Rent	15	0	0	5	5	5
Administration	10	10	10	10	10	11
Non-current assets	0	20	0	0	0	17

Required:

(a) Summarise the differences for each category of receipt and payment between the forecast and the actual data, and suggest possible causes for each difference.

(b) Assuming that the actual and budgeted bank balance on 1 April is zero, calculate the bank balance at 30 June for both the budgeted and actual cash figures. Reconcile the difference between these two figures using the variances calculated in Part (a).

4.5 A cash budget has been prepared for Zizzors Ltd for the next five periods.

The budget was prepared based on the following sales volumes and a selling price of £12 per item.

Period	Sales volume (items)
Period 1	2,300
Period 2	2,400
Period 3	2,460
Period 4	2,520
Period 5	2,600

The pattern of cash receipts used in the budget assumed 50% of sales were received in the month of sale and the remaining 50% in the month following sale.

In the light of current economic trends Zizzors Ltd needs to adjust its cash budget to take account of the following:

- The selling price from period 1 will be reduced by 15% per item.
- The pattern of sales receipts changes to 25% of sales received in the month of sale, 50% in the month following sale and the remaining 25% two months after sale.

Required:

(a) Use the table below to calculate the effect of the changes in the forecast sales for periods 1 to 5, and the timing of cash receipts for periods 3, 4 and 5:

	Period 1 £	Period 2 £	Period 3 £	Period 4 £	Period 5 £
Original value of forecast sales	27,600	28,800	29,520	30,240	31,200
Original timing of receipts			29,160	29,880	30,720
Revised value of forecast sales					
Revised timing of receipts					

(b) Zizzors Ltd has managed to negotiate extended payment terms with its suppliers. The original budget was prepared on the basis of paying suppliers in the month following purchase. The revised payment terms allow for settlement of 40% in the month following purchase with the remaining payment two months after purchase. The original budgeted purchase figures were:

Period	**Budgeted purchases £**
Period 1	8,480
Period 2	9,600
Period 3	9,820
Period 4	10,940
Period 5	11,110

Use the table below to calculate the effect of the changes in the timing of purchase payments for periods 3, 4 and 5:

	Period 3 £	**Period 4 £**	**Period 5 £**
Original timing of payments			
Revised timing of payments			

(c) Using your calculations from Parts (a) and (b), complete the table to show the net effect of the changes to sales receipts and purchase payments for Periods 3, 4 and 5.

	Period 3 £	**Period 4 £**	**Period 5 £**
Changes in sales receipts			
Changes in purchase payments			
Net change			

4.6 The quarterly budgeted and actual figures for Joe Green Enterprises are shown below. Negative figures are shown in brackets.

	Budgeted	Actual
	£	£
Receipts from receivables	88,426	84,622
Cash sales	15,350	16,790
Payments to payables	(42,618)	(44,791)
Cash purchases	(7,600)	(7,450)
Capital expenditure	–	(32,000)
Wages and salaries	(18,200)	(18,600)
General expenses	(24,500)	(22,464)
Net cash flow	10,858	(23,893)
Opening bank balance	4,200	4,200
Closing bank balance	15,058	(19,693)

Required:

(a) Using the table below, prepare a reconciliation of budgeted cash flow with actual cash flow for the quarter.

Select the appropriate description for each entry, and show + or – signs to denote increased or reduced cash. Ensure that the reconciliation balances.

	£
Budgeted closing bank balance	
Surplus/Shortfall in receipts from receivables	
Surplus/Shortfall in cash sales	
Increase/Decrease in payments to payables	
Increase/Decrease in cash purchases	
Increase/Decrease in capital expenditure	
Increase/Decrease in wages and salaries	
Increase/Decrease in general expenses	
Actual closing bank balance	

(b) Which of the following actions, if used in isolation, could the organisation have taken to avoid an overdrawn bank balance?

(a)	Chased customers to pay sooner and delayed payments to suppliers	
(b)	Increased cash sales through better marketing	
(c)	Delayed capital expenditure	
(d)	Negotiated lower wages payments to employees	

(c) Variances between budget and actual cash flows can occur for a number of reasons. There are also a variety of courses of action available to minimise adverse variances or benefit from favourable variances.

Match each cause of a variance listed in the table below with one of the following possible courses of action and enter the course of action in the right-hand column of the table.

Improve credit control **Change suppliers** **Reduce overtime working**

Negotiate early settlement discount **Improve the product**

Labour costs have increased	
Sales volumes have decreased	
Payments to suppliers are being made earlier	
Customers are taking more days to settle their debts	
Prices of raw materials have increased	

4.7 A company has forecast the following sales of a new product that will commence sales in Month 1:

	Month 1 £	Month 2 £	Month 3 £	Month 4 £	Total £
Forecast Sales	103,500	108,000	106,800	102,400	420,700

The expected receipts from sales are that:

- 20% is received in the month of sale (cash sales)
- 30% is received in the month following the sale
- 50% is received two months following the sale

This has produced the following initial forecast of receipts:

	Receipts from Sales in:				
	Month 1 £	**Month 2** £	**Month 3** £	**Month 4** £	**Total** £
Month 1 Sales	20,700	31,050	51,750		
Month 2 Sales		21,600	32,400	54,000	
Month 3 Sales			21,360	32,040	
Month 4 Sales				20,480	
Forecast receipts	20,700	52,650	105,510	106,520	285,380

The company is now considering offering a discount of 4% to credit customers who pay in the month following sale. This is expected to change the receipts profile to the following:

- 20% of sales is received in the month of sale (cash sales)
- 60% of sales is received in the month following the sale
- 20% of sales is received two months following the sale

All solutions should be shown to the nearest £ where appropriate.

(a) Complete the following table to show the expected receipts if the settlement discount is offered.

	Receipts from Sales in:				
	Month 1 £	**Month 2** £	**Month 3** £	**Month 4** £	**Total** £
Month 1 Sales					
Month 2 Sales					
Month 3 Sales					
Month 4 Sales					
Forecast receipts					

(b) Calculate the increased or reduced receipts in months 1 to 4 by completing the following table and using + or – signs.

	Month 1 £	**Month 2** £	**Month 3** £	**Month 4** £	**Net Total** £
Change in cash flow					

(c) Calculate the amount of discount that will be allowed on the sales made in months 1 to 4 based on the above assumptions.

5 The UK financial system and liquidity

this chapter covers...

So far in this book we have looked in detail at the way in which organisations set up cash flow budgets to plan for future inflows and outflows of cash and estimate their liquidity. Organisations need to be able to manage their liquidity and deal with:

- *shortages of cash – by borrowing from banks*
- *surpluses of cash – by placing deposits with banks*

This chapter provides the background knowledge needed to place this process of liquidity management in context and provide an understanding of how interest rates are arrived at, and how they affect organisations.

The chapter covers:

- *an outline of liquidity management and some legislation that can have an impact on it*
- *the structure of the banking system and the way in which banks themselves raise funds from the money markets*
- *the way in which the Government's monetary policy is carried out by the control of the amount of money in circulation in order to provide stability in the economy and to stimulate growth of Gross Domestic Product*
- *the effects of the financial crisis of 2007 and the policy of Quantitative Easing (QE)*
- *the influence of economic trends on an organisation's own liquidity management*

THE BASIS OF LIQUIDITY MANAGEMENT

why is liquidity important?

the liquidity of a business is the availability of cash or assets which can easily be turned into cash

Without cash or liquidity a business can experience cash flow problems by running out of money to meet day-to-day requirements, for example – payments to payables, paying wages and reducing the bank overdraft when requested to do so.

In a worst case scenario the business can be bankrupted (made insolvent) because payables – including the bank – who are not paid on time can take legal action as a result of which the court can repay payables by selling the assets of the business.

Remember that cash is crucial. A common saying worth bearing in mind is:

Turnover is vanity, profit is sanity, but cash is king!

liquidity management

It is crucial that a business **manages** its liquidity. **Liquidity management** involves:

- the management of cash inflows and outflows
- the arrangement of finance at the best terms obtainable when there is a cash shortfall
- the appropriate investment of any cash surplus to achieve maximum return for an acceptable level of risk

In larger organisations the strategic control of liquidity is managed by the **treasury department**. Its role is concerned with managing the money and financial risks of the organisation. This includes making sure that the organisation has the capital (both long term and working capital) that it needs, and helping to develop its long term strategy and policies. A lot of its work involves deciding how and where to borrow or invest money while managing the associated risks. We will see later how this must be carried out within a range of external regulations and internal policies.

legislation impacting on treasury management

There are two specific laws that you need to be familiar with that can have an impact on borrowing, investing, or both.

- The Bribery Act 2010 contains several offences connected to bribery:
  - active bribery – the offering, promising or giving of a bribe;

  - passive bribery – the requesting, agreeing to receive or accepting a bribe;
  - bribery of a foreign public official in order to obtain or retain business or an advantage in the conduct of business;
  - failing to prevent bribery on behalf of a commercial organisation.

  The legislation could therefore apply where an inducement is offered to an individual who is responsible for borrowing or investing corporate funds in order to encourage them to borrow or invest in a certain way or with a certain organisation. In addition, the organisation must ensure that it has systems in place to prevent any form of bribery taking place.

- Money Laundering Regulations apply to a number of business sectors, including financial and credit businesses, accountants, solicitors and estate agents. Money laundering means exchanging money or assets that were obtained criminally for money or assets that are 'clean', and don't have an obvious link to any criminal activity. Organisations that the regulations apply to must:
  - assess the risk of the business being used by criminals to launder money;
  - check the identity of customers and the beneficial owners of companies with which they do business;
  - monitor customers' activities and report anything suspicious to the National Crime Agency (NCA);
  - ensure that management control systems and employee training are in place, and retain relevant documentation.

  The regulations could apply in certain circumstances when another organisation was intending to lend money to your organisation, or invest in it in another way. It would then be important to ensure that appropriate checks were carried out before going ahead with any transactions.

In the earlier chapters of this book we have examined the way in which organisations such as businesses set up cash budgets to forecast shortages and surpluses of cash over a period of time. As we have seen, these fluctuations can to some extent be smoothed out by managing timing efficiently, for example by scheduling payments to suppliers so that they are covered by receipts from customers. The raising of finance and the investment of surplus funds are also aspects of liquidity management, and will be dealt with in the following two chapters.

First, however, it is important to put the individual business in the context of the financial system as a whole – in short, the workings of the banks and the setting of the level of interest rates which can seriously affect planning and operations.

BANKS AS FINANCIAL INTERMEDIARIES

the need for a banking system

It is easy to take banks for granted. But consider what would happen if they did not exist. Think again about the problems of cash flow and liquidity: suppose Business A needed £10,000 for the period of a month and Business B had £10,000 surplus cash. Would Business B lend to Business A? There are a number of problems:

- Business A might be a poor credit risk as a borrower
- Business B might only have the money available for two weeks
- they would need to work out the 'cost' of the loan which Business A would pay to Business B

It can be seen from this that banks form the useful function of **financial intermediaries** – they come between (they 'intermediate') between depositors and borrowers, accepting deposits and making loans.

There are many advantages to this arrangement:

- the **amounts** deposited and borrowed can be very flexible – Business A does not have to look around for someone who has £10,000 to lend, the loan from the bank may be funded by a number (an aggregate) of smaller deposits
- the **time period** of the loan does not have to rely on the time period of the deposit – there is what is known technically as 'maturity transformation'
- the **risk** to the depositor is normally regarded as being low – until the financial market crisis of 2007, bank failures had been very rare events in the UK and Europe
- **known cost and reward** – the interest payable on the loan and the interest received for the deposit will be based on established market rates, providing a fair deal for borrower and depositor

Banks are therefore very efficient financial intermediaries. The banking system not only provides its traditional service of money transmission, it also helps to provide a stable source of liquidity. You should note that Building Societies are also financial intermediaries, although they mostly deal in the narrower field of personal savings and house finance.

The banking system as a whole includes a variety of institutions – and groups of companies – carrying out different functions:

- retail 'High Street' banks such as RBS and HSBC
- 'investment' banks or merchant banks, which deal with major company financing, investment advice and share issues, eg Barclays (formerly 'Barclays Capital')

The banking system, as we will see in the next section, has an important relationship with the UK Central Bank, the Bank of England.

THE BANK OF ENGLAND AND BANK LIQUIDITY

role of the Bank of England

The Bank of England is the UK's Central Bank. It carries out a number of functions, for example:

- it is banker to the Government – it holds accounts for Government departments
- it is banker to other banks – it holds accounts for other banks
- it is responsible for note printing, gold and foreign currency reserves
- it helps to influence interest rates in the economy – these rates are set with the aim of controlling the rate of inflation (see page 162)

If you want to find out more about the Bank of England, visit www.bankofengland.co.uk, a very helpful and informative website.

the financial market crisis in the UK

The financial market crisis of 2007 led to rescues by the UK Government through nationalisation of Northern Rock (bought by Virgin Money in 2012) and Bradford & Bingley (now part of Santander). In addition, the Government took substantial stakes in RBS and in a new entity formed through the merger of LloydsTSB and HBOS, now Lloyds Banking Group. The composition of the UK banking industry has therefore been altered radically by the crisis and, as a result, banks are now operating in a more tightly regulated environment than before.

banks and the Bank of England

The banks operating in the banking system provide each other with liquidity – ie cash balances – as they are regularly making large volumes of payments to each other. This source of liquidity is very important because a bank needs a 'cushion' of liquidity if customers lose confidence in the bank and demand their deposits back (as happened with Northern Rock).

Because of this danger, the banks need a fail-safe source of liquidity in case of liquidity shortages in the system. If banks cannot borrow from other banks they can obtain funds when needed on a daily basis from the Bank of England. This is done by the Bank of England buying from the banks a variety of short-term securities (paper 'certificates') which are traded in the London **money markets.** These markets need some explanation.

UK money markets

A **money market** is what the term suggests – a market for borrowing money and investing money. Nothing, of course, is free: the cost of the money is the interest rate charged on the amount borrowed. Trading is carried out largely through **inter-dealer brokers** (also known as **money brokers**).

The major sterling money market is the **interbank market**, which, as the name suggests, involves banks and other large institutions lending to each other on an **unsecured** basis over short periods, for example overnight or over one, three or six months. There are no certificates issued for these loans.

Secured money markets, on the other hand, involve the issue of a variety of what are essentially IOU 'securities' or 'certificates' issued by reputable institutions, both governmental and commercial (retail and investment banks, insurance companies, pension funds), when raising money. The institution agrees to pay a fixed interest rate on the certificates, which can then be 'sold' as an investment in the money markets before the maturity (repayment) date. Whoever has the certificate when it matures will receive the face value of that certificate from the issuer.

These secured markets are shown in the table below. The term 'short-term' typically applies to three or six month certificates. Notice that these securities are listed in the order of risk.

UK money markets in tradeable securities

Type of market	*Issuer of security*	*Description*
treasury bills	UK Government	91 day certificates issued to provide short-term Government funding
gilts	UK Government	'gilts' (short for 'gilt-edged stock') are Government securities, ie certificates issued in return for long-term Government borrowing
local authority bills	local authorities	short-term bills issued by local authorities (eg County Councils, Metropolitan Councils in the UK)
certificates of deposit (CDs)	banks	short-term certificates issued by the banks for deposits received
bills of exchange	companies	short-term bills, normally guaranteed by banks (often merchant banks)
corporate bonds and commercial paper	companies	debt certificates (higher risk than bills)

a note on 'bills'

The table on the previous page mentions the term 'bill'. This is an abbreviation of **bill of exchange**, a traditional method of settling debt between traders, and another form of marketable security in the London money markets. A bill of exchange is a document which sets out the amount and payment date of a debt. It can be sold – at a discount – before the date the debt is due to be paid so that the person/institution that buys it will receive the money on the due date.

a note on inter-dealer brokers (money brokers)

The London inter-dealer brokers (also known as 'money brokers') have a wide product base which has grown from routine foreign exchange and money market loans and deposits to include bonds, shares and commodities. These brokers are important because they enable the dealing markets to operate efficiently together.

the need for bank liquidity

Each day the UK banks pass between themselves a large volume of payments relating to customer transactions, eg BACS payments and cheques. They trade on the inter-bank market (see previous page) making 'wholesale' deposits and borrowing short-term, according to their **liquidity needs**.

Banks also invest funds in the 'marketable security' money markets, eg in gilts, treasury bills, CDs, and other types of bill. These investments are made so that the banks can remain liquid – they are in a position to be able to repay customer deposits because they are holding marketable securities which they can sell at short notice if they need to.

The statement of financial position of a bank is therefore likely to contain the following elements:

elements of a bank statement of financial position (simplified)

liabilities	assets
customer deposits (amounts due to customers)	loans (amounts due from customers)
other payables, including: • interbank and other wholesale deposits by companies and overseas residents	investments, including: • inter-bank market deposits • marketable securities from the London money market
capital & reserves	accounts with the Bank of England notes and coins

bank borrowing in times of need

Banks are able to borrow from the **Bank of England** (the Bank) when they are in need of funds, through a range of facilities, which have been developed and extended in response to the financial crisis of 2007. Through its **Operational Standing Facilities**, the Bank of England lends overnight funds in order to alleviate short-term technical or operational problems that may cause imbalances between banks.

Through its **Open Market Operations (OMOs)**, the Bank of England can add or drain funds from the banking system. **OMOs** take two forms:

1. Outright purchases or sales of securities (eg gilts) from or to banks.
2. More normally, funds are provided using **repo** (repurchase) agreements, in which the Bank buys securities (including a wider range of high quality securities) from the banks, with a simultaneous agreement to sell them back at a later date. Effectively, these are **secured loans from the Bank to the banking system**.

Since 2010, OMOs have been long-term arrangements in which funds are offered monthly with an interest rate indexed to Bank Rate (see next page). These OMOs normally have maturities of three or six months.

In addition, through the **Discount Window Facility** banks can borrow gilts from the Bank, against a wide range of types of security. This provides banks with a means of improving the liquidity of their statements of financial position, by giving them access to assets that are easy to convert to cash.

In short, if the banking system needs liquidity (cash) in times of crisis, the Bank of England is there to provide it.

THE BANK OF ENGLAND AND MONETARY POLICY

Monetary policy involves the control of the money supply (the amount of money) in the economy which in turn affects the rate of inflation.

By contrast, **fiscal policy** is the use by UK Government (not the Bank of England) of how much it spends and how it applies taxes to help control the economy. The direct and indirect effects of fiscal policy can impact on personal spending, capital expenditure, exchange rates and deficit levels.

High inflation can be damaging to the functioning of the economy. Low inflation – which results in price stability – can encourage sustainable long-term economic growth. The main long-term overall objectives of an effective monetary policy are therefore to:

- maintain **price stability**, as defined by the inflation target set by the Government
- achieve the economic goal of a stable level of **employment**

- achieve **economic growth** measured in terms of Gross Domestic Product, also known as 'GDP'
- avoid the economy slipping into **recession**

GDP and recession

An important aim of Government economic policy is to maintain or increase **Gross Domestic Product (GDP)**. 'Real' GDP (ie GDP adjusted for the effects of inflation) is an accurate indicator of economic activity and is defined as:

the market value of goods and services produced by a country over a given period of time

In other words, GDP is the total value of what a country produces. If GDP is stable or increasing, Government economic and monetary policy is working; if on the other hand GDP falls, the country may be entering into **recession** and Government policy will be open to criticism.

Recession is the situation in which GDP has fallen over two successive quarters.

Recession is not good for business liquidity. Inflows of cash are restricted in two ways:

- customers may fall behind in paying invoices or even become insolvent so that the amounts owing become irrecoverable debts
- reduced demand for products is likely to reduce revenue from sales

the Bank of England and Bank Rate

The Bank of England has traditionally aimed to meet the Government's inflation target by setting short-term interest rates. Interest rate decisions are taken by the Monetary Policy Committee (MPC) of the Bank of England.

Each month, the MPC sets **Bank Rate**, which is the rate paid on reserve balances held by commercial banks at the Bank of England overnight.

Bank Rate is also the rate applied to lending by the Bank to commercial banks and that rate affects the whole pattern of rates set by commercial banks for their savers and borrowers. This, in turn, affects spending and output in the economy, and eventually costs and prices.

the Bank of England and recession

In March 2009, following the effects of the 2007 financial crisis, Bank Rate fell to 0.5% and at the time of writing remains at that figure. The UK economy was entering a period of low or no growth. As a consequence of this the Bank of England policy of controlling the supply of money through interest rates became less effective and it needed to find another way of injecting cash into the financial system. In March 2009 the Bank added a new policy response, known as **Quantitative Easing (QE)**.

Quantitative Easing

The aim of Quantitative Easing is to increase the amount of money circulating and being spent in the economy directly, through purchases by the Bank of high quality assets, mainly gilts (Government Stock) from private sector institutions, financed by the creation of central bank reserves. For example, when the Bank purchases £100 million of gilts from an insurance company, it credits the company's bank account with £100 million.

Quantitative Easing has various secondary effects that, it is hoped, will boost spending in the economy. By January 2010, Quantitative Easing asset purchases by the Bank had reached £200 billion, and in July 2012 the total had almost doubled to £375 billion.

The intention of the Government with this policy is that the process will be reversed when the economy has recovered sufficiently.

HOW CHANGES IN INTEREST RATES AFFECT BUSINESSES

As already noted in this chapter, Organisations such as businesses often find it disruptive if interest rates fluctuate.

the effect of a rise in interest rates on a business

If interest rates rise, financial planning is made more difficult:

- the cost of borrowing will increase – interest charges will increase and investment in the business will be discouraged
- a rise in interest rates is often associated with a rise in inflation, leading to a rise in the cost of raw materials and an increase in overheads
- the value of the currency will tend to rise in the short term, making exports less competitive but imported raw materials cheaper

On the other hand, if the business is very liquid and has funds to invest, the return will be greater as interest rates rise.

the effect of a fall in interest rates

If interest rates fall, the effects are generally positive – which is what the Government is aiming for:

- the cost of borrowing will decrease – interest charges will go down, borrowing will be cheaper and investment in the business will be encouraged, all of which is symptomatic of a healthy economy
- the rate of inflation will stabilise or even fall, leading to price stability or even a fall in the costs of raw materials and overheads

THE IMPACT OF EXCHANGE RATES AND COMMODITY PRICES

Both exchange rates and commodity prices are the result of supply and demand.

- Exchange rates between currencies move because one currency is seen as more attractive. This could be, for example because of the strength of the national economy, or an increase in national interest rates. When a currency becomes stronger (ie more expensive to purchase using another currency) the businesses that operate in that currency will find it harder to export. Imports will, however, become cheaper.
- Commodity prices (for example oil) increase as either demand increases, or the supply diminishes. The change in prices will make businesses that sell the commodity more valuable, but add to the costs of organisations that buy and use the commodity. The price of commodities like oil will obviously have an impact on transport costs (which form part of the cost of most things), but will also influence industries which are concerned with synthetics including plastics. It will also have an impact on tax revenue in the countries of producers and users of oil are located as company profits are influenced.

Stable exchange rates and stable commodity prices enable businesses to plan more effectively. Volatile rates and prices make the financial markets nervous and prices of shares in affected companies will also tend to be volatile, adding additional risk to investments.

Chapter Summary

- Sufficient liquidity – the availability of cash or near-cash assets – in an organisation such as a business is essential for its survival.
- Liquidity management involves the careful timing of cash inflows and outflows, the arrangement of finance where required and the investment of surplus funds where appropriate.
- Legislation that can affect treasury management includes the Bribery Act 2010 and Money Laundering Regulations.
- The Bank of England carries out a number of important roles: banker to the Government, banker to the banks, note printing, maintaining gold and currency reserves, influencing interest rates as part of the monetary policy of the Government.
- Banks and other institutions trade actively in the UK money markets where money can be borrowed or invested, normally over the short term. The money markets include the interbank market (unsecured wholesale money deposits) and markets in tradeable securities, for example Government stocks, CDs, bills of exchange, and commercial paper (see Key Terms for fuller details).
- Banks can raise funds from the Bank of England by borrowing overnight, by selling securities to the Bank, and, most importantly, by trading marketable securities in return for cash on the basis that they will repurchase equivalent securities at a future date (most commonly one week ahead) from the Bank. This is known as a 'repo' transaction and is charged by the Bank of England at what is known as the 'repo' rate of interest.
- One of the Bank of England's functions is to help administer the monetary policy of the Government. This policy aims to adjust the supply of money in the economy in order to control the rate of inflation and the stability of the currency.
- Monetary policy was traditionally carried out by the Bank of England influencing interest rates (under the direction of the Monetary Policy Committee) through setting the rate at which the Bank of England lends to the financial system.
- Quantitative Easing (QE) was introduced by the Bank of England to increase the quantity of money in the economy by purchasing gilts and other securities from private sector institutions.
- Organisations such as businesses are affected by the economic and financial environment which results from the operation of monetary policy. Generally speaking low interest rates are associated with low inflation and are beneficial – they enable businesses to borrow and invest in growth, which in turn is a sign of a healthy and stable economy.
- Movements in exchange rates and commodity prices can impact directly on businesses and through the value of investments that they hold.

Key Terms

liquidity	the availability of cash or assets which can easily be turned into cash
liquidity management	the management of cash inflows and outflows, ensuring that finance is arranged where there is a cash shortfall and surplus funds are invested to achieve a return
treasury management	the function within an organisation which deals with borrowing, investing and managing the associated risks
Bribery Act 2010	the legislation that created various offences concerned with bribery
Money Laundering Regulations	the rules that apply to certain organisations to help prevent criminal organisations using their facilities to 'launder' money
retail bank	a bank that offers financial services to the general public, also known as a 'High Street' bank
merchant bank	a bank that deals with company financing and investments, also known as an 'investment' bank
money market	a market in which institutions invest and raise 'money', either in the form of straightforward money balances or through tradeable securities (see below)
tradeable securities	certificates issued by institutions (including the Government) in return for money received for a certain period of time; these certificates (see below for the different types) can be 'sold' to other institutions in the money markets before maturity
gilts	also known as 'Government stock' or 'gilt-edged stock', gilts are certificates issued in return for money borrowed by the Government over the long term (ie periods of years)
treasury bills	91 day certificates issued to raise short-term funding for the Government
certificates of deposit (CDs)	short-term certificates issued by the banks in return for money deposited with them
repo agreement	a 'repurchase' agreement made between the Bank of England and banking institutions whereby the Bank of England buys acceptable

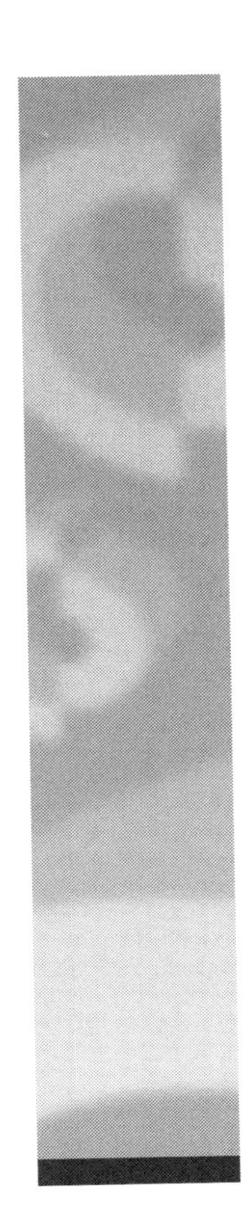

tradeable securities on the basis that the banks will repurchase equivalent securities from the Bank of England at a later date

repo rate the rate of interest charged by the Bank of England on a repo agreement

monetary policy Government policy which is used to adjust the amount of money in the economy

Bank Rate is set by the Bank of England's Monetary Policy Committee at the same rate as repo rate and is intended to influence rates of interest for borrowers and savers in the economy generally

Gross Domestic Product Gross Domestic Product (GDP) is the inflation-adjusted market value of goods and services produced by a country over a given period of time and when positive an indicator of economic prosperity

recession a period of time in which Gross Domestic Product has fallen for at least two successive quarters

quantitative easing increasing the amount of money circulating and being spent in the economy directly, through purchases by the Bank of England of high quality assets (mainly gilts) from private sector institutions

Activities

5.1 A inter-dealerbroker (also known as a money broker) is best described as someone that:

(a)	Deals only with company shares and insurance	
(b)	Deals only with company shares and mortgage loans	
(c)	Deals with a wide range of money and currency deposits	
(d)	Deals with a wide range of money deposits and insurance	

Which **one** of these options is the most accurate description?

5.2 Complete each of the gaps in the sentences set out below with one of these financial instruments:

treasury bill **certificate of deposit** **gilt-edged security** **corporate bond**

(a) A [ ] is a tradeable investment to fund longer-term Government borrowing.

(b) A [ ] is a form of investment issued by a commercial company.

(c) A [ ] is a short-term tradeable investment issued in respect of a deposit received by the bank.

(d) A [ ] is a short-term tradeable investment to fund Government borrowing.

5.3 Liquid assets shown in a UK bank's statement of financial position are likely to contain:

(a)	Customer deposits, notes and coins, investments on the interbank money market	
(b)	Notes and coins, treasury bills, certificates of deposit	
(c)	Customer deposits, treasury bills, certificates of deposit	
(d)	Customer loans, borrowing on the interbank money market, treasury bills	

Which **one** of these options is correct?

5.4 Complete the gaps in the following text by using the following phrases:

repo (repurchase) **Bank of England** **Open Market Operations**

The Bank of England can add to or take funds out of the banking system using [ ]. Using this system, funds are provided using [ ] agreements, in which the [ ] buys tradeable securities from the banks, with a simultaneous agreement to sell them back at a later date.

5.5 Bank rate is an interest rate which is:

(a)	Set by the UK Treasury and is the minimum rate at which banks can lend to customers	
(b)	Set by the Bank of England and is the minimum rate paid on bank deposits in the interbank market	
(c)	Set by the Monetary Control Committee and is the rate which sets the pattern for commercial bank lending rates	

Which **one** of these options is correct?

5.6 Quantitative easing is a policy which involves the Bank of England buying easily saleable investments such as gilts from private sector institutions such as insurance companies. Its main aim is to:

(a)	Increase the amount of money circulating in the economy and hence the amount of spending in the economy	
(b)	Decrease the amount of money circulating in the economy and hence the amount of spending in the economy	
(c)	Increase the amount and type of non-current assets held by banks and other lenders	
(d)	Decrease the amount and type of non-current assets held by banks and other lenders	

Which **one** of these options is correct?

5.7 Complete the following text by using the following words and phrases:

raw materials **healthy** **rise in the rate of inflation** **interest charges**

cheaper **borrowing**

If the level of interest rates rises in the UK economy, the result is likely to be associated with a

[ ] and the cost of [ ]

This will mean a rise in costs for businesses because of higher [ ] but a possible fall in the cost of imported [ ]. If interest rates fall, on the other hand, borrowing will be [ ] the economy will become more [ ].

6 Raising short-term and long-term finance

this chapter covers...

Liquidity management involves the accurate predicting of shortages and surpluses of cash through the use of a cash budget, which will indicate any need for short-term financing. This can be provided by:

- *bank overdrafts for short-term day-to-day requirements*
- *other short-term financing options such as factoring and invoice discounting*

An organisation will also have to plan for long-term financing of its assets and expansion plans. It will need liquidity to repay that financing. Forms of long-term finance include:

- *bank long-term loans and commercial mortgages*
- *operating and finance leases and hire purchase*
- *the issue of further equity capital to investors, eg shares, loan stock and bonds*

It is important to consider a number of factors when deciding on the form of financing:

- *the accounting implications of the finance, eg how it will affect the financial statements of the business and its gearing*
- *the cost of the finance in terms of interest and fees*
- *the need for businesses to provide security to cover borrowing*

This chapter also examines the legal aspects of financing:

- *the documentation involved in financing and taking of security*
- *the need for companies and public sector organisations to comply with legislation when raising finance*

TYPES OF FINANCE

In this chapter we start by describing and illustrating the two main classifications of financing:

- short-term finance
- long-term finance

You will need to appreciate that financing can be obtained not only from banks and other financial services companies but also from the issue of new shares. Both have a very different effect on the gearing of the borrower.

SHORT-TERM FINANCE – BANK OVERDRAFT

There are various interpretations of what 'short-term' means. In this chapter we will use the term to refer to periods of up to twelve months. A common form of short-term finance is the **bank overdraft**.

bank overdraft

An overdraft is an arrangement ('facility') between a bank and a customer which allows the customer to borrow money on a current account up to a specified amount ('limit').

Overdrafts are available to personal and to business customers. Negative figures on the bottom of a cash budget indicate an overdraft.

The **features** of an overdraft include:

- interest is calculated on a daily basis and charged at an agreed rate (usually a fixed percentage above the bank's 'base' rate) monthly or quarterly, but only on the amount that is borrowed
- the customer is also likely to have to pay an arrangement fee based on a percentage of the overall 'limit', ie the maximum amount that can be borrowed
- the overdraft 'facility' is agreed for a set time period, often six or twelve months, after which it can be reviewed by the bank and renewed with an appropriate limit to reflect activity on the current account
- business overdrafts for small and medium-sized businesses will normally need to be secured, eg a charge over the customer's business or private assets or a guarantee (see page 188); larger businesses (eg listed companies) may not need to provide security

- a business overdraft is nowadays normally a **committed overdraft**, ie it is granted for a fixed period of time and is only repayable on demand if the borrower becomes insolvent

The main **advantage** of an overdraft is that it is very flexible:

- the borrower only borrows what is needed for the short-term
- the borrower only pays interest on what is borrowed, which helps reduce the overall interest charge
- the overdraft limit may be raised by the bank with the minimum of formality if the borrower needs extra working capital, or consolidated into a term loan if the borrowing becomes 'hard core'

The often-quoted disadvantage of an overdraft is that it is repayable on demand. But, as mentioned on the previous page, this is only likely to happen with a business overdraft if the bank considers that the business is becoming insolvent.

Another **disadvantage** of an overdraft is that the interest rate is likely to be set at a set percentage over bank base rate and so could rise to a high level if base rate goes up. This interest rate risk potentially makes an overdraft **expensive** in comparison to a bank loan with a fixed or capped interest rate (see page 174).

SHORT-TERM FINANCE – FACTORING AND INVOICE DISCOUNTING

The most common form of short-term financing is the bank overdraft, but businesses can also take advantage of other forms of financing which will ease the problems of working capital shortages and also enable the business to grow. These include **factoring** and **invoice discounting**.

factoring

Factoring is a financial arrangement in which a business sells its accounts receivable (its invoices) for cash to a factoring company, which carries out the debt management and collects the debts when they are due.

The 'factoring company' is often a subsidiary company of a bank and so factoring services are often offered by banks as part of a financing package. The features of a typical factoring arrangement are:

- a percentage of the value of invoices issued to customers (typically 85%) is paid into the bank account of the business within 24 hours
- the remainder (typically 15%) is paid to the seller when the invoice is due, less the factoring company's charges

- the factoring company takes on the debt management for the seller, including credit checks and debt chasing

The **advantages** of factoring are:

- it turns unpaid invoices into immediately available working capital
- it helps to avoid irrecoverable debts through efficient debt collection
- some factoring companies will also provide debt insurance cover

The **disadvantages** of factoring are:

- it costs money – but for the small and growing business this could be money well spent in avoiding the dangers of overtrading and not having time to run the sales ledger efficiently
- security may be required (see pages 187-189)

invoice discounting

Invoice discounting is factoring without the debt management service.

Invoice discounting means that the invoice finance company provides the up-front cash, but leaves the sales ledger function of processing and pursuing debts to the seller. With **factoring**, the seller hands over its credit control function to the invoice finance company.

The **advantages** of invoice discounting are:

- it turns unpaid invoices into immediately available working capital
- it enables the seller to maintain better contact with its customers

The **disadvantages** of invoice discounting are:

- the cost
- the need to maintain an efficient sales ledger
- security may be required (see pages 187-189)

LONG-TERM FINANCE – BANK LOANS

It is important when raising finance to **match the finance to the need**. We have already seen that an overdraft is ideal for a short-term borrowing requirement: it is flexible, a business borrows what it needs, when it is needed and can repay the borrowing when it is able to do so. Longer-term borrowing will require a different type of finance.

bank loans

If a business is purchasing assets which will be retained in the business for a year or more, it will have to make a choice from different types of non-current asset finance. A common choice is the **bank loan**.

Businesses will need to acquire new non-current assets as part of expansion plans, eg computers, equipment, vehicles, and property.

The normal practice is to pay back the cost of the assets over the period for which they are retained. For example, computer and vehicle finance may be repaid over one to three years whereas if a business is buying land and property a commercial mortgage loan for up to twenty-five years would be a sensible choice. There are two main forms of bank loan for businesses:

- **business loans**
- **commercial mortgages**

We will describe each of these in turn.

bank business loan

A **business loan** is longer-term financing to cover items of expense such as new equipment, premises expansion or a new project. Each bank will have its own products but the typical features of a bank business loan are:

- loan amounts can range from £1,000 to £250,000
- a bank loan can be granted for up to ten years, but a normal term would be for five years
- the loan is often repaid in regular instalments (monthly, quarterly or annually); the capital amount borrowed may also be repaid in full at the end of the loan period – these loans are known as 'bullets'
- sometimes a **repayment holiday** can be arranged if the loan is for an asset from which the income generated will be subject to a delay, for example a major capital project which will take time to get into operation
- security is likely to be required to cover the loan (see pages 187-189)
- interest rates can be:
  - **fixed** for the period of the loan, which helps the financial planning processes of the business
  - **variable**, at a fixed percentage over the bank **base lending rate**
  - **variable** at a fixed percentage over **LIBOR** (London Interbank Offered Rate), which is the interest rate at which banks will borrow on the London **interbank market**; LIBOR linked loans are for larger amounts, typically for £500,000 and above
  - **capped** – ie the bank will guarantee a maximum rate and will carry the risk if the market interest rates rise above the upper 'capped' limit
- an arrangement fee is charged at the beginning of the loan – it is typically around 1% of the amount borrowed

The **advantages** of bank business loans are:

- repayments can be scheduled to suit the life of the asset
- repayment may be delayed if required (the 'repayment holiday')
- the regularity of repayments helps the business in its financial planning processes
- interest rates can be lower – eg fixed or capped rates – than interest rates for overdraft borrowing; in other words, long-term borrowing can be cheaper than overdraft financing

commercial mortgage

A commercial mortgage is a loan for up to twenty five years to cover the purchase of property (the business equivalent of a 'home loan' mortgage).

- a mortgage is an arrangement in which the property is used as security for borrowing; if the business defaults on the loan, the bank can sell the property to get its money back
- banks can provide finance for the purchase of commercial property, normally up to 70% of its market value
- interest may be paid:
  - at a rate fixed at the beginning of the mortgage
  - at a variable rate in line with market rates during the lifetime of the mortgage
  - at a capped rate

The main advantage of a commercial mortgage is that of cost: it is repayable over a long period of time and the interest costs are lower than an overdraft.

LONG-TERM FINANCE – LEASING

If a business wishes to make use of non-current assets, finance is also available from finance companies (often owned by banks) in the form of operating leases, finance leases and hire purchase (HP), a type of finance lease.

what is a lease?

A **lease** is an arrangement where the owner of an asset (the **lessor**) gives another person or body (the **lessee**) rights of use and possession of that asset for a specified period of time in return for rental or lease payments. Assets that are often leased include computers, company cars and property.

There are two main types of lease – an **operating lease** (mainly short-term rentals) and a **finance lease,** which, as the name suggests, is a method of financing longer-term assets.

operating lease and finance lease – the differences

What is the difference between these two types of lease?

- an **operating lease** is a **short-term** arrangement where:
  - the lessee 'rents' the asset from the lessor (a leasing company) but is not given the rights of ownership
  - when the lease comes to an end the lessor will expect the assets to retain some value so that they can be sold or leased out again – this is known as 'residual value'; assets such as cars and aircraft are often leased out on operating leases
  - as it is a shorter-term arrangement, with the asset having a residual value, the rental payments are likely to be lower than a finance lease (see below)
  - the lessee will be expected to carry out the maintenance of the asset unless it is carried out by the lessor under a contract
- a **finance lease** is a lease that is a method of raising finance to pay for an asset over the **long term** (its economic life) where:
  - the lessee (the person using the assets) takes responsibility for the risks and rewards of ownership, but not the ownership
  - the total cost of the assets is normally covered by the rental payments over the period of the lease
  - at the end of the lease the lease agreement may allow the lessee to retain or purchase the assets which by this time may not be worth much (unlike the assets under an operating lease)

Hire Purchase (HP)

A hire purchase (HP) contract is a type of finance lease where the user will usually retain the use and take ownership of the asset at the end of the hire period, often for a relatively small sum.

As with the finance lease the user of the asset enjoys the risks and rewards of ownership.

For both **HP** and **finance leases** of at least 5 years the lessee has the right to claim capital allowances for plant and machinery under tax rules. This contrasts with **operating leases** where the lessor claims these allowances and the lessee sets the revenue cost of renting the asset against tax.

accounting treatment of leases – the differences

The accounting treatment of operating and finance leases is quite different. The lessor (the person giving the lease) under an **operating lease** continues to own the asset and needs to account for it as such in financial statements. The lessee records the lease payments in the statement of profit or loss as a rental expense. Operating leases do not result in the lease arrangement being recorded on the lessee's statement of financial position as an asset or a liability representing the amounts due to be paid.

The classification of leases as **finance leases** is very important and very different. With a finance lease (and hire purchase) the relevant assets (and liabilities) **must** be shown on the statement of financial position of the lessee. The asset is recorded at the lower of fair value and the present value of the minimum lease payments. A corresponding liability is set up and interest is calculated on the outstanding liability and charged to the statement of profit or loss each year.

leases – the effect on gearing

Keeping the asset and the liability off the statement of profit or loss can significantly improve the lessee's financial ratios, eg gearing, the relationship between external borrowing and equity.

The formula to use for calculating gearing when studying this Unit is:

$$\frac{\textit{total debt (ie non-current liabilities + overdrafts)} \ \times \ 100\%}{\textit{total debt + equity}}$$

The higher the gearing the less attractive it becomes for a lender to grant further finance.

Study and memorise the table below which summarises and highlights the differences between operating and finance leases. Remember:

lessor = the leasing company providing the asset

lessee = the business using the asset

	Finance lease	**Operating lease**
Who owns the asset?	Lessor	Lessor
Length of lease?	Economic life of asset	Only a part of the economic life
Who is responsible for upkeep of asset?	Lessee	Lessee (unless lessor agrees to maintain asset under contract)
Statement of financial position?	Non-current asset and non-current liability	Not recorded
Statement of profit or loss?	Interest paid recorded Depreciation recorded	Lease repayments recorded
Effect on gearing ratio (debt/equity)?	Higher ratio (lease is part of long-term debt)	No effect
Effect on risk profile to lender?	Higher risk (higher gearing)	No effect on gearing but reduced profit due to lease payments

sale and leaseback arrangements

Another form of long-term financing based on leasing is **sale and leaseback**. This is where an asset is sold by a business but then leased back on a long-term basis. This means that the business no longer owns the asset but can continue to use it. **Sale and leaseback** is used for non-current assets, for example commercial property, planes and trains. The main advantages of sale and leaseback are the use of the funds available from the sale and the fact that the lessor will have the responsibility of maintaining the asset.

LONG-TERM FINANCE – CAPITAL FINANCING

The final form of financing you will need to know about is limited company long-term finance in the form of new **equity share capital** and the issue of **fixed interest stock**. The specific types of financing that we will describe are the issue of:

- equity shares
- preference shares
- loan stock
- bonds

equity shares

Limited company equity shares represent the investment by individual investors in that company. The majority of the shares are likely to have been issued when the company was first formed and may represent the individual injections of capital by the first directors.

You will know from your study of limited company Statements of Financial Position that the Equity section normally starts with the share capital. These 'Equity shares' are also known as 'ordinary shares' and are the most common form of shares. If a company is undertaking a substantial expansion plan it may raise finance directly from investors in **new issue** of equity shares. The only downside to this is that the earnings and control of the existing shareholders may be diluted if there are new investors involved.

preference shares

Preference shares are similar to ordinary equity shares in that they represent an investment in a company. Where they differ is in the rights they confer on the investor and the type and level of return they provide:

- at times when there is little profit for distribution preference shareholders are first in the queue for dividends; they will be paid in **preference** to the ordinary equity shareholders who may not receive anything at all

- if the company becomes insolvent, the preference shareholders will get 'first slice' of the money available to pay back to the investors; in other words they get **preference** over the ordinary equity shareholders
- the percentage rate of dividend paid on preference shares is **fixed** whereas equity shareholders receive a dividend at a rate which **varies** according to the performance of the company

Preference shares do not confer voting rights at company meetings and are generally treated as long-term debt on a company's statement of financial position. Raising finance in this way will therefore **increase gearing**.

loan stock

Limited companies can also raise funds for expansion or acquisition of other companies by issue of **loan stock**. It is normally the larger public limited companies that issue loan stock as the stock will be traded on the stock markets. Loan stock:

- pays a fixed rate of interest
- can be secured or unsecured

A secured loan stock may also be called a convertible loan stock if the loan stock can be directly converted to ordinary equity shares at a later date.

Loan stock is classed as a non-current liability on the statement of financial position of the company.

corporate and zero coupon bonds

A bond is a general term used to describe a lump sum invested in a stock issued by a company at a fixed interest rate for a fixed term. At the end of the term the original value is repaid in full. In the meantime the stock can be bought and sold at any time at the market price on the stock markets.

Bonds issued by large companies quoted on the stock markets are known as **corporate bonds**. An example of a bond at the time of writing is Barclays 5.75% redemption date 14 September 2026.

Some bonds do not pay any interest at all but are issued at a substantial discount to their face value which is the amount that will be repaid on the redemption date. These bonds are known as **zero coupon bonds**.

the effect of capital financing on gearing

Gearing is the relationship of external borrowing to equity. We have seen with leasing finance that a **finance lease** requires the lessee to record the lease as a non-current liability. This will **increase gearing**.

Raising finance through an issue of **equity share capital**, on the other hand, increases the total of equity funding and this will effectively **reduce gearing** and improve the company's credit rating. This in turn will make it easier for the company to raise further finance if the need arises.

Note that preference shares, loan stock and bonds all count as **external financing** and will be non-current liabilities on the statement of financial position of the borrower. Raising finance in this way will **increase gearing.**

Study and memorise the table below.

capital financing – the effect on gearing (debt/equity)		
Type of finance	**Statement of financial position**	**Effect on gearing**
Equity shares	Equity	Reduction
Preference shares	Non-current liability	Increase
Loan stock	Non-current liability	Increase
Bonds	Non-current liability	Increase

The Case Study that follows shows how a business deals with a choice between different forms of long-term finance.

The text that follows the Case Study explains the comparative costs to a business of taking out different forms of financing.

SCION PRINTING: LONG-TERM FINANCING

situation

Scion Printing is a printing company based in Exeter. The directors, who between them own all the ordinary share capital of the company, are planning to expand the company's production facilities by acquiring a new digital processing printer. They calculate that they will need £300,000 for a state-of-the-art machine.

The finance director is weighing up the advantages and disadvantages of different means of financing the project. He is concerned that the company is highly geared and only an average credit risk for a lender.

He is considering three options for raising the £300,000:

Option 1: A finance lease for 8 years

Option 2: An operating lease for 4 years

Option 3: An issue of new ordinary share capital to the five directors

required

You are to draw up briefing notes for the Finance Director which:

- list the main features of each option
- set out the effects each option will have on the statement of profit or loss and the statement of financial position
- summarise the effect each option will have on the company's gearing

solution

Option 1: A finance lease for 8 years

(a) Main Features

- A finance lease will enable Scion to lease the equipment and pay for it over 8 years.
- If the equipment is still useful after this period there may be the possibility of purchasing it from the leasing company.
- The cost of the finance over this period will be much the same as the outright purchase cost plus the interest charge.
- The equipment will remain the property of the leasing company.
- Scion will be responsible for repairs and maintenance during the term of the lease agreement.

(b) Accounting and Financial implications

- The equipment will be shown on the statement of financial position as an asset at its full purchase price.
- The balance of the lease payments outstanding will be shown as a liability on the statement of financial position. The amount due within one year will be included with current liabilities and the balance with non-current liabilities.
- The interest on the payments will be included in the statement of profit or loss.
- The balance of the lease payments outstanding in current and non-current liabilities is classed as debt and will be included in the gearing calculation.
- The gearing of the company will increase which could affect the company's credit rating and ability to raise additional finance.

Option 2: An operating lease for 4 years

(a) Main Features

- Scion will have use of the asset for the period of the lease and the option to purchase it at the end of the 4 years.

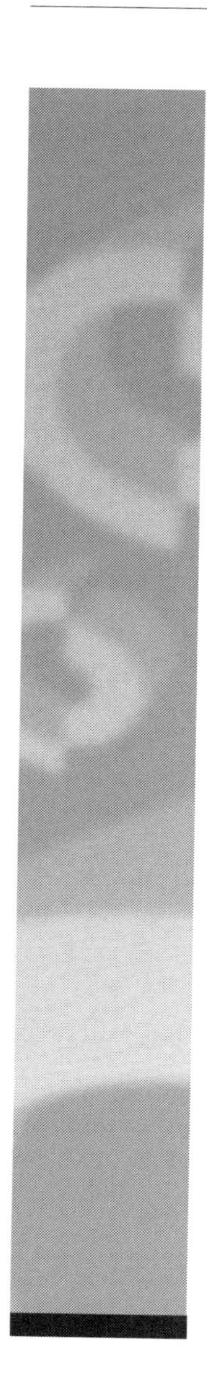

- Payment for the lease will be by way of instalments over the 4 years.
- The leasing company will retain ownership of the asset.
- Scion will be responsible for repairs and maintenance during the term of the hire purchase agreement, unless it is contracted to the lessor.

(b) Accounting and Financial implications

- The lease payments are included in Scion's statement of profit or loss.
- Scion will show reduced profits due to the lease payments.
- The equipment is not included as an asset in the statement of financial position and the liability to pay for the lease is not included in the liabilities.
- There is therefore no effect on the gearing of Scion.
- If it wishes to raise further finance Scion will be a better credit risk as the lease is not shown in the statement of financial position.

Option 3: An issue of ordinary share capital to the directors

(a) Main Features

- Scion will raise the £300,000 from the directors of the business, who are happy to make the extra investment.
- This financing will be used to purchase the equipment outright.

(b) Accounting and Financial implications

- The new equipment will be included in the non-current assets on Scion's statement of financial position.
- There will not be any associated expenses (repayments or interest) recorded on the statement of profit or loss.
- The equity position on the statement of financial position will increase and consequently gearing will be lower.
- Scion will be in a stronger position to raise additional finance with lower gearing and the plant available as security.

THE COST OF FINANCE

When a business is applying for finance for working capital or for asset purchase it should bear in mind a number of factors:

- can the business afford to repay the proposed financing?
- what is the cost of the finance in terms of interest and fees?

We will deal with each of these factors in detail on the next page.

'can the business afford to repay the financing?'

This factor is central to the feasibility of the project planned by the business. A business that wants to borrow will be asked by the lender to produce a number of financial statements, including the statement of profit or loss and statement of financial position and a cash budget. It is the cash budget that will indicate to the lender whether the business can generate the cash which will initially keep the overdraft within its set limit and provide the funds for repayment of a loan.

'what is the cost of the interest and fees?'

If a business is planning to raise and repay finance, it must take account of the interest and fees that it will have to pay. It will also have to make sure that it is getting the best deal from the lender by investigating all the different forms of loan and any specialised finance that may be available, and then weighing up the advantages and disadvantages.

overdraft interest

Interest is payable both on loans and overdrafts. Generally speaking, **overdrafts** carry higher interest rates, but as interest is only paid on exactly what is borrowed, they are more efficient forms of financing for short-term needs. The interest cost can be calculated as follows:

average overdraft (£) x average annual interest rate (%)

For example, if the balance of an overdraft averages £10,000 and the average annual interest rate is 6%, the annual cost will be £10,000 x 6% = £600. This would work out at £50 a month (ie £600 divided by 12).

the cost of borrowing – flat rate

There are various ways of calculating the percentage rate of interest paid on borrowing. The problem is that different methods produce very different results and so the borrower must be aware of the method of calculation used. One type of interest rate used is the **flat rate**:

a flat rate of interest is based on the total amount borrowed (the principal) over the whole period of the loan and ignores any repayments made

For example: a business borrows £10,000 over 4 years which it repays in four equal annual instalments. It is charged interest at 5% of the total of £10,000. The **total interest** charged using the flat rate interest formula is:

P (Principal, ie the loan amount) x R (Rate of Interest) x T (Time period)

This works out at £10,000 x 5/100 x 4 years = £2,000, ie £500 a year.

As the loan is repaid by instalments at the end of each year there will only be £2,500 of the principal outstanding in the final (fourth) year but the business will be charged £500 interest in that year under the flat rate calculation shown above. Borrowers should therefore beware of flat rates.

calculating a flat rate of interest

The flat rate charged on a loan can be calculated by:

- working out the total interest by comparing the principal borrowed with the total amount repaid over the period of the loan
- dividing this total interest by the number of years of the loan
- expressing the result as a percentage of the principal borrowed

For example, a loan of £6,000 is offered to a business to be repaid over 3 years, based on 36 payments of £200 each:

- total interest is therefore (£200 x 36) – £6,000 = £1,200
- dividing the total interest by 3 years gives £1,200 ÷ 3 = £400
- expressing this as a percentage of the principal:

  £400 ÷ £6,000 x 100 = 6.67%

comparing the cost of borrowing – APR

APR (Annual Percentage Rate) was introduced to provide a far more accurate way of comparing the costs of borrowing by taking into account factors such as the reducing balance of a loan over time and the added fees and interest costs on **an annual basis**. The principle of APR is different from the **flat rate** (see previous page), which calculates the interest on the whole loan (principal) over the period of the loan, ignoring the fact that the balance will be reducing and that there may be fees to pay.

The example that follows provides an illustration of why an APR rate is cheaper than a loan which is quoted on the terms of flat rate interest.

A business is looking for a 6 year loan of £10,000. One loan quotes a flat rate of 5%, and the other an average APR of 6%. Which is the cheaper form of finance? Remember:

- the flat rate is applied to the whole of the **loan principal** every year
- the Annual Percentage Rate is calculated on the **amount outstanding**, which is reducing each year and includes fees

The table on the next page shows on an approximate basis the interest payments the business would make using the two different calculations.

Year	Flat rate 5%	APR 6%
1	£500	£600
2	£500	£500
3	£500	£400
4	£500	£300
5	£500	£200
6	£500	£100
Total interest paid	£3,000	£2,100

As you will see from the table the business will pay total interest of £3,000 on a 5% flat rate loan and £2,100 on an APR of 6%. The APR rate loan is in fact £900 cheaper over the six years.

'simple' rate of interest – a note

The term 'simple interest rate' is sometimes used to differentiate a flat rate from a compound interest rate. The APR is based on a compound interest rate. You will not be required to calculate an APR in your assessment.

fees

The main type of fee which has to be considered when working out the cost of the finance is the **arrangement** fee. The fees paid will vary according to whether you have a loan or an overdraft:

- For a **loan**, the procedure is simple: you pay an arrangement fee at a fixed percentage of the total amount borrowed, eg 1%. This is a 'one-off' fee charged for setting up the loan in the first place, and payable when you take the loan.
- For an **overdraft** you are likely to pay a fixed percentage **arrangement fee** charged as a percentage of the overdraft limit (ie the amount up to which you can borrow). You may also have to pay a fixed percentage **renewal fee** when the overdraft is renewed at the end of twelve months.

The Case Study which follows explains how the cost of borrowing can be calculated for bank borrowing.

MATRIX LIMITED: FINANCING CHOICES

situation

Matrix Limited makes electronic measuring equipment. The directors are planning to expand the company's production facilities within its premises at The Enigma Science Park in Rugby.

These expansion plans will involve:

- new production machinery costing £150,000
- an estimated working capital injection of £20,000

The expansion program will take approximately nine months to complete.

The directors have come up with two possible plans for funding this expansion, and need advice on which plan to adopt.

Plan A

This proposal, which has already been discussed with the company's bank, is that the company should apply for a £150,000 bank business loan to finance the new production machinery.

The loan should be over five years with repayments in equal annual instalments at the end of each year. The interest rate will be fixed at 5% per annum on the reducing balance and will be paid with each of the annual instalments and calculated on the loan amount outstanding immediately before the repayment.

An arrangement fee of 1% is payable at the time the loan is first drawn down (ie paid over to Matrix by the bank).

The bank is also offering an overdraft facility of £20,000 at an annual rate of 8%.

The cash flow projections estimate that the average overdraft over the year will be at a level of £15,000. The arrangement fee is 1.5% of the overdraft limit.

Plan B

This proposal, made by a couple of the directors who have approached another bank, is that the total borrowing requirement of £170,000 (the expansion cost and working capital) should be covered by a fixed five year loan to be repaid by equal instalments at each year-end.

The interest rate will be fixed at 6% for the first year but will be charged at 5% over bank base for the remaining four years.

An arrangement fee of 1.5% is payable at the time the loan is first drawn down.

You are to:

(a) Calculate the cost of the bank finance for the two proposals (ie the interest and fees) **for the first year**.

(b) State which option the directors should choose on the basis of the total first year cost of finance.

Note: normally the cost over the period of the whole loan would be used to make a fully valid comparison.

solution

(a) You draw up a table for the calculations that you have made:

	Loan interest £	Arrangement fees £	Overdraft interest £	Total cost £
Plan A	7,500	1,800	1,200	10,500
Plan B	10,200	2,550	-	12,750

(b) Plan A is preferred because the total fee and interest cost is £10,500 for the loan and the overdraft, as opposed to £12,750 for the loan from the other bank.

SECURITY FOR FINANCING

the need for security

Lenders normally require business customers to provide security to cover borrowing. The basic principle involved is that providers of finance quite rightly view lending to business customers as having an element of risk. They need to have the reassurance that if the business becomes insolvent and defaults on the loan or overdraft, they will have rights over assets (such as property) that they can sell, or some form of guarantee that they can rely on in order to get some or all of their money back.

types of security – an introduction

The business managers and owners will have to consider a number of issues when offering security:

- if the business is a limited company, there may be **business assets** available to put down as security – for example, premises, equipment, inventory held; if this is the case, the company could give a **fixed and floating charge**, or a **mortgage** if the finance was a commercial mortgage for premises
- if the people providing security are company directors, they may be asked to sign **guarantees** covering the company debt; they will also have to pledge their own personal assets to support the guarantees
- if the people borrowing are partners or sole traders they will be asked to **mortgage** their personal assets (normally their home) as security; note that if the people raising finance are partners or sole traders, they cannot give guarantees as they **are** the business and it is a nonsense to guarantee yourself

The main types of **security** are set out below.

mortgage

A **mortgage** is a legal document signed by a borrower pledging his/her property to a lender. If the borrower fails to repay, the lender (eg a bank) is given the the legal right to sell the property in order to get the money back.

A mortgage is the form of security normally taken by banks and building societies to secure loans for the purchase of property.

Note that the term 'mortgage' is often used to describe a house loan. Strictly speaking, however, the 'mortgage' is not the money borrowed but the security document signed by the borrower which enables the lender to sell the property if the borrower defaults on the loan.

guarantee

A **guarantee** is a document signed by Person A which states that if Person B (or Company B) does not pay up, Person A will have to do so instead.

A bank will often take the guarantees of company directors to secure their company borrowing, and then back up the guarantees with mortgages over the directors' houses or other investments. This means that if the company defaults on its borrowing, the bank can demand that the directors pay up instead, and will be able to sell the directors' property to repay the loan if the directors cannot come up with the money in any other way.

fixed charge

A **fixed charge** is a document signed by a company borrower which states that if it defaults on a loan, the bank can sell company property specified in the document (eg company premises or equipment) to repay the debt.

floating charge

A **floating charge** is a document signed by a company which states that if the company does not pay up to the bank on demand, the bank can sell or claim from the company's 'floating assets' (eg its inventory and cash balances) which happen to be in the company's possession when the claim is made. These assets are 'floating' because they are changing from day-to-day.

fixed and floating charge

Banks lending to limited companies will normally take a combined fixed charge and floating charge in a single document – a **fixed and floating charge** – a charge over all of the company's assets:

- the **fixed charge** will enable the bank to sell off a company's non-current assets if the bank puts in its claim
- the **floating charge** will enable the bank to sell off what are basically the current assets of the company

a note on 'loan to value'

Lenders will sometimes use a **loan to value** calculation to decide whether or not to provide finance for the purchase of assets. The formula is:

$$\frac{\textit{amount of loan} \times 100}{\textit{value of asset}} = \textit{loan to value percentage}$$

For example, a business wanting to borrow £300,000 to buy a warehouse valued at £600,000 will produce a loan to value of 50%. The lender will set its own criteria as to whether this 50% is an acceptable risk. 'Loan to value' calculations are widely used by lenders providing property mortgages.

THE LEGAL ASPECTS OF RAISING FINANCE

facility letters from lenders

Legal rights and duties are set out in the formal documentation which is signed by a lender and the borrower when the lender provides finance. These legal agreements are commonly known as **facility letters**, ie they are 'letters' which provide borrowing 'facilities'.

The extracts which follow are taken from a bank business loan facility letter for a partnership. Study them and read the notes that accompany them. Osborne Books is grateful to the Royal Bank of Scotland for kindly giving permission for the reproduction of extracts from its loan documentation.

THIS IS AN IMPORTANT DOCUMENT. YOU SHOULD TAKE INDEPENDENT LEGAL ADVICE BEFORE SIGNING AND SIGN ONLY IF YOU WANT TO BE LEGALLY BOUND.

THIS AGREEMENT is made between:-

(1) **The Royal Bank of Scotland plc** (the "**Bank**"); and

(2) ******* and ******* (the "**Customer**") being the partners of ****** (the "**Partnership**")

to set out the terms and conditions on which the Bank is pleased to make available to the Customer a loan of £****** (the "**Loan**").

1 **Purpose**

The Loan shall be utilised to ********.

2 **Preconditions**

2.1 The Bank shall not be obliged to provide the Loan unless the following conditions are satisfied on the date on which the Loan is drawn:-

(a) the Bank has received the duplicate of this Agreement signed by the Customer;

(b) any security to be granted in terms of Clause 8 is valued and completed to the satisfaction of the Bank;

(c) the availability as security for the Loan of any existing security is confirmed to the satisfaction of the Bank; and

(d) the Bank is satisfied that no default event as outlined in Clause 11 (an "**Event of Default**") (or event which may result in an Event of Default) has occurred or may occur as a consequence of the Loan being drawn.

3 **Drawdown**

3.1 The Loan will require to be drawn down in one amount within 3 months from the date this Agreement is signed on behalf of the Bank.

This introductory part sets out basic details such as the name of the borrower, the amount and purpose of the loan and when it has to be taken ('drawdown').

10 **Undertakings**

10.1 The Undertakings in this clause shall remain in force until the Loan has been repaid in full.

10.2 The Customer shall immediately notify the Bank in the event of an Event of Default occurring.

10.3 The Customer shall not:-

(a) grant any security to any third party;

(b) other than in the ordinary course of business, sell, transfer, lease or otherwise dispose of any assets;

(c) enter into any obligation, whether by way of borrowing from another source, leasing commitments, factoring of debts, granting of guarantees or by any other means;

(d) make any change in the nature of business conducted by the Partnership;

without the prior written consent of the Bank.

Here the customer agrees to certain **undertakings** or **covenants** such as not giving security to any other person without the consent of the bank and complying with all laws, regulations and environmental requirements.

The extract shows how a customer might **default** on the loan, which would then immediately make the loan repayable on demand to the bank.

11.1 If any Event of Default occurs, then the Bank may by written notice to the Customer declare the Loan, all interest accrued and all other sums payable by the Customer under this Agreement to be immediately due and payable and/or terminate the obligations of the Bank under this Agreement. Each of the following events is an Event of Default:-

(a) the Customer fails to pay any amount payable under this Agreement on the due date;

(b) the Customer fails to comply with any provision of this Agreement and, where capable of remedy, such failure is not remedied to the reasonable satisfaction of the Bank within 7 days of the Bank giving notice to the Customer requiring the Customer to remedy the same;

(c) the Customer or any other grantor of the Security fails to comply with any provision of the Security and, where capable of remedy, such failure is not remedied to the reasonable satisfaction of the Bank within 7 days of the Bank giving notice to the Customer/other grantor requiring the Customer/other grantor to remedy the same;

(d) any information given or warranty or representation made by, or on behalf of, the Customer to the Bank proves inaccurate;

(e) any procedure is used against the Customer to attach or take possession of any property for payment of a debt;

(f) any insolvency proceedings are commenced against the Customer or the Partnership in any jurisdiction or the Customer makes arrangements with its creditors;

(g) the death of the Customer;

(h) a default arises under any other liability of the Customer to the Bank or to any other creditor or any such liability is not paid when due or when a demand has been made;

(i) any distress, execution, attachment or other legal process affects the whole or a material part of the assets of the Customer or the Partnership;

(j) any application is made, or other steps are taken, for the appointment of an administrator in relation to the Partnership;

(k) the dissolution of the Partnership;

(l) if applicable the cancellation of, or failure to renew, for whatever reason, any Policy(ies) of Assurance effected in connection with the Loan or any premium payable thereunder remains unpaid for a period of 7 days or more or there is any reduction in the amount of any premium payable thereunder;

(m) there is a significant drop in the value of the Customer's business or the Security; and

(n) any other circumstances arise which may reasonably lead the Bank to believe that the Security might be prejudiced or that the Customer's obligations to the Bank under this Agreement will not be met.

12 **Miscellaneous**

12.1 Without any obligation upon the Bank to do so, the Bank shall be entitled to allow the Customer extended time to pay or grant any other indulgence to the Customer without affecting any of the rights of the Bank in whole or in part.

COMPLIANCE WITH LEGAL REGULATIONS

All organisations, both private and public sector, must ensure that legal requirements and internal regulations are complied with when raising finance.

legal compliance by limited companies

Limited companies are regulated by the **Companies Acts** which require that every company adopts a set of rules (Articles) which govern the powers of **directors** acting on behalf of the company. The 'Model Articles' state:

'The directors are responsible for the management of the company's business, for which purpose they may exercise all the powers of the company.'

These powers will include:

- the raising of loans
- the issue of shares to raise finance

You should note that directors, as well as being expected to be competent at their job, have a **fiduciary duty of care** when acting on behalf of the company. This means that they should act:

- in good faith and honestly
- in the best interests of the company rather than in their own interest or for profitable gain

'Fiduciary' means that you rely on someone else (eg a doctor, solicitor, financial adviser) to act in **good faith** and not take advantage of their position for their own profit or advantage. You should also note that **employees** are bound by the fundamental principles of professional ethics to act in the same way, with integrity and professionalism.

legal requirements by public sector organisations

Public Sector organisations such as County Councils are governed by 'Standing Orders' which can include 'Financial Standing Orders' operated by executives known as 'Strategic Directors' who are responsible for raising finance and spending. The section 'External Funding' of a typical set of Standing Orders states:

'External funds are a significant proportion of the Council's budget. Whatever the source, funding conditions need to be carefully considered to ensure that they are compatible with the authority's aims and objectives.'

The public sector Strategic Directors are therefore directly comparable with company directors and employees in their need to act in good faith and honestly and in the best interests of the organisation that employs them.

Chapter Summary

- A business may need to raise finance to provide the necessary liquidity for its day-to-day operations and also for planned expansion.
- The finance raised should be for the appropriate purpose and time period (short-term or long-term) and it should be for the right amount.
- A bank overdraft is very suitable for short-term financing. It allows an organisation to borrow on its current account up to a defined limit, paying interest only on what is borrowed. The facility provides a very flexible source of liquidity.
- Further short-term financing can be provided by setting up factoring or invoice discounting facilities with financial companies.
- Long-term finance is used to finance non-current asset purchases. 'Long-term' can mean anything from twelve months to twenty five years.
- Bank loans and commercial mortgages provide long-term finance for assets such as equipment, land and buildings. Loans are normally tailored to suit the expected life of the asset. Banks will normally require security for loans.
- Leasing is another form of long-term finance. There are various forms of leasing: operating lease, finance lease and hire purchase (a form of finance lease).
- Companies can raise further long-term funds through the issue of shares, loan stock and bonds.
- Most forms of long-term financing have an effect on the gearing of a company (the debt/equity ratio) because they increase the debt position. The exceptions include operating leases (which are essentially rental arrangements) and the issue of new equity shares (which improve the gearing).
- Businesses assessing the suitability of financing should calculate and compare the cost of different types of finance. This cost is made up of interest charges on loans and overdrafts, and fees such as arrangement fees.
- Businesses borrowing from a financial institution will be asked to provide security to cover the borrowing. If the business fails, the bank will be able to recover all or part of its money from the selling of its security.
- Companies and public sector bodies needing to borrow or raise funds must comply with the necessary legislation and regulations (external and internal) requiring that they act in good faith and honestly.

Key Terms

overdraft	an arrangement ('facility') between a bank and a customer which allows the customer to borrow money on a current account up to a specified amount ('limit')
business loan	a long-term bank loan for asset purchase or project finance
commercial mortgage	a long-term bank loan for the purchase of property
factoring	a financial arrangement in which a business sells its accounts receivable (its invoices) for cash to a factoring company, which collects the debts when they are due
invoice discounting	factoring (see item above) without the debt management service
operating lease	a short-term rental arrangement for an asset – it does not appear on the statement of financial position of the business
finance lease	a longer-term rental arrangement for an asset which does appear on the statement of financial position of the business
hire purchase	a form of finance lease where the lessee normally takes possession of the 'hired' asset at the end of the rental period
equity shares	ordinary shares of a limited company appearing in the equity section of the statement of financial position – a new issue reduces gearing
preference shares	shares which give the owner a fixed dividend and which are treated as a non-current liability in the statement of financial position – a new issue increases gearing
loan stock and bonds	fixed rate stock issued by a company which is traded on the Stock Markets and treated as a non-current liability – a new issue increases gearing

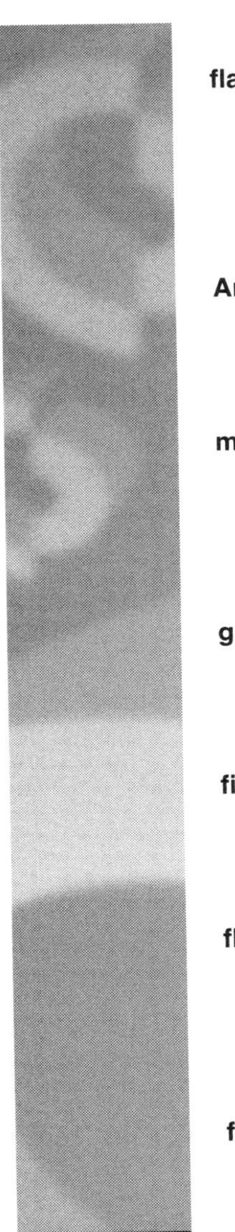

flat rate interest a rate based on the whole amount borrowed over the period of the loan and ignoring any repayments made – it can seem deceptively cheap – the formula is:

***P**rincipal x **R**ate of interest x **T**ime period (years)*

Annual Percentage Rate the annual cost of finance including interest and fees, taking into account the effect of the reducing balance of the loan each time a repayment is made

mortgage a document signed by a borrower pledging property as security for the borrowing from a lender; the document allows the lender to sell the property if the borrower defaults on the loan

guarantee a document signed by person A which states that person A undertakes to repay the debt of person B if person B fails to pay up on demand

fixed charge a document signed by a company which states that if it fails to pay up on demand to the bank, the bank can sell specified assets owned by the company to recover the debt

floating charge a document signed by a borrowing company which states that if it defaults on the borrowing, the bank can sell 'floating' assets (basically current assets) owned by the company at that particular time in order to recover the debt

fixed and floating charge a combination of a fixed charge and a floating charge which covers all the non-current and current assets of the company

Activities

6.1 The features of a business overdraft include the following (tick the correct option):

(a)	Interest is only paid on what you borrow, the interest charge is very low	
(b)	Repayments are by monthly instalments, the interest charge is very low	
(c)	Security is not required, the account must always be in debit	
(d)	Security is sometimes required, interest is only paid on what you borrow	

6.2 A business loan is normally (tick the correct option):

(a)	A form of finance for working capital requirements	
(b)	A form of finance for asset purchase	
(c)	A loan that fluctuates regularly from debit to credit	
(d)	Provided for periods of up to one year	

6.3 An interest rate that is capped is one that (tick the correct option):

(a)	Is only available for overdrafts	
(b)	Remains the same for the whole of the loan period	
(c)	Has an upper limit for the interest rate	
(d)	Has a lower limit for the interest rate	

6.4 Tomas Hanx, a sole trader, wishes to borrow £50,000 from the bank in the form of a loan to finance the expansion of his business. The bank will need to obtain security from Tomas to support the lending. It will be able to obtain its security if the customer signs a (tick the correct option):

(a)	A guarantee	
(b)	A fixed and floating charge	
(c)	A mortgage over his property	
(d)	A repurchase agreement	

6.5 A bank has offered to lend Strauss Ltd £160,000 to be repaid in 12 monthly instalments of £13,800 per month.

The flat rate of interest being charged is: ☐ per cent.

6.6 A bank has provided a customer with a quotation for a fixed rate loan as follows:

Amount borrowed	£16,500.00
Term	12 months
Monthly repayments x 12	£1,409.65
Flat rate of interest	2.52%
Annual Percentage Rate (APR)	4.9%

(a) What is the total amount that will be paid by the customer? £ ☐

(b) The reason why the APR is nearly twice as high as the flat rate of interest is because (tick the correct option):

(a)	It is the average rate of interest charged by the bank for this particular type of loan	
(b)	It allows for any possible early repayment of the loan	
(c)	It takes into account all the financial costs of the loan and the fact that the balance will be reducing over the twelve months	
(d)	It reflects the fact that the borrowing rate may fluctuate over the period of the loan	

6.7 Artemis PLC plans to acquire a new fleet of delivery vehicles. It realises that the cost price of the vehicles will be £500,000 and wishes to reduce this cost, bearing in mind the high rate of depreciation of the assets.

The Finance Director is considering either Hire Purchase or an Operating Lease as a means of finance.

He asks you to prepare for him some notes setting out:

1 the main features of the two financing options

2 the effect each of the two options will have on the company's financial statements and gearing

6.8 Marriner Limited manufactures boat equipment and is planning to expand its operations over the next two years. It will need £150,000 for new production machinery and has projected an additional working capital need of £30,000.

The directors are considering raising finance from the bank in the form of a business loan for £150,000 to finance the machinery and an overdraft for £30,000 to cover the working capital requirement.

The bank offers the directors of Marriner Limited two alternative methods of financing:

Option 1

A five year business loan of £150,000 with equal annual repayments, paid at the end of each year. The interest rate is fixed at 5% and interest is calculated on the loan amount outstanding at the time of the repayment.

An arrangement fee of 1.25%, payable at the time the loan is made by the bank to the customer.

The bank is also offering an overdraft facility of £30,000 at an annual rate of 7%. The cash flow forecast estimates that the average overdraft for the first year will be at a level of £20,000. The arrangement fee will be 1.5% of the overdraft limit.

The security requested is a fixed and floating charge over the assets of Marriner Limited.The assets are sufficient to cover the fixed and floating charge.

Option 2

A variable rate business loan of £180,000 to cover both the cost of the expansion and also the working capital requirement. The loan will be repaid over six years with equal annual repayments paid at the end of each year. The interest rate will be bank base rate plus 5%. For the first year, bank base rate is forecast to average 1%.

An arrangement fee of 1% is payable at the time the loan is made by the bank to the customer.

The security requested is the personal guarantees of the six directors, supported by mortgages over their family homes.

You are to:

(a) Calculate the cost of the finance (interest and fees) for each option for the first year, setting out your findings in the following table:

	Loan interest £	Arrangement fees £	Overdraft interest £	Total cost £
Option 1				
Option 2				

(b) State which option the directors should choose on the basis of the total first year cost of the finance.

(c) State which option the directors should prefer on the basis of the security requirements.

In the case of (b) and (c) give brief reasons for your answers.

7 Investing surplus funds

this chapter covers...

Organisations are likely from time-to-time to have money to invest over short-term periods and also long-term periods. The word 'organisation' used here refers not only to businesses but also to public sector bodies such as local authorities and NHS trusts.

Organisations will try to obtain the best return on their investments, but need to exercise caution when it comes to risk (higher risk investments normally offer a better return). Organisations in both the public and private sectors will therefore be subject to strict internal controls which will ensure that:

- *investments are made only by employees who are authorised to do so*
- *investments are 'safe', ie reasonably risk-free*

Skills that are needed when making investment decisions include:

- *calculating the yield (return) on the investment*
- *calculating the investment amount needed to produce a required rate of return*
- *dealing with early cash-in penalties and bonus interest rates*

Typical investments include:

- *government securities ('gilts') and treasury bills*
- *money market accounts, certificates of deposit and deposit accounts*
- *listed and unlisted shares and bonds*

Higher risk investments include assets such as property and precious metals, eg gold.

INVESTMENT DECISIONS – RISK, RETURN AND LIQUIDITY

factors affecting investment decisions

When a person or organisation is planning to invest money, a number of factors will always be certain:

- the **amount** of money to be invested
- the length of time for which that money will be **available**

The first factor to be borne in mind by the **investing organisation** relates to any legal, ethical or procedural constraints imposed; in other words, is the organisation (or its employees) allowed to make this type of investment?

There are also other factors which will need to be weighed up by the investor in choosing the 'best' investment for the surplus funds. These can be summarised as '**risk**, **return** and **liquidity**'.

risk

Risk is the level of uncertainty the investor is willing to accept in making the investment, for example:

- is the investment safe?
- can it fall in capital value?
- can the return made on the investment decline over time?

An investor who is not willing to take a risk is said to be **risk averse**, whereas an investor willing to take more of a risk is **risk seeking**.

return and liquidity

An organisation will normally want to invest its cash surpluses so that it earns a return on the amount invested. Certain rules apply to the level of return (income or capital gain) available on investments.

Generally speaking the rate of return will be **higher**:

- for **larger amounts**
- for **less liquid amounts**, ie for amounts invested for longer fixed periods or with longer notice requirements
- if there is **more risk** attached to the investment

The rate of return will generally be **lower**:

- for **smaller amounts**
- for **more liquid amounts**, ie for 'no notice' or 'call' accounts
- if there is **less risk** attached to the investment

For example, £10 deposited for one day on a current account with a reputable bank will probably earn nothing at all: it is a relatively small amount, it is there for a very short period of time and there is little or no risk attached.

On the other hand, £1 million invested for a fixed six month period with an overseas bank with a low credit rating is likely to earn a higher rate, but there is a greater risk of the bank failing and the money being lost (see page 187).

It is important therefore for organisations to have clear guidelines indicating the level of **risk** they are allowed to take and the level of **exposure** to which they can commit themselves. Exposure is a term normally applied to lending, but it can also apply to the amount invested with any one institution or type of investment.

the effect of economic and financial trends

Organisations which are investing over the longer term will need to be aware of the effect of trends in the economy, and particularly the effects of **inflation** and interest rates. Rising inflation can bring about a rise in interest rates; this is good for investors as it will increase their rate of return. But it is not good for the economy as it will deter businesses from borrowing to expand their operations and helping to increase Gross Domestic Product (GDP).

Investors also need to be aware of the effects of **recession** and its associated economic (and sometimes political) instability. In times like these investors are likely to need to take a 'low risk'approach which will inevitably lower their rates of return. Interest rates will also tend to be lower which will also result in a lower rate of return. There is clearly a danger investing long-term when interest rates are low. An organisation may invest at a low fixed rate and then find that market rates start to rise.

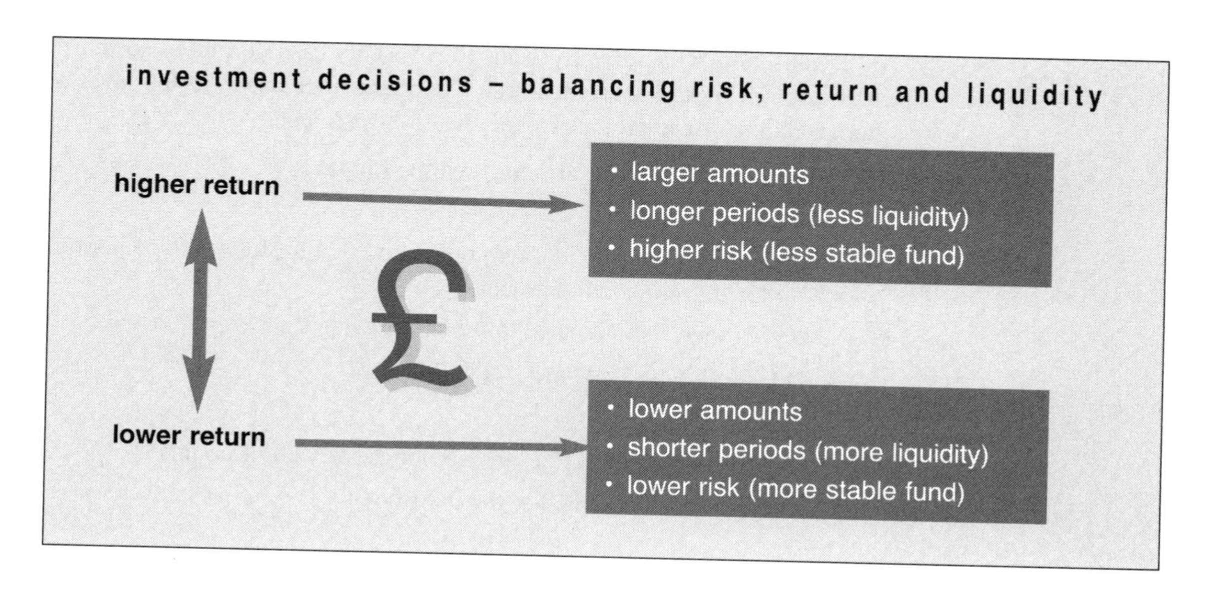

TYPES OF SHORT-TERM INVESTMENT

We will now describe in detail some of the liquid funds in which private or public sector Treasuries may invest on a day-to-day basis.

We will look in more detail at the way in which private or public sector Treasuries are guided by internal policies and regulations relating to investment on pages 216-217. The investments we will describe include:

- money market interbank deposits
- certificates of deposit
- treasury bills
- bank deposit accounts

We have already explained and defined many of these investments in Chapter 5. In this chapter we take a more practical view and explain the decisions that have to be made by a senior employee working in a private or public sector Treasury. We will first deal with short-term investments and then with longer-term securities.

short-term money markets

The treasurer will normally have online access to market rates. The data below has been adapted from rates shown in the Financial Times. The time periods range from overnight to one year. Study the variations in the rates and then read the explanations of the various investments that follow.

UK interest rates (short-term money markets)

	Overnight	7 Days notice	One month	Three months	Six months	One year
	%	%	%	%	%	%
Interbank	0.40	0.44	0.45	0.55	0.76	1.20
CDs			0.58	0.67	0.88	1.16
Treasury Bills				0.51		

interbank market

The **interbank** market is made up of short-term deposits placed by banks with each other. Company and local authority treasurers place deposits with their bank on 'money market' accounts and these are then consolidated with other liquid funds helds by the banks and are placed on the interbank market.

The deposits are referred to by company and public sector treasuries as **money market deposits** and earn very competitive rates of interest. These deposits can be:

- **call accounts** which allow immediate withdrawal of funds; this liquidity means that the rate is **lower** than the interest rate for the same amount invested for a longer time period
- **fixed-term deposits** which will mature on a certain date, eg in one month or three months' time, or in the shorter term in one or seven days time – normally **the longer the period the higher the interest rate**
- **notice deposits** which are invested and can be withdrawn when advance notice is given, eg seven days or one month's notice – normally **the longer the notice period, the higher the interest rate**

Money market accounts held at banks are for large sums (normally £50,000 minimum). The features of money market accounts offered by a typical UK bank are as follows (figures correct at time of writing):

money market accounts held at a typical UK bank		
	Fixed Term	**Call/notice**
Access to funds	Fixed term of overnight to 5 years	Immediate (call) 7 or 14 days' notice 1,3 or 6 months' notice
Minimum balance	£250,000 (overnight to 6 days) £50,000 (7 days to 5 years)	£50,000
Maximum balance	No maximum	No maximum

In conclusion, the main features of money market deposits are:

- **risk** – this is low as the banks are generally seen as a good risk and the interbank market is essential to the Bank of England for implementing its monetary policy and for the fixing of bank lending rate
- **return** – this will be higher than the rates for bank deposit accounts (see next page) as the amounts invested are higher
- **liquidity** – this will vary according to the type of account (call, notice, fixed term); the higher the liquidity the lower the interest rate

certificates of deposit (CDs)

Certificates of Deposit (usually known as 'CDs') are tradeable securities issued by banks, certifying that a sum of money, normally a minimum of £50,000, has been deposited and will be repaid on a set date, often six months later. They can be bought and sold on the market (at a discount) and whoever holds the CD on the repayment date will receive the amount stated on the certificate. As they are issued by banks normally rated to be a good risk, they are classed as reasonably low risk investments.

Treasury Bills

Treasury Bills are three month tradeable certificates issued by the UK Debt Management Office (DMO) and backed by the Government. They are sold to banks and other dealing institutions at a discount and the eventual holder will be repaid in full on the due date. As you will see from the table of rates on page 203, the Treasury Bill offers the lowest three month rate. This is because it is backed by the Government and is seen to be a **low risk**.

bank deposit accounts

Treasuries or business owners having smaller amounts to deposit (typically less than £50,000) can invest these in **deposit accounts** offered by individual banks and other financial institutions. These can be in the form of **fixed term**, **notice**, or **immediate access** accounts and can be operated online. As with money market accounts, deposit accounts will offer different interest rates depending on the amount deposited and the liquidity (notice period for withdrawal) required.

The main features of deposit accounts are:

- **risk** – this is low as the banks are generally seen as a good risk (although the financial crisis of 2007 shook public confidence in banks)
- **risk and the FSCS** – for any small businesses (turnover up to £6.5M, and up to 50 employees at the time of writing) the UK Government's Financial Services Compensation Scheme (FSCS) guarantees repayment of deposits of up to £85,000 (at the time of writing) if the financial institution fails
- **return** – this will be low as the amount invested and the risk level are both likely to be low; it will increase as liquidity is reduced (see below)
- **liquidity** – this will vary according to the type of account (instant access, notice, fixed term); the higher the liquidity the lower the interest rate

In short, the usual investment principles apply: the longer the period, the lower the liquidity and the higher the amount, the better the interest rate.

other short-term investments – commercial paper

The investments described on the last two pages are the normal secure short-term investments which fulfil the 'safety' requirement of a company or local authority Treasurer. There are other investments which may be more risky, but which nevertheless sometimes feature in investment portfolios. These include **Commercial paper** (CP), which represents short-term lending to first class quoted commercial companies. The securities issued by the companies through a bank take the form of loan notes (value £100,000 and above) with maturities mainly between seven days and three months.

LIQUIDITY MANAGEMENT IN PRACTICE

Each working day the company or local authority Treasurer (or delegated authorised staff) will have to perform complex calculations and take decisions to ensure that there will be sufficient liquidity not just for that day or week, but for months ahead. The following data will need to be collected and analysed:

- the final cleared balance of the bank account the previous day
- details of maturing deposits and investments
- daily cash flow projections of sales receipts and payments

Any surplus funds can then either be placed on a money market account with the bank overnight (if it will be needed the next working day) or alternatively be placed in other short-term markets for periods such as one month, three months, six months or a year to meet longer-term requirements. This will all be done in accordance with the organisation's guidelines for risk and exposure management.

If the organisation is smaller and does not have a dedicated Treasury function, the work will be carried out within an Accounting Department or just by the finance manager in the case of a much smaller business. The amount of liquid funds may be less but the same investment principles apply and the same investment expertise will be required.

LONGER-TERM INVESTMENTS

Government stock – gilts

One of the safest ways of investing for the longer term is to provide money to help fund Government debt. Investors can purchase '**Government stock**', also known as 'gilt-edged' stock or '**gilts**' for short, on account of its prestige and security. Gilts are often given the title 'Treasury' or 'Exchequer' stock to link them to the Government Department they are funding.

Gilts are popular longer-term investments for businesses and public sector organisations. They are more or less risk-free, they provide a regular income and they can always be sold 'second hand' in the stock markets. Their prices are reported daily in the financial press.

Gilts are mostly at a **fixed interest** rate, for example Treasury 4% 2016, although some are index-linked, ie the return is linked to the Retail Price Index. The interest rate is often referred to as the 'coupon'.

Gilts are also mostly for a **fixed period**, for example the Treasury 4% 2016 mentioned above, although some are undated. War Loan 3.5%, for example, was issued during the Second World War in the hope that people would buy them as a patriotic gesture, perhaps never to have them repaid!

The maturity periods of gilts are classified as follows:

shorts	up to 5 years
mediums	5 to 15 years
longs	more than 15 years

As mentioned above, **gilts** can be traded, and the price will reflect market conditions at the time. Gilts are normally quoted in terms of £100, but can be traded in any amount. £1 of stock will be worth £1 on the maturity date. In the interim, however, gilts with an interest rate ('coupon') higher than prevailing rates will trade for more than £1, and gilts with a low coupon will trade at a lower price. For example, if you wanted to buy (at the time of writing) Treasury 4% 2016, you would have to pay £1.1247 per £1 of stock. If you held the stock until the 'redemption' (repayment) date in 2016, you would receive just £1 per £1 of stock. £1 is known as the stock's 'par value'.

gilts and yields

An investor wanting to know the return on gilts should examine and compare the **yield** each stock provides. Yield means the same as 'expected return', but measuring it is not straightforward because:

- the price of each stock fluctuates
- the length of time before the redemption date (when the stock is repaid) will vary

There are two main yields which an investor should look at:

- The **interest yield** is the annual return for the investor based on the price of the stock and the interest rate stated on the gilt (the coupon rate). Using the example of Treasury 4.5% 2034, the calculation is as follows:

  $$\frac{\text{interest rate}}{\text{market price}} = \frac{4.5\%}{£1.2602} = 3.57\%$$

  In other words, because the market price of £1.2602 is higher than the nominal value of £1, the effective interest rate reduces from 4.5% to 3.57%.

- The **redemption yield** (the 'yield to maturity') takes into account the change in price of the stock to redemption (maturity). It involves:
  - the price paid for the stock

- the interest rate stated on the gilt (the coupon rate)
- the period of time which has to run before the stock is repaid (remember that the price returns to £1 per £1 of stock at the redemption date, affecting the yield)

The redemption yield is very useful because it allows stock with differing redemption dates to be meaningfully compared. It also enables the yield to be compared with the percentage rates offered by other investments. The current redemption yield for the Treasury 4.5% 2034 is 2.87%. You will not be required to calculate redemption rates in your assessments.

INVESTMENT IN SHARES

Investment in **gilts** can be seen by the Treasuries of public and private sector organisations as a comparatively secure risk – the investment is backed by the Government itself, which should be relatively secure. Investment in the **shares** of companies listed on the Stock Exchange is however a much more risky affair and should be approached with caution by Treasuries. Prices can fluctuate according to market sentiment and shares can occasionally become worthless in the case of the company invested in going 'bust'.

types of shares – listed shares

It is important to be able to distinguish between different types of company share and their levels of risk and return. Shares can either be **listed** or **unlisted**.

UK and some overseas 'listed' shares issued by companies are traded on the London Stock Exchange. There are two main markets:

- the **Main Market,** on which the larger and well-established and reputable company shares are listed and traded
- the **Alternative Investment Market (AIM)** on which smaller and more recently established companies are traded

The main types of listed shares are described in detail in Chapter 6 (page 174). The two main types of share that are suitable for investment are:

- **equity** shares – which pay **dividends** to investors, the amounts being dependent on the profits made by the company
- **preference shares** – which pay a fixed rate of interest to investors

preference shares – yield calculation

Calculating the **return** on **preference shares** is straightforward because they are fixed interest stock, and the yield is calculated in the same way as interest yield on gilt-edged stock.

For example if a 5% Preference stock 2015 issued at £10 a share is now trading at £12 a share, the following calculation is used:

$$\frac{\text{interest (£) x 100}}{\text{market price (£)}} = \frac{5\% \text{ x £10 x 100}}{\text{£12}} = 4.17\%$$

In other words, if the market price is higher than the issue (face value) price and the same interest amount is paid regardless of the market price, the effective interest rate will be lower.

equity shares – dividend yield calculation

The return on equity shares is based on the variable amount of dividend paid by the company on its equity share capital. Calculating the **return** on **equity shares** is the calculation of **dividend yield**. The formula is as follows (note that the calculation is based on pence):

$$\frac{\textit{dividend per share (pence) x 100}}{\textit{market price of share (pence)}} = \textit{dividend yield (percentage)}$$

If a company pays a dividend of 25p per share and the market price is £5.00 (ie 500 pence), the calculation of the **dividend yield percentage** is therefore:

$$\frac{25 \text{ x } 100}{500} = 5\%$$

This dividend yield expressed as a percentage is therefore useful as a comparison of the return on, say, a bank deposit account.

the main features of listed shares

- **risk** – this can be high because share prices are subject to market fluctuations and some shares can be worthless if the company goes into liquidation; the risk factor can be reduced by investing in a portfolio of shares with different risk profiles, or in **managed funds** which invest in a wide range of shares in a particular area, for example different geographical areas, technology companies, mining and commodities
- **return** – shares are often held for the long term as their value will generally increase; if they are held for the short term the return may even be negative if they fall in value; also note that the costs of dealing in shares can be high and should be offset against the return received from capital gain and dividend income
- **liquidity** – most shares can be sold at very short notice to realise cash, but because of the reasons stated above, this could result in a loss being made, and therefore shares are normally viewed as being a long-term investment

types of shares – unlisted shares

Where a company is not listed on the UK Stock Exchange, any foreign recognised Stock Exchange or alternative market, its shares and securities are classified as **unlisted**.

Unlisted shares are the shares of **private companies** where the ownership is in private hands. Many of these are smaller companies, for example family businesses. But there are also large unlisted companies, the Virgin Group founded and headed by Richard Branson is a good example. Unlisted shares are not normally available as an investment, the main exception being if they are purchased by another company carrying out a merger or an acquisition. The valuation in this case will be based either on a multiple of annual turnover or on profits. As far as treasury management is concerned therefore, unlisted shares are considered as being 'off limits'.

INVESTING IN ASSETS – LAND, GOLD AND COMMODITIES

Land, **gold** and **commodities** such as silver, oil and wheat have traditionally provided a return on investment but market fluctuations (the oil price is a good example) can have a major effect on their risk factor.

land as an investment

For many businesses land and buildings are commercial premises, a non-current asset and useful security if the business wishes to borrow. If an organisation wishes to purchase land as a form of **investment**, it will normally do so in the expectation of having an established tenant paying market rate rent and also ensuring a better price on resale. The yield on property leased out to a tenant is calculated as:

$$\frac{\textit{rent per year x 100}}{\textit{property value}} = \textit{yield on property}$$

The 'risk, return and liquidity' profile of land is as follows:

- **risk**
  - commercial property in some areas has fallen significantly in value over recent years, so the risk factor is high
  - income from leased property is only guaranteed if the tenant remains in occupation and solvent, so there is the risk of the loss of rental
- **return**
  - capital values have historically risen over time so there is a possibility of capital appreciation, but it will be unquantifiable
  - rent received from a tenant (eg 6%) may be higher than the interest paid on the same amount invested in a deposit account (eg 3%)

- **liquidity**
  - selling property can take an extremely long time
  - there is no 'sell by' or maturity date attached to land and so it can be put up for sale at any time
  - the problem could be finding a buyer, particularly in a time of economic recession when the asking price may have to be dropped, resulting in a capital loss to the investor

gold as an investment

Investment in gold has been traditionally made by buying and taking responsibility for the storage of the physical metal (bullion) in the form of **gold bars** or **coins** (eg Krugerrands). This has meant that the investor has to ensure the physical security of the investment, and pay the costs of secure storage.

More recently investors in gold have been able to invest in **Exchange Traded Funds (ETFs)** which are a type of Exchange Traded Product (ETP). **ETFs** are shares which track the performance of a market index. For example, the share could track the FTSE All-Share index, currencies or commodities such as gold. There are two types of gold ETFs:

- a **'physical' ETF** which actually owns and arranges for the storage of the gold – this is the safer but more expensive option
- a **'synthetic' ETF** which uses derivatives (financial contracts) to replicate the performance of the gold index – this is the riskier option

The 'risk, return and liquidity' profile of gold is as follows:

- **risk**
  - gold is a commodity which used to be seen as a safe store of value
  - the market value of gold has recently has been volatile, which makes it a high risk investment in the short term
  - if an ETF is used, a 'physical' ETF is less risky than a 'synthetic' ETF
- **return**
  - gold, although it does not provide any income, has traditionally increased in capital value over time, but this return is unpredictable
- **liquidity**
  - gold is very liquid and can be sold in physical form through a bullion dealer, or in ETF (share) form through a stock broker
  - the price of gold, however, is completely unpredictable, which makes it a more suitable long-term investment rather than a liquid fund

commodities as an investment

'Commodities' is a term used to describe tradeable resources such as:

- metals such as silver, copper and gold (see also previous page)
- crops such as wheat and coffee
- natural resources such as oil and gas

Investors do not buy the actual commodities but can invest in exchange-traded funds (ETFs). The risk factor can be very high.

We will now look at a Case Study of a company Treasury and some of the ways in which it can invest surplus funds, both short-term and long-term.

Case Study

AUREA PLC: SHORT-TERM AND LONG-TERM INVESTMENTS

situation

Your name is Dick Brodey and you work as a trainee in the Treasury Department of Aurea PLC. You report to Assistant Treasurer Mario Polo. Your section deals with the investment of short-term funds on the money markets and also with long-term investments for the company.

On Tuesday Mario shows you three investment possibilities, the first is for a short-term investment of £100,000 and the other two are for long-term investment.

1. A quote for depositing £100,000 for six months (fixed) on a money market account with HZBS Bank at an interest rate of 2.00% p.a. This is higher than the online deposit account which is instant access but pays only 1% p.a. interest.

2. Purchasing £500,000 Treasury 8% 2021 at £1.37 per £1 of stock. Interest yield 5.84%, redemption yield 3.96%. This will be held for at least 12 months.

3. Purchasing a £500,000 warehouse which has just been built as part of a new and popular business park. The company intends to lease it out to another business. The projected annual yield to valuation percentage is 6%, produced from an annual rental income of £30,000.

Mario asks you to provide investment profiles for the three proposed investments. The company's *Treasury Policies and Procedures Manual* requires that the three main criteria of risk, return and liquidity should be covered in full.

solution

1. **£100,000 – MONEY MARKET ACCOUNT WITH HZBS BANK**

   risk

   There is little risk attached to this investment, partly because it is short-term and also because the bank is unlikely to be allowed to fail by the Government.

return

A rise in interest rates before the end of the month in which the deposit is made might result in a very short-term reduction in potential earnings from interest, but it is likely that the 2% rate given on the deposit will have discounted any interest rate rise. The 2% return is twice as much as the 1% paid on the online account.

liquidity

The funds are a fixed deposit for six months and early withdrawal would result in penalty fees. The company must ensure that its cash projections will allow this amount to be invested for a full six months.

2 £500,000 – TREASURY 8% 2021

risk

The risk is low because the gilt-edged stock is issued on behalf of the Government. There could be a risk of loss of capital value, however, if interest rates rose and gilts prices fell as a result.

return

The interest yield relates the price paid for the stock with its stated interest rate and provides an acceptable return at 5.84%.

The redemption yield at 3.96% is a more useful point of comparison with other investment schemes as it takes into account the fall in value of the stock as it reaches the redemption (repayment) date in 2021.

A rise in interest rates would cause the market price of the stock to fall and the return for existing holders of stock will be reduced.

liquidity

The stock is very liquid because it can be sold at any time. This type of investment, however, is normally held for the long-term because it is a very low risk investment.

3 £500,000 – WAREHOUSE PROPERTY INVESTMENT

risk

The risk is high because the commercial property market is vulnerable in periods of recession and prices can fall. Also, the company is dependent on finding a tenant with a successful business to provide the rental income.

return

Property values have historically risen over time, and so a capital gain is a possibility rather than a certainty. The 6% yield from the rental income of £30,000 is acceptable, and the lease will provide for periodic rental reviews.

liquidity

Property can be sold at any time, but the process is expensive and can be protracted. Finding a buyer could be a problem, especially if the economy is in recession and the asking price has to be dropped. Property is best viewed as illiquid and a long-term investment.

INVESTMENTS – RETURN CALCULATIONS

In this Section we explain:

- the terminology associated with calculating the return on investments
- the various formulas used in carrying out those calculations

You will need to memorise these for your assessment.

types of interest rate

There are a number of different types of interest rate which can be applied to investments (and also to borrowing, as we saw in the last chapter). These will have to be considered carefully when calculating the return on the investment.

Another factor to bear in mind when assessing investment possibilities is that when calculating the return on an investment the investor must be aware that there can be **penalty fees for early withdrawal** of money.

- **fixed rate** – an interest rate fixed for the period of the deposit; this makes calculation of the return very straightforward, but the investor runs the risk of fixing at a low rate and then finding that rates rise; if the investor wants to cash in early, there may be penalty fees payable
- **variable rate** – a fixed percentage added to the variable bank lending rate to produce a rate that varies in line with other interest rates in the economy; this is less risky because there is no danger in being caught out by a general interest rate rise
- **bonus rate** – an introductory extra percentage paid on an investment, usually for the first year of the deposit to attract the investor as a 'sweetener'; the investor will have to beware here as the interest rate will then fall after the period of the bonus (often the first year)

calculations using interest rates and yields

In your assessment you may be asked to perform some simple calculations relating to:

- the amount needed for an investment when you are given the figures for the interest amount and the interest rate
- yields on gilts (Government Stock)
- yields on shares

The first of these calculations is new to this chapter, the last two are revision from previous pages. It is important in each case to:

- remember the formula
- take great care over decimal places

worked example:

calculating an investment amount required for a given return

How much will an investor need to invest in order to earn £1,500 interest, assuming a fixed annual interest rate of 2.5%?

The formula to use is:

$$\frac{\textit{Interest amount} \times 100}{\textit{rate of interest}} = \textit{amount needed for the investment}$$

answer

In this case the calculation will be:

$$\frac{1{,}500 \times 100}{2.5} = \text{£60,000 investment}$$

worked example:

calculating an interest yield on a gilt

Calculate the interest yield (to two decimal places) on Treasury 4.5% 2034 (market price £1.26)

The formula to use is as follows:

$$\frac{\textit{interest rate}}{\textit{market price}} = \textit{interest yield\%}$$

answer

In this case the calculation will be:

$$\frac{4.5}{\text{£}1.26} = \text{3.57\% interest yield}$$

worked example:

calculating a dividend yield on a share

Calculate the dividend yield (to two decimal places) on Bonanza PLC ordinary shares (market price £6.80, dividend paid 30p per share). The formula to use is as follows:

$$\frac{\textit{dividend per share (pence)} \times 100}{\textit{market price per share (pence)}} = \textit{dividend yield\%}$$

answer

In this case the calculation will be:

$$\frac{30\text{p} \times 100}{680\text{p}} = \text{4.41\% dividend yield}$$

ORGANISATIONAL REGULATIONS FOR INVESTMENT

So far in this chapter we have discussed in general terms investment by 'organisations'. These organisations with cash balances to invest include:

- **private sector** businesses of all sizes
- **public sector** organisations such as local authorities and NHS trusts

private sector investment policy

In the **private sector,** large businesses will have an Accounts Department or Treasury which will have a section dealing with liquidity management and investment of funds.

In smaller businesses, it is likely to be the Accounts Manager/Supervisor or, in the case of a sole trader business, the proprietor. Larger businesses such as limited companies will have a set of regulations – **Policies and Procedures** – setting out, for example:

- the various authorities and responsibilities given to employees in day-to-day liquidity management, ie who can invest in what, and up to what limit
- the types of investment that are permissible and advisable
- a minimum requirement for highly liquid funds (eg overnight bank deposits)

In this way, sufficient liquidity will be maintained and risk minimised.

This risk limitation forms part of the duties required by 'corporate governance' set out in The Turnbull Report published by the Institute of Chartered Accountants in England & Wales (www.icaew.co.uk). This report states that 'a company's system of internal control has a key role in the management of risks that are significant to the fulfilment of its business objectives'.

public sector investment policy

In the **public sector**, large organisations such as County Councils operate a Treasury function under the control of a County Treasurer. The Treasury will have a section dealing with day-to-day investment along the same lines as the corporate treasury in the private sector.

The public sector body (eg the County Council) will have a set of **Standing Orders** (regulations) which will similarly set out the authorities and responsibilities given to its employees and will dictate the types of investment which are permissible. These regulations should be covered in a '**Statement on Internal Control**' drawn up by the local authority in order to comply with the requirements of The Accounts and Audit Regulations.

Guidance on this subject is provided by the Chartered Institute of Public Finance and Accountancy – CIPFA (www.cipfa.org.uk).

One notable example of a situation where public sector organisations were found to have been lax in their Treasury management occurred when a number of local authorities were caught short when investing large sums of liquid funds in **Icelandic banks** which offered attractive interest rates on deposits but then went 'bust'.

An extract from a report at the time following an investigation by the Audit Commission is quoted below. The Audit Commission is the body which regulates the proper control of local authority financial management in the UK. The lesson is obvious!

> *The Audit Commission (the local government spending watchdog) said the councils breached accountancy procedures and failed to follow their own protocols when they deposited £32.8m in the Glitnir and Landsbanki banks between 1 and 3 October. The banks collapsed on 7 October.*
>
> *Most councils responded to warnings from credit agencies about the increased risk of investing money in Icelandic banks and removed more than £1bn in spring and summer last year. Yet 127 English local authorities still had £954m deposited with the two banks when they went into administration. This amounted to 3.1% of the total funds held on deposit by English authorities.*
>
> *The Icelandic banking collapse exposed the "variable" standards of treasury management in local authorities, the commission said. "Good treasury managers recognised those risks and managed them appropriately. Others either did not appreciate the risks, or underestimated their significance."*

Now read the Case Study that follows, illustrating how a private sector business Treasury operates an investment policy.

Case Study

LAURICO PLC: TREASURY INVESTMENT POLICY

situation

Laurico PLC is a large public limited company which has a Treasury which runs a strict investment policy. The investment manual of the Treasury Department includes the following policy for investing **short-term** surplus funds:

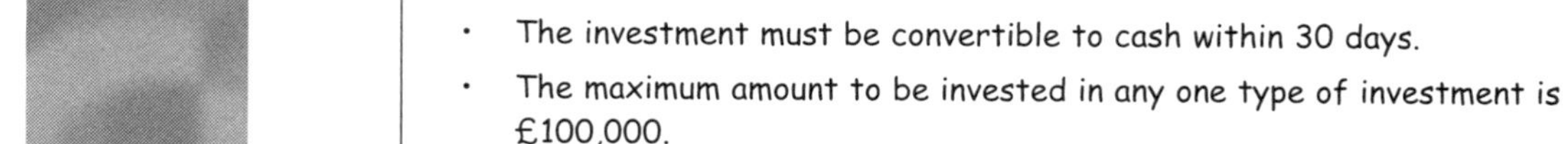

- The investment must be convertible to cash within 30 days.
- The maximum amount to be invested in any one type of investment is £100,000.
- The interest rate must be at least 1% above bank base rate.
- The investment must not include any form of investment in shares - direct or indirect.
- Only low or medium risk investments are to be selected.

The Treasury is reviewing its investment options at the beginning of the month and has selected four options for £100,000 it has available for the month. Bank base rate is currently 1%

Option 1 - Fidex mixed fund

Investment in a 30-day notice period fund; medium risk; investment portfolio includes shares; interest rate is 2.8% per annum, lowest investment £50,000.

Option 2 – National Bank plc money market account

Minimum investment allowed is £50,000; 7-day notice period; interest rate is 1.5% above base rate; low risk; does not include investment in shares.

Option 3 – Peregrino Banking Corporation (overseas investment)

Investment with overseas bank; high risk; projected interest rate is 5% and a minimum investment of £40,000 is required; 7 day notice period.

Option 4 – Soldi Bank online Treasury Account

Online account with well-rated international bank; no notice period (immediate withdrawals); interest rate is 1.5% above base rate; low risk; does not include investment in shares. Minimum investment £250,000.

required

(a) Complete the table below for each of the four options, writing 'yes' if the investment meets Laurico policy requirements and 'no' if it does not.

(b) State which of the four options should be chosen for the £100,000 available for investment.

	Convertible within 30 days?	Available for up to £100,000?	Interest rate high enough?	Not including shares?	Acceptable risk?
Option 1					
Option 2					
Option 3					
Option 4					

solution

(a)

	Convertible within 30 days	Available for up to £100,000?	Interest rate high enough?	Not including shares?	Acceptable risk?
Option 1	yes	yes	yes	no	yes
Option 2	yes	yes	yes	yes	yes
Option 3	yes	yes	yes	yes	no
Option 4	yes	no	yes	yes	yes

(b) Option 2: National Bank plc money market account

FURTHER INVESTMENT CONSIDERATIONS

In addition to the organisational regulations for investment that we have just examined, there are various other issues that should be taken into account when considering either individual investments or drawing up an investment policy.

the portfolio effect

This is concerned with the limitation of risk that comes from holding a diversified portfolio of investments. It is the investment equivalent of avoiding having 'all your eggs in one basket'. Where investments (eg shares or debentures) are made across a range of organisations and business sectors the damage will be limited if one company fails or if one business sector encounters a down-turn. The risk to the capital invested and the return generated is therefore minimised, although the reward will typically be reduced as returns are averaged out.

impact of the Financial Services Compensation Scheme (FSCS)

The FSCS is available to assist individuals and some small businesses to reduce the losses from certain investments. Great care must be taken to find out whether the scheme would cover the investment situation that is being considered, and if so to what extent.

expertise of the Treasury Department

Consideration must always be given to the expertise within the organisation's own treasury function when making investments. There have been many examples published in the last few years of complex and unsuitable investment products being sold to investors who did not fully understand the risks involved. Staff should be professionally qualified, and advice should only be accepted from trusted organisations that are fully regulated. The dangers of external inducements being offered to staff to tempt them to act improperly by investing in unsuitable products (and therefore committing an offence under the Bribery Act 2010) should not be ignored, and procedures should be in place to avoid this.

investing locally or world-wide

It should be easier to carry out fact finding exercises about potential UK or local investments than those based overseas. UK based investments will always be subject to UK laws, which should provide some assurance. Knowledge of the business practices of the prospective investment company should also be easier to determine.

The range of investments considered must always be within the expertise of the staff concerned within the treasury function, and the economy of the country within which the investment operates must be taken into account. However there are many major international organisations that are well known enough for some investors to consider suitable.

business practices of investment companies

Where investment is being considered in companies or institutions, there should be a match between the ethics of both organisations. For example, if an organisation had developed a brand identity that shows particularly strong ethical ethos, it would be foolish to invest in a company that routinely used child labour. Apart from the mismatch of ethical ideals, if the investment were made and subsequently became public knowledge the reputation of the investing company could suffer considerable damage.

The type of industries that, although quite legal, are not always considered ethical include (for example) armaments and tobacco. Environmental issues and sustainability are other areas where organisations would want to match their own ethos to those of any companies that they invested in.

Investments can be made in 'ethical funds' that list the type of industries that will not be included in their portfolio, and such an investment would give some reassurance. If investment in individual companies is preferred, it would be easier to appraise the business practices of a local company than one operating in a foreign country.

Apart from investment in individual companies, the choice of banking partner can be linked to ethical issues. There is a considerable amount of public data available about the practices of all the major banks to help inform such a decision.

A NOTE ON TREASURY HOUSEKEEPING

Another function of the Treasury or Accounts Department is one of simple housekeeping – looking after cash and investment certificates.

cash handling

Cash in the form of notes and coins is a security risk and most organisations will have **Policies and Procedures** for dealing with it.

These range from the petty cash procedures for small balances held in an office to procedures laid down for the security of the large amounts of cash handled, for example, by the supermarkets. Whatever the extent of the risk, the procedures must be strictly adhered to at all times. Adequate insurance must also be maintained.

looking after investment certificates

The use of certificates for investments is nowadays very much on the decline as electronic records are becoming normal practice. Certificates of Deposit, for example, are stored in paper and electronic format by the Central Money Markets Office, within the Bank of England. Nevertheless, investments in the form of paper certificates are still used and need to be stored carefully.

This is particularly important in the case of what are known as 'bearer' certificates where the name of the owner is not recorded on the certificate; the certificate belongs to whoever is holding it at the time – just like a bank note. It belongs to the 'bearer'. The security risk is clearly high in this case.

Chapter Summary

- Risk, return and liquidity have to be weighed up carefully when making an investment decision. Organisations need to minimise risk when investing both for the short term and the long term.

- Organisations must take into account external economic and financial considerations when making investment decisions. Care must be taken when investing at fixed rates when interest rates and inflation are rising, as the return on the investment will fall.

- The range of 'safe' investments for short-term liquidity surpluses includes: money market deposits, certificates of deposit and bank deposit accounts (see Key Terms for explanations of these securities).

- Longer-term investments for a Treasury include Government stock ('gilts'), listed and unlisted shares, land and gold. These vary in terms of risk, return and liquidity (see Key Terms for explanations of these securities).

- The rate of return on investments generally increases in line with the amount deposited, the period of the deposit and the risk involved. Sensible liquidity management involves obtaining the best rate of return possible on a 'safe' range of investments.

- The rate of return on investments involves a number of calculations which require knowledge of different types of interest rate (fixed, variable and bonus) and yields on investments such as shares and gilts.

- Liquidity management by a private or public sector Treasury takes place on a daily basis. Data used will include the previous day's bank balance, deposits and investments maturing and daily cash flow projections of sales receipts and payments.

- Both public sector and private sector organisations have internal regulations which set down guidelines for maintaining liquidity of investments. They are also bound by external legislation and regulations in the areas of risk management and internal control.

- Further investment considerations include diversifying the portfolio, whether any FSCS compensation would be available in the event of losses, the expertise within the treasury function, the geographical spread of investments, and the ethical business practices of investment companies.

- Organisations which deal with cash and investment certificates need to establish procedures for the secure handling, storage and insurance of these valuables.

Key Terms

exposure	the amount of money invested by an organisation in any one institution or type of investment
risk averse	avoiding high-risk investments
risk seeking	tolerating high-risk investments
interbank market	short-term deposits made by banks with each other
money market accounts	accounts for short-term deposits made by customers with banks; the surplus money is then used by the banks to place deposits in the interbank market
certificates of deposit	tradeable certificates issued by banks, certifying that a sum of money, normally a minimum of £50,000, has been deposited and will be repaid on a set date
treasury bills	three month tradeable certificates issued by the Debt Management Office and backed by the Government, sold to banks and other institutions at a discount and repayable at the full price on maturity
bank deposit accounts	interest-bearing accounts offered by the banks for smaller amounts; they can be fixed or variable interest rate, notice or instant access
gilts	also known as 'Government stock' or 'gilt-edged stock' are investments which provide funds for Government borrowing and are tradeable 'second hand' at a price determined by the market; they represent a secure longer-term form of investment
interest yield	the yield on gilts which represents the annual return for the investor; it is based on the market price of the stock and the interest rate stated on the gilt
redemption yield	the yield on gilts which takes into account the fact that gilts change in value in the period up to the redemption date; it usefully compares the yield of the gilt with the yields offered by other investments
listed shares	shares listed, bought and sold on the Stock Exchange
unlisted shares	private company shares – not listed and not freely bought or sold
land	the asset of property – bought for use by a business or held as an investment to provide rental income
gold	a marketable commodity, subject to market volatility, available in physical bullion form or through Exchange Traded Funds (ETFs)

Activities

7.1 The rate of return on an investment will be affected by a variety of factors. Complete the gaps in the text below with the correct word taken from the following:

better **longer** **larger** **lower**

The rate of return on an investment will be higher if the investment is made for a [ ] period of time and for a [ ] amount. The risk will be [ ] if the institution being invested in has a [ ] credit rating.

7.2 Economic trends can often affect investment decisions. There is a danger for an investor in fixed interest rate funds at a time when the rate of inflation is rising. Indicate below whether this second statement is true or false:

True	
False	

7.3 The table below shows the rates for a number of short-term funds in which a private sector company or a local authority might invest. Study the table and complete the text which follows from the words given.

	Overnight	7 Days notice	One month	Three months	Six months	One year
	%	%	%	%	%	%
Interbank	0.41	0.45	0.46	0.56	0.77	1.22
Certificates of Deposit (CDs)			0.59	0.68	0.89	1.18
Treasury Bills				0.52		

high risk **Certificate of Deposit** **low risk** **lower** **interbank** **Treasury Bill** **higher**

The [ ] market is made up of short-term deposits placed by banks with each other. The longer the period of the investment, the [ ] the return. The [ ] market is based on tradeable certificates issued by the Government-run Debt Management Office and the rate is lower than the interbank market because the risk is [ ]. The [ ] market trades certificates issued by banks and is also a [ ] market compared with shares, which can be [ ].

7.4 The table below displays the type of data which investors in Government stock (gilts) will need when making investment decisions. Study the table and answer the questions that follow.

Stock	Price £1 of stock (pence)	Interest yield %	Redemption yield %
Treasury 4% 2016	104.25	3.84	3.30
Treasury 4.75% 2020	106.80	4.45	3.94

Tick the correct answer from the options given:

(a) For what type of investment are gilts better suited?

(a) Shorter-term investment	
(b) Longer-term investment	

(b) What is the correct definition of 'redemption yield'?

(a) The yield taking into account the period to run before the stock is repayable	
(b) The yield which takes into account the current bank base rate	

(c) What is the correct definition of 'interest yield'?

(a) The annual percentage return based on the quoted price of the stock and the stated interest rate of the stock	
(b) The stated interest rate of the stock	

(d) What is the interest yield on the Treasury 4% 2016 if the price rose to £1.06?

(a) 4.24%	
(b) 3.77%	

7.5 How much will an investor need to invest in order to earn £2,500 interest a year, assuming a fixed annual interest rate of 2%? Enter your answer in the box below.

£ [ ]

7.6 Which of the following statements best describes a bonus rate of interest? Tick the correct option.

(a) An increase in the interest rate each year that you have invested the money	
(b) An increase in the interest rate when you invest more money in the account	
(c) An increase in the interest rate for the first period of the investment to encourage you to set up the account in the first place	

7.7 A successful private company has £200,000 to invest over the next eight years. You have been asked to write a set of notes to the directors, who hold the majority of the shares, setting out clearly the risk, return and liquidity aspects of investing in:

- gilt-edged stock
- listed shares
- property

7.8 Barsetshire County Council has a Treasury which has a strict investment policy set out in a set of Standing Orders (regulations). These establish the authorities and responsibilities given to its employees and the types of investment which are permissible. The investment manual of the Treasury includes the following policy for investing **short-term** surplus funds:

- The risk level must be low.
- The investment must be convertible to cash within 30 days.
- The maximum amount to be invested in any one type of investment is £100,000.
- The interest rate must be at least 1% above bank base rate.
- No deposits should be placed with financial institutions outside the UK.

The County Treasury is reviewing its investment options at the beginning of the month and has selected four options for £100,000 which it has immediately available for an investment over one month. Bank base rate is currently 1%.

Option 1 - Bibco Mining Fund

A Treasury Manager has been given a recommendation by a financial broker for an investment in a managed fund which is based largely on the shares of international gold mining companies. He reckons the fund could yield 10% over the year and could prove a good short-term investment, but ideally would have to be kept for at least a year. There is a high risk factor. £100,000 could be invested.

Option 2 – Western Bank plc money market account

UK bank money market based product; minimum investment allowed is £100,000; no notice period (immediate withdrawals); interest rate is 1.5% above base rate; low risk.

Option 3 – National Mutual Bank bond

Investment in UK bank; low risk; projected interest rate is 5% and a minimum investment of £500,000 is required; one year fixed period.

Option 4 – State Bank of Ruritania Treasury Account

Money market account with well-rated international bank; no notice period (immediate withdrawals); interest rate is 2.0% above UK base rate; medium risk. Minimum investment £100,000.

Required:

(a) Complete the table below for each of the four options, writing 'yes' if the investment meets County Treasury policy requirements and 'no' if it does not.

	Convertible within 1 month	Available for £100,000	Interest rate 1% over base	Overseas investment	Level of risk
Option 1					
Option 2					
Option 3					
Option 4					

(b) State which of the four options should be chosen for the £100,000 available for investment.

(a) Option 1	
(b) Option 2	
(c) Option 3	
(d) Option 4	

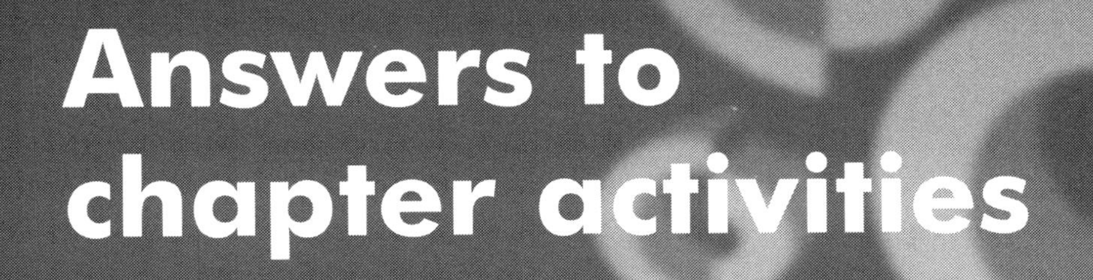

Answers to chapter activities

CHAPTER 1 – MANAGING CASH FLOWS

1.1

	£
Operating profit	84,000
Change in inventory	–1,500
Change in trade receivables	–7,300
Change in trade payables	+2,200
Adjustment for non-cash items	+13,700
Purchase of non-current assets	–33,000
Payment of Corporation Tax	–10,000
Net change in cash position	+48,100
Budgeted cash position 1 Jan 20-5	–29,000
Budgeted cash position 31 Dec 20-5	+19,100

1.2 The correct answer is (d) Inventory; Receivables; Cash; Payables; Inventory

Inventory is sold to customers and the amounts owed become receivables; the customers pay and the receivables become cash; the cash is used to pay suppliers (payables); suppliers deliver more inventory.

1.3 **(a)** Line diagram as shown below. Cash cycle = 5 months.

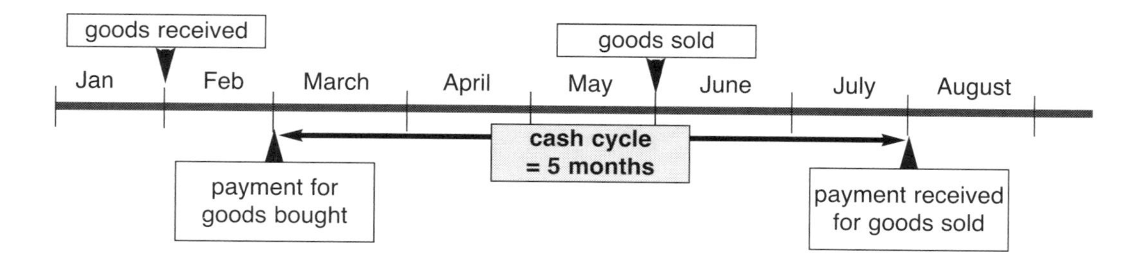

(b) Cash cycle = 3 months.

1.4 Overtrading can occur when a business has **insufficient** working capital.

Overcapitalisation can occur when a business has **too much** working capital.

Signs of overtrading include **rapidly increasing** sales volumes, **reducing** profit margins, and **longer** creditor payment periods.

1.5 The credit controller's absence accounts for an increase in receivables of £40,000, and an equal reduction in the bank balance.

The early delivery accounts for increased inventory of £20,000 and an increase in payables of the same amount.

The additional goods bought account for an increase in inventory of £10,000, and a reduction in the bank balance of the same amount since the goods have been paid for.

These three issues together account for the differences between the budgeted and actual positions.

1.6 Statements 2, 3, and 5 are true. The others are false.

1.7 Performance Limited:

(a) Working Capital = Current Assets – Current Liabilities

= £415,000 – £145,000

= £270,000

(b) Inventory holding period $= \frac{\text{inventory}}{\text{cost of sales}} \times 365$

$= \frac{£160{,}000}{£480{,}000} \times 365$

= 122 days

Receivables collection period $= \frac{\text{receivables}}{\text{credit sales}} \times 365$

$= \frac{£230{,}000}{£800{,}000} \times 365$

= 105 days

Payables payment period $= \frac{\text{payables}}{\text{purchases}} \times 365$

$= \frac{£145{,}000}{£500{,}000} \times 365$

= 106 days

Cash Cycle = 122 days + 105 days – 106 days = 121 days

1.8 Capital payments = payments that relate to the acquisition of non-current assets (2).

Regular revenue receipts = income received from the operating activities of the business that are expected to occur frequently (6).

Drawings = payments made to the owners of the business (3).

Exceptional payments = payments that do not arise from the operating activities of the business and that are not expected to occur frequently (11).

CHAPTER 2 – FORECASTING DATA FOR CASH BUDGETS

2.1

	Selling price £.p	**Gross profit** £.p
Mark-up of 20%	88.20	14.70
Mark-up of 22%	89.67	16.17
Margin of 15%	86.47	12.97
Margin of 17%	88.55	15.05

2.2 **(a)** (b) Selling prices are decreasing each year by a fixed percentage

(b) (c) £13

The price is decreasing each year by 20%.

2.3 **(a)** As can be seen from the workings, this example has a regular trend, increasing by £5 each day, and seasonal variations that are consistent, with each set of 5 totalling zero.

(b) The forecast for week 4 is calculated as follows:

	Forecast trend £		**Seasonal variations**	**Forecast £**
Tues	1,065 + (3 x 5)	= 1,080	–90	990
Wed	1,065 + (4 x 5)	= 1,085	–50	1,035
Thurs	1,065 + (5 x 5)	= 1,090	+25	1,115
Fri	1,065 + (6 x 5)	= 1,095	+60	1,155
Sat	1,065 + (7 x 5)	= 1,100	+55	1,155

Workings:

	Week / Day	Sales £	5-Point moving average (trend)	Seasonal variations
Week 1	Tues	915		
	Wed	960		
	Thurs	1,040	1,015	+25
	Fri	1,080	1,020	+60
	Sat	1,080	1,025	+55
Week 2	Tues	940	1,030	–90
	Wed	985	1,035	–50
	Thurs	1,065	1,040	+25
	Fri	1,105	1,045	+60
	Sat	1,105	1,050	+55
Week 3	Tues	965	1,055	–90
	Wed	1,010	1,060	–50
	Thurs	1,090	1,065	+25
	Fri	1,130		
	Sat	1,130		

2.4 **(a)** Average trend movement is difference between last and first trend figures, divided by number of movements:

= (6,290 – 5,800) ÷ 7 = +70

(b) If trend is increasing at an average 70 units per quarter, then by:

Year 3 quarter 3 it will be 6,290 + (3 x 70) = 6,500, and by

Year 3 quarter 4 it will be 6,290 + (4 x 70) = 6,570.

Adjusting these figures by the seasonal variations (which were identical for both years) gives:

Year 3 quarter 3 forecast of (6,500 + 880) = 7,380

Year 3 quarter 4 forecast of (6,570 – 100) = 6,470.

2.5 (a)

	Sales volume *(units)*	**Trend**	**Monthly variation** *(volume less trend)*
August	18,720		
September	11,880	13,680	–1,800
October	10,440	14,040	–3,600
November	19,800	14,400	5,400
December	12,960		

The monthly sales volume trend is +360 units.

(b)

Forecast trend	15,120
Variation	–3,600
Forecast sales volume	11,520
Forecast sales (£)	46,080
Forecast purchases (£)	18,432

Workings:

Forecast trend	14,400 (Nov) + 360 + 360 = 15,120	
Variation (3 month cycle)	–3,600	
Forecast sales volume	11,520	
Forecast sales	11,520 x £4	= £46,080
Forecast purchases	£46,080 x 40%	= £18,432

(c) (a) £7,365 *Working:* £6,220 x (386 ÷ 326)

2.6 (a) Original cost: £240,000 ÷ 20,000 kilograms = £12.00 per kilogram

Forecast cost: £12.00 x (221 ÷ 196) = £13.53 per kilogram

(b) Total cost: £13.53 x 22,500 kilograms = £304,425

2.7

20-2 Quarter	Trend calculation	Trend £	S V Calculation	S V £	Forecast £
1	(28 x £1,500) + £62,000	104,000	£104,000 x (–10%)	–10,400	93,600
2	(29 x £1,500) + £62,000	105,500	£105,500 x (+70%)	+73,850	179,350
3	(30 x £1,500) + £62,000	107,000	£107,000 x (+25%)	+26,750	133,750
4	(31 x £1,500) + £62,000	108,500	£108,500 x (–85%)	–92,225	16,275

2.8 (a)

Period	Sales units	4 point averages	Centred averages	Seasonal variations
Year 1				
Qtr 1	1,000			
Qtr 2	860			
		770		
Qtr 3	660		760	–100
		750		
Qtr 4	560		740	–180
Year 2		730		
Qtr 1	920		720	+200
		710		
Qtr 2	780		700	+80
		690		
Qtr 3	580		680	–100
		670		
Qtr 4	480		660	–180
Year 3		650		
Qtr 1	840		640	+200
		630		
Qtr 2	700		620	+80
		610		
Qtr 3	500		600	–100
		590		
Qtr 4	400		580	–180
Year 4		570		
Qtr 1	760		560	+200
		550		
Qtr 2	620		540	+80
		530		
Qtr 3	420			
Qtr 4	320			

(b) Forecast for Year 5:

Period	Forecast Trend	Forecast S.V.	Forecast Sales
Qtr 1	480	+200	680
Qtr 2	460	+80	540
Qtr 3	440	–100	340
Qtr 4	420	–180	240

2.9

Month	Jan	Feb	March	April	May	June
Price £	1.45	1.48	1.41	1.52	1.55	1.57
Index	95.39	97.37	92.76	100.00	101.97	103.29

CHAPTER 3 – PREPARING CASH BUDGETS

3.1 (a) Sonita's Business – Cash budget for first four months' trading

	1 *£000*	**2** *£000*	**3** *£000*	**4** *£000*
Receipts				
Initial Investment	35			
Receipts from Sales	10	10	10	10
Total Receipts	45	10	10	10
Payments				
Purchases	9	–	8	7
Expenses	2	2	2	2
Non-current Assets	30	–	–	–
Drawings	1	1	1	1
Total Payments	42	3	11	10
Cash Flow for Month	3	7	(1)	0
Bank balance b/f	0	3	10	9
Bank balance c/f	3	10	9	9

(b)

	£
Budgeted Profit for Period	5,000
Add non-cash expenditure used in calculation of profit:	
Depreciation	2,000
Add cash receipts not used in calculation of profit:	
Capital Invested	35,000
Deduct cash payments not used in the calculation of profit:	
Purchase of Equipment	(30,000)
Payment of Drawings	(4,000)
Adjust for changes in inventory:	
Deduct increase in inventory	(5,000)
Adjust for changes in payables:	
Add increase in payables	6,000
Increase in cash	9,000

3.2 Jim Smith's Business – Cash budget for first six months' trading

	Jan	Feb	Mar	Apr	May	Jun
	£	£	£	£	£	£
Receipts						
Capital	10,000					
Receivables	–	1,250	3,000	4,000	4,000	4,500
Total receipts	10,000	1,250	3,000	4,000	4,000	4,500
Payments						
Van	6,000					
Payables	–	4,500	4,500	3,500	3,500	3,500
Expenses	750	600	600	650	650	700
Total payments	6,750	5,100	5,100	4,150	4,150	4,200
Cash flow for month	3,250	(3,850)	(2,100)	(150)	(150)	300
Bank balance b/f	0	3,250	(600)	(2,700)	(2,850)	(3,000)
Bank balance c/f	3,250	(600)	(2,700)	(2,850)	(3,000)	(2,700)

3.3 (a)

Sarah's Business:
Cash budget for the first three months' trading

	Month 1 £	Month 2 £	Month 3 £
Receipts			
Initial investment	40,000		
Receipts from sales (1 month credit)	0	7,500	12,000
Receipts from sales (2 month credit)	0	0	2,500
Total receipts	40,000	7,500	14,500
Payments			
Purchases	0	10,000	14,000
Rent	4,000	0	0
Expenses	2,000	2,000	2,000
Non-current assets	32,000	0	0
Drawings	2,000	2,000	2,000
Overdraft interest	0	0	65
Total payments	40,000	14,000	18,065
Cash flow for month	0	(6,500)	(3,565)
Balance b/f	0	0	(6,500)
Balance c/f	0	(6,500)	(10,065)

(b)

	£
Original Budgeted Profit for Period	11,000
Less overdraft interest*	(65)
Revised Budgeted Profit	10,935

* In this activity the overdraft interest is considered to be the amount to be paid in the period. An alternative approach would be to also adjust for the interest based on the Month 3 closing cash balance as an accrual. This would also mean incorporating an additional adjustment in the reconciliation statement that follows.

(c)

	£
Revised Budgeted Profit for Period	10,935
Add non-cash expenditure used in calculation of profit:	
Depreciation	2,000
Add cash receipts not used in calculation of profit:	
Capital Invested	40,000
Deduct cash payments not used in the calculation of profit:	
Purchase of Equipment	(32,000)
Payment of Drawings	(6,000)
Rent Prepayment	(3,000)
Adjust for changes in inventory:	
Deduct increase in inventory	(10,000)
Adjust for changes in trade receivables:	
Deduct increase in trade receivables (1)	(28,000)
Adjust for changes in trade payables:	
Add increase in trade payables (2)	16,000
(Decrease) in cash	(10,065)

Notes:

(1) Trade receivables at end of Month 3:

25% of Month 2 Sales (25% x £16,000)	£4,000
100% of Month 3 Sales	£24,000
Total	£28,000

(2) As purchases are made on 1 month's credit, trade payables at the end of Month 3 equal the purchases made in Month 3.

3.4 (a)

Month:	Sep £	Oct £	Nov £	Dec £	Jan £	Feb £
Receipts						
Cash sales	7,200	7,200	8,000	12,000	5,400	5,400
Credit sales	800	800	800	2,000	8,000	600
Total receipts	8,000	8,000	8,800	14,000	13,400	6,000
Payments						
Cash purchases	2,940	2,940	7,350	3,675	2,205	2,205
Credit purchases	3,000	3,000	3,000	7,500	3,750	2,250
Wages, rent and expenses	2,000	2,000	2,000	2,000	2,000	2,000
Total payments	7,940	7,940	12,350	13,175	7,955	6,455
Cash flow for month	60	60	(3,550)	825	5,445	(455)
Bank balance b/f	(1,050)	(990)	(930)	(4,480)	(3,655)	1,790
Bank balance c/f	(990)	(930)	(4,480)	(3,655)	1,790	1,335

Tutorial note:

The cash purchases are shown in the cash budget after the 2% discount has been deducted.

(b) The cash budget shows that Antonio is over his limit in November and December. This is largely caused by his cash purchases of £7,350 in November which have placed a strain on the bank account. This could best be avoided by negotiating credit terms on some of these purchases. If this is not possible, the only solution is for Antonio to inject some funds or someone else to make a loan to the business during November.

3.5 Solution

	£
Sales receipts	167,720
Purchases payments	12,731
Wages paid	60,400
Rent paid	12,660
Office expenses	17,540
Van expenses	7,572
Van depreciation	0

Workings:

Sales receipts	165,200 + 18,620 – 16,100
Purchases payments	13,140 + 715 – 1,124
Wages paid	No adjustments
Rent paid	12,000 – 1,200 + 1,860
Office expenses	17,600 + 180 – 240
Van expenses	7,550 – 501 + 523
Van depreciation	Non-cash item

3.6 (a)

	ACTUAL		**FORECAST**			
	January	**February**	**March**	**April**	**May**	**June**
Total sales	37,000	42,600	45,800	50,000	55,600	61,700
Cash sales	5,550	6,390	6,870	7,500	8,340	9,255
Credit sales	31,450	36,210	38,930	42,500	47,260	52,445

(b)

	CREDIT SALES £	**CASH RECEIVED** February £	March £	April £	May £	June £
January	31,450	22,015	9,435			
February	36,210		25,347	10,863		
March	38,930			27,251	11,679	
April	42,500				29,750	12,750
May	47,260					33,082
Monthly credit sales receipts			34,782	38,114	41,429	45,832

3.7

PAYMENTS	October £	November £	December £
Purchases	51,720	52,800	54,000
Wages	12,300	12,300	12,750
Expenses	7,490	8,830	7,656
New machine	12,000	12,000	12,000
Total payments	83,510	85,930	86,406

3.8 **Pete Still Cash Budget for January – April 20-6**

	January £	February £	March £	April £
Receipts				
Receipts from 20-5 sales	12,000	9,000		
Receipts from 20-6 sales:				
Cash sales	4,800	3,600	4,500	5,100
Credit sales (1 month's credit)		5,600	4,200	5,250
Credit sales (2 months' credit)			5,432	4,074
Total receipts	16,800	18,200	14,132	14,424
Payments				
Purchases made in 20-5	4,000	–		
Purchases made in 20-6:				
Current month	4,704	5,292	5,880	6,468
Following month		3,200	3,600	4,000
Power, light & heat	400	400	400	400
Insurance		3,120		
Telephone & postage	450	450	450	450
General expenses	300	300	300	300
Non-current assets	30,000			
Drawings		2,000		2,000
Total payments	39,854	14,762	10,630	13,618
Cash flow for month	(23,054)	3,438	3,502	806
Balance b/f	10,000	(13,054)	(9,616)	(6,114)
Balance c/f	(13,054)	(9,616)	(6,114)	(5,308)

Notes:

Receipts from sales are calculated as follows using January sales as an example:

	£
Cash Sales (£16,000 x 30%)	4,800
Credit Sales Received February (£16,000 x 70% x 50%)	5,600
Credit Sales Received March (£16,000 x 70% x 98.5%) – £5,600	5,432

Payments for purchases are calculated as follows, using January purchases as an example:

	£
Paid January after discount (£8,000 x 60% x 98%)	4,704
Paid February (£8,000 x 40%)	3,200

Power, Light & Heat is calculated as £1,850 + £300 – £550 = £1,600. £1,600 ÷ 4 = £400 per month.
Insurance is calculated as £1,030 – £250 + £2,340 = £3,120, paid in February.
Telephone & Postage is calculated as £1,890 – £90 = £1,800. £1,800 ÷ 4 = £450 per month.

3.9

	£
Operating profit	163,000
Change in inventory	–10,500
Change in trade receivables	+2,700
Change in trade payables	+13,200
Adjustment for non-cash items (1)	+38,000
Proceeds from disposal of non-current assets (2)	+11,500
Payment of Corporation Tax (3)	–66,000
Net change in cash position	+151,900
Budgeted cash position 1 Jan 20-5	–44,000
Budgeted cash position 31 Dec 20-5	+107,900

(1) Non-cash items:
Depreciation £33,500 + Loss on Disposal £4,500 = £38,000

(2) Carrying Value of Assets Disposed of:
£180,000 – £33,500 – £130,500 = £16,000

Proceeds:
£16,000 – £4,500 = £11,500

(3) Payment of Corporation Tax:
£55,000 + £79,000 – £68,000 = £66,000

3.10

	Period 1	Period 2	Period 3	Period 4	Period 5
	units	*units*	*units*	*units*	*units*
Raw materials usage	1,960	2,202	2,300	2,150	2,200
– opening inventory	555	603	701	489	600
+ closing inventory	603	701	489	600	Not known
= raw materials purchases	2,008	2,300	2,088	2,261	

		Payments in Periods:			
	Total	Period 2	Period 3	Period 4	Period 5
	£	£	£	£	£
Period 1 purchases	140,560	70,280	56,224	14,056	
Period 2 purchases	161,000		80,500	64,400	16,100
Period 3 purchases	146,160			73,080	58,464
Total purchase payments			136,724	151,536	

CHAPTER 4 – USING CASH BUDGETS

4.1

	January	February	March	April
	£	£	£	£
Changes to receipts	–	–	(5,000)	(4,000)
Changes to payments for non-current assets	26,000	(24,000)		
Revised:				
Cash flow for month	(24,820)	21,640	(7,080)	(1,240)
Bank balance b/f	10,000	(14,820)	6,820	(260)
Bank balance c/f	(14,820)	6,820	(260)	(1,500)

4.2 **Revised cash budget (extract) for the period July – October**

	July	August	September	October
Payments	£	£	£	£
Purchases	25,000	28,000	26,650	24,600
Labour	19,000	17,000	18,000	20,700
Rent	21,000	–	–	–
Expenses	10,080	10,093	10,133	10,140

4.3

Month	January £	February £	March £	April £
Calculation of Changes to Receipts:				
Old receipts	8,500	7,500	5,000	9,000
New receipts – cash	2,375	4,275	4,750	5,700
New receipts – credit	8,500	7,500	2,500	4,500
Change	2,375	4,275	2,250	1,200
Changes to payments for purchases	0	0	0	210
Revised:				
Cash flow for month	4,755	5,915	170	3,750
Balance b/f	10,000	14,755	20,670	20,840
Balance c/f	14,755	20,670	20,840	24,590

4.4 (a)

Receipts from Cash Sales: No overall difference.

There is no difference in total, but each month's figures are a little different to the budget. It may be that an average figure has been used for the budget, and this seems to be proving accurate overall.

Receipts from Trade Receivables: No overall difference.

This appears to be a timing difference, as the shortfall in earlier months' receipts is made up in June.

Payments for Purchases: £3,000 less payments than budgeted.

Since the payments have been regular, unlike the budget, it may be that an anticipated inventory increase did not take place as planned.

Payment for rent: No overall difference.

It appears that the budgeted rent amount (presumably including a prepayment) has instead been paid in three equal monthly amounts.

Payment for Administration: £1,000 more than budgeted.

Since the increased payment is in the last month of the budget period it is impossible to tell whether this is the start of a trend, or an early payment of a July amount.

Payment for Non-current Assets: £3,000 less than budgeted.

The payment seems to have been delayed in comparison with the budget. The amount of payment is less than budget which could indicate that a cheaper non-current asset has been acquired. However the smaller payment may not be the whole position, as further payments could occur in the next month.

4.4 (b)

	£000
Budgeted closing bank balance	47
Variance in cash sales	0
Variance in receipts from trade receivables	0
Variance in payments for purchases	3
Variance in payments for wages	0
Variance in payments for rent	0
Variance in payments for administration	–1
Variance in payments for non-current assets	3
Actual closing bank balance	52

4.5 (a)

	Period 1 £	**Period 2 £**	**Period 3 £**	**Period 4 £**	**Period 5 £**
Original value of forecast sales	27,600	28,800	29,520	30,240	31,200
Original timing of receipts			29,160	29,880	30,720
Revised value of forecast sales	23,460	24,480	25,092	25,704	26,520
Revised timing of receipts			24,378	25,092	25,755

Working: timing of receipts

		£
Period 3 receipts:	25% x £23,460 (period 1)	5,865
	50% x £24,480 (period 2)	12,240
	25% x £25,092 (period 3)	6,273
		24,378
Period 4 receipts:	25% x £24,480 (period 2)	6,120
	50% x £25,092 (period 3)	12,546
	25% x £25,704 (period 4)	6,426
		25,092
Period 5 receipts:	25% x £25,092 (period 3)	6,273
	50% x £25,704 (period 4)	12,852
	25% x £26,520 (period 5)	6,630
		25,755

(b)

	Period 3 £	**Period 4** £	**Period 5** £
Original timing of payments	9,600	9,820	10,940
Revised timing of payments	8,928	9,688	10,268

Working: revised timing of payments

		£
Period 3 payments:	60% x £8,480	5,088
	40% x £9,600	3,840
		8,928
Period 4 payments:	60% x £9,600	5,760
	40% x £9,820	3,928
		9,688
Period 5 payments:	60% x £9,820	5,892
	40% x £10,940	4,376
		10,268

(c)

	Period 3 £	**Period 4** £	**Period 5** £
Changes in sales receipts	–4,782	–4,788	–4,965
Changes in purchase payments	+672	+132	+672
Net change	–4,110	–4,656	–4,293

4.6 (a)

	£
Budgeted closing bank balance	15,058
Shortfall in receipts from receivables	–3,804
Surplus in cash sales	+1,440
Increase in payments to payables	–2,173
Decrease in cash purchases	+150
Increase in capital expenditure	–32,000
Increase in wages and salaries	–400
Decrease in general expenses	+2,036
Actual closing bank balance	–19,693

(b) (c) Delayed capital expenditure

All the other actions would have helped the position, but none would be sufficient, in isolation, to avoid an overdraft.

(c)

Labour costs have increased	Reduce overtime working
Sales volumes have decreased	Improve the product
Payments to suppliers are being made earlier	Negotiate early settlement discount
Customers taking more days to settle their debts	Improve credit control
Prices of raw materials have increased	Change suppliers

4.7 (a)

	Receipts from Sales in:				
	Month 1 £	**Month 2** £	**Month 3** £	**Month 4** £	**Total** £
Month 1 Sales	20,700	59,616	20,700		
Month 2 Sales		21,600	62,208	21,600	
Month 3 Sales			21,360	61,517	
Month 4 Sales				20,480	
Forecast receipts	20,700	81,216	104,268	103,597	309,781

(b)

	Month 1 £	**Month 2** £	**Month 3** £	**Month 4** £	**Net Total** £
Change in cash flow	0	+28,566	–1,242	–2,923	+24,401

(c) £420,700 x 60% x 4% = £10,097

CHAPTER 5: THE UK FINANCIAL SYSTEM AND LIQUIDITY

5.1 (c) Deals with a wide range of money and currency deposits

5.2 **(a)** A **gilt-edged security** is a tradeable investment to fund longer-term Government borrowing.

(b) A **corporate bond** is a form of investment issued by a commercial company.

(c) A **certificate of deposit** is a short-term tradeable investment issued in respect of a deposit received by the bank.

(d) A **treasury bill** is a short-term tradeable investment to fund Government borrowing.

5.3 (b) Notes and coins, treasury bills, certificates of deposit

5.4 The Bank of England can add to or take funds out of the banking system using **Open Market Operations**. Using this system, funds are provided using **repo (repurchase)** agreements, in which the **Bank of England** buys tradeable securities from the banks, with a simultaneous agreement to sell them back at a later date.

5.5 (c) Set by the Monetary Control Committee and is the rate which sets the pattern for commercial bank lending rates

5.6 (a) Increase the amount of money circulating in the economy and hence the amount of spending in the economy

5.7 If the level of interest rates rises in the UK economy, the result is likely to be associated with a **rise in the rate of inflation** and the cost of **borrowing.** This will mean a rise in costs for businesses because of higher **interest charges** but a also possible fall in the cost of imported **raw materials.** If interest rates fall, on the other hand, borrowing will be **cheaper** and the economy will become more **healthy.**

CHAPTER 6: RAISING SHORT-TERM AND LONG-TERM FINANCE

6.1 (d) Security is sometimes required, interest is only paid on what you borrow

6.2 (b) A form of finance for asset purchase

6.3 (c) Has an upper limit for the interest rate

6.4 (c) A mortgage over his property

6.5 3.5%

6.6 **(a)** £16,915.80

(b) (c) It takes into account all the financial costs of the loan and the fact that the balance will be reducing over the twelve months

6.7 Hire Purchase (HP)

1
- HP is a form of finance lease
- Artemis PLC will retain the use of the assets and is likely to take ownership at the end of the hire period
- Artemis PLC will be liable for the maintenance and repairs of the vehicles
- interest is charged on the reducing balance of the finance
- Artemis PLC will have the benefit of tax allowances on the assets

2
- the relevant assets (and liabilities) will be shown on the statement of financial position of the lessee; the asset must be valued at full cost and the liability figure must represent all repayment and interest cost and the interest will be charged to the statement of profit or loss
- gearing will be increased as the finance will be shown as a non-current liabiity

Operating lease

1
- an operating lease is a hire contract where the hirer retains the ownership of the asset
- at the end of the lease the asset will retain significant value known as 'residual value'
- payments are likely to be lower than those of an HP contract
- Artemis PLC, depending on the contract, may be responsible for the maintenance and repairs of the vehicles

2
- the assets will remain the property of the leasing company and so will not be shown on the statement of financial position of Artemis PLC, nor will there be any non-current liability; the relevant lease payments will be charged in the statement of profit or loss
- gearing will not be affected as the statement of financial position is not affected
- profit will be reduced as a result of the lease payments being charged in the statement of profit or loss

6.8 (a)

	Loan interest	Arrangement fees	Overdraft interest	Total cost
	£	£	£	£
Option 1	7,500	2,325*	1,400	11,225
Option 2	10,800	1,800	-	12,600

*workings: £1875 + £450

(b) Option 1 is less expensive in terms of interest and fees cost. The fees are more expensive than Option 2, but the loan fee of £1,875 is only payable in the first year and so will only impact on that year. Option 1 is the recommendation.

(c) The choice of security is clear. Option 1 is again preferable because the assets to be pledged are those of the company. If the security for this option has to be realised it will affect the company shareholders (including probably the directors) but if Option 2 is chosen, the directors may have to sell their own assets, including possibly their homes, to repay the bank under their personal guarantees.

CHAPTER 7: INVESTING SURPLUS FUNDS

7.1 The rate of return on an investment will be higher if the investment is made for a **longer** period of time and for a **larger** amount. The risk will be **lower** if the institution being invested in has a **better** credit rating.

7.2 True. Interest rates tend to rise in times of rising inflation. This means that an investor in a fixed rate investment would find that the rate of return would become increasingly unattractive if the rate of inflation increased and other schemes with better rates came onto the market.

7.3 The **interbank** market is made up of short-term deposits placed by banks with each other. The longer the period of the investment, the **higher** the return. The **Treasury Bill** market is based on tradeable certificates issued by the Government-run Debt Management Office and the rate is lower than the interbank market because the risk is **lower**. The **Certificate of Deposit** market trades certificates issued by banks and is also a **low risk** market compared with shares, which can be **high risk**.

7.4
(a) (b) Longer-term investment
(b) (a) The yield taking into account the period to run before the stock is repayable
(c) (a) The annual percentage return based on the quoted price of the stock and the stated interest rate of the stock
(d) (b) 3.77%

7.5 £125,000

7.6 (c) An increase in the interest rate for the first period of the investment to encourage you to set up the account in the first place

7.7 **GILT-EDGED STOCK**

risk

Risk is very low because the gilt-edged stock is issued on behalf of the Government and so carries state-owned risk.

There is an economic risk if interest rates rise to a higher level than was expected by the market as this will reduce the return on the investment.

return

The two indicators that need to be examined are:

- the interest yield which relates the price paid for the stock with its stated interest rate
- the redemption yield which takes into account the fall or rise in value of the stock as it reaches the redemption (repayment)

A rise in interest rates would cause the market price of the stock to fall and the return for existing holders of stock will be reduced.

liquidity

The stock is very liquid because it can be sold at any time. This type of investment, however, is normally held for the long-term because it is a very low risk investment.

LISTED SHARES

risk

Shares have a recognised risk element, which will depend on the shares being purchased:

- share prices are subject to market fluctuations
- the investment could be lost if the company goes into liquidation
- risk can be reduced by investing in a portfolio of shares with different risk profiles or in managed funds which invest in a wide range of shares in a particular area

return

Shares are often held for the long term as their value will generally increase in line with the stock market indices.

If shares are held for the short term the return may be negative if they fall in value.

The costs of dealing in shares can be high and will need to be offset against the return received from capital gain and dividend income.

liquidity

Shares can be sold at short notice to realise cash and this could result in a loss being made.

Shares are normally viewed as being a long-term investment.

PROPERTY

Note: it is assumed that property investment is related to property purchased to make a return rather than to expand the premises of the business itself.

risk

The risk is high because the commercial property market is vulnerable in periods of recession and prices can fall.

The investing company is dependent on having a tenant in occupation with a successful business and a long lease to provide the rental income.

return

Property values have historically risen over time, and so a capital gain is possible, but not guaranteed.

Rental income is the main return on property, and can be regularly reviewed.

liquidity

Property can be sold at any time.

Selling property is expensive and can take a long time.

Finding a buyer will be difficult if the economy is in recession and the asking price has to be dropped.

Property is best viewed as illiquid and as a long-term investment.

7.8 (a)

	Convertible within 1 month	Available for £100,000	Interest rate 1% over base	Overseas investment	Level of risk
Option 1	no	yes	yes	no	no
Option 2	yes	yes	yes	yes	yes
Option 3	no	no	yes	yes	yes
Option 4	yes	yes	yes	no	no

(b) (b) Option 2 (Western Bank plc money market account).

Index

for your notes

for your notes

for your notes

for your notes

for your notes

for your notes

for your notes

for your notes

for your notes